'A book to pique the curiosity as well as the appetite – a riveting read, full of lovely recipes I can't wait to try.'

Felicity Cloake, food writer, *Guardian*

'Sybil's book has taken the complicated subject of the multi-sensory approach to cooking and made it both approachable and fun. This is a definitive guide to the "building blocks" of creating dishes that speak on many levels and tap into our conscious and unconscious enjoyment of them.'

**Kyle Connaughton, chef/owner
Single Thread Farm-Restaurant-Inn**

'Sybil Kapoor's books are the most well-thumbed on my kitchen shelf, and this one is already acquiring a heavy patina of spatters. I love, love, love the food in this book, and the thoughtful commentary that comes with it. From Kapoor I learnt that eating chapatti and paneer with my fingers would enhance my perception of its texture, and that some dishes, such as spiced pea and potato frittata taste better (and more silky) just-warm.'

Victoria Moore, wine correspondent, *Daily Telegraph* and *BBC Good Food*

'Sybil has bridged the gap between food science and everyday cuisine. It's great to see there is an easier approach for home cooks like you and me, and encouragement to explore and look at food from a different point of view.'

**Tony Conigliaro,
founder of the Drink Factory**

For Raju with Love

First published in the United Kingdom in 2018 by
Pavilion
43 Great Ormond Street
London WC1N 3HZ

ISBN 978-1-91159-567-0

A CIP catalogue record for this book is available from the British Library

10 9 8 7 6 5 4 3 2 1

Reproduction by Mission Productions Ltd, Hong Kong
Printed and bound by 1010 International Printing Ltd, China

This book can be ordered direct from the publisher at
www.pavilionbooks.com

Neither the author nor the publisher can accept responsibility for any injury or illness that may arise as a result of following the advice contained in this work. Any application of the information contained in the book is at the reader's sole discretion.

Note for American readers

Best substitutions for UK ingredients are marked where necessary within the recipes in this book. Caster sugar sold in the UK is a fine form of granulated sugar. In most instances this can be replaced by US granulated sugar which is similarly fine. For some baking or pâtisserie recipes, US superfine sugar is a better substitute and is indicated on the page. In the UK, granulated sugar tends to have quite large granules so is not suitable for baking.

A New Way to Cook

SIGHT

SMELL

TOUCH

TASTE

SOUND

Sybil Kapoor

PAVILION

Contents

The Theory

'My fountain pen is full of ink; I have fresh sheets of paper before me. I love my book because I am writing it for you. I feel that I need only let my pen run on and I shall make myself clear. And my ideas move more quickly still.'

COOKING IN TEN MINUTES by Edouard de Pomiane, 1948

Edouard de Pomiane's words capture the intense pleasure I feel on writing a new book, and none more so than this book. It's the culmination of many years of cooking, travelling, thinking and writing. It started with a simple question: what makes a recipe delicious?

Cooking is the creation of dishes using different techniques and ingredients. Thus, you might think that the answer depends on who you are, where you live and what sort of food you like to eat. True, but underlying our preferences are our senses. We all share the senses of sight, smell, touch (texture and temperature), taste and sound. They're integral to our experience of eating, no matter where we live in the world.

Taste, flavour, texture, temperature and appearance are the building blocks of all cookery, regardless of whether you are making a pickle in India or porridge in Scotland. And so, this book was born. If I could understand how these five elements work together and how they affect me, then I, and therefore you, should be able to make consistently delectable dishes.

The first step of writing always lies in research. Much has been written on each of our gustatory senses, including a good deal of flim-flam within the foodie world. Does it really matter whether you expect something to taste sharp because it's coloured green? It may be that asparagus and coffee share certain flavour compounds, but which cook really thinks that they taste good together as a result?

Since this is a cookery book and not a scientific manual, I've only woven in scientific information that brings insight. It's not necessary to be a scientist to cook well, but it is important to be sensitive to your different senses. Eat one chewy toffee, for example, and it tastes gorgeous; eat a bagful of toffees and you stop appreciating their caramel flavour and sweet bitter taste. Your attention lessens with prolonged exposure to any one taste or flavour and you stop registering it.

I divided the book into five chapters, starting with taste and following with flavour, texture, temperature and appearance. This allows you to learn the fundamentals, step by step, so that by the time you reach temperature, for example, you will understand how it might alter your perception of taste, flavour and texture. A warm Basil Custard (p.174), for instance, has more basil aroma when tepid, but will taste less sweet if chilled, added to which the colder its egg-thickened milk becomes, the more it will coat your mouth.

Mattar Paneer (p.140), Chapattis (p.142) and Indian Lemon and Ginger Pickle (p.149)

Sticky Asian Beef Kebabs with Cucumber Dip (p.92)

It was at this stage that the project became daunting. Each chapter could have easily become a book in its own right. I've had to cut and condense everything down to the basics. Use the introduction and notes of each chapter as guides, which can lead you into new territories beyond these pages.

The recipes that follow are subdivided into sections that illustrate how the chapter's chosen element can be used within cookery. This varies according to the subject matter. 'Taste' tackles the basics of how you apply different tastes, such as by marination, combination or layering. Whereas 'Texture' is designed to illustrate how different aspects of touch can alter the eating experience – from the anticipatory feel of salt on hand-held chips, to the noise of chewing a squeaky Thai salad; the chapter includes sections on learning about textures, changing texture, fat sensitivity, sound, transferring food from hand to mouth, and challenging textures.

Every recipe has been written to illustrate a particular point, albeit from my subjective viewpoint. The best way to learn is through practical experience. Trust your own senses – they don't lie. Lift an aromatic glass of Mint Julep (p.63) to your mouth and you will understand how scent can be used to heighten anticipation. Try eating a Plum Tarte Tatin (p.180) warm, and then cold, and you will appreciate how different temperatures radically change the buttery texture of the sugary juices and flaky pastry.

The hardest chapter to write was 'Appearance'. Your cooking is as much a statement of who you are, as your choice of clothes. It's equally subject to changing fashions, from those of restaurant food to the influence of Instagram. Rather than illogically stating 'this is an attractive way to plate something', I decided to explore what makes us want to create something beautiful and how we might construct it. It helps to take into account the context of eating before drawing on seasonal influences and memories. In practical terms, it also means utilizing texture, colour and space, as well as utensils.

Throughout the book, you'll also find easy experiments and provocative tests to help you decide what you think works. There is no right or wrong in cooking, only likes and dislikes. The more you look, sniff, taste, feel and listen to the world around you, the more intensely you will experience life, from the dapple of summer sunlight to the scent of an Indian takeaway drifting down the street.

The more you are conscious of each of your senses, the more creative you will become as a cook and the more intensely you will enjoy eating. After all, life and food are forever entwined, and every aspect of cooking is guided by our senses. The downy touch of a peach skin, the scent of freshly picked basil, the shock of sour lemon juice, the pleasure of drinking cool water, or the desire to capture the beauty of a full-blown rose. Every experience influences us and, little by little, changes how we cook and eat.

A brief note about the recipes
Wherever possible I use organic ingredients. I always use fine sea salt, naturally brewed soy sauce and unwaxed fruit. A few ingredients, such as tapioca seed pearls and soft white corn tortillas are not widely available, but they can be found online or in specialist stores. Both metric and imperial measurements (plus US cups) appear on the page, however it is important to work with one set of measurements and not alternate between the two within a recipe. Be aware that oven temperatures vary between appliances and adjust if necessary.

• • •

Taste

Taste Recipes

Marination
infusing an ingredient with different tastes

Combination
combined tastes released as one

Layering
releasing different tastes through texture

Dressing
coating ingredients uniformly with chosen tastes

Saucing
dipping introduces variety of taste

Accompanying
the influence of side dishes

Taste

'The first thing I remember tasting and then wanting to taste again is the grayish-pink fuzz my grandmother skimmed from a spitting kettle of strawberry jam. I suppose I was about four.'

THE GASTRONOMICAL ME
by M F K Fisher, 1943

Taste lies at the heart of all good food. Every cook begins by thinking about what they feel like eating before they set to work in the kitchen. Our cravings are usually led by the memory of a particular taste: perhaps the bitter taste of early morning coffee or the savoury taste of a lunchtime toasted-cheese sandwich.

Yet, what is taste? The word has many different meanings, including flavour. In the interests of clarity within this book, I'm going to restrict the meaning to the five tastes; sweet, sour, bitter, salt and umami (savoury). These can only be detected in your mouth from water-soluble compounds. As soon as you place something in your mouth, your saliva begins to dissolve the food, releasing certain chemicals called 'tastants', which in turn stimulate your taste cells through the taste pores. These are located in the taste buds, which are situated on your tongue and soft palate.

Flavour, which I explore in the next chapter, is primarily detected from airborne compounds that are picked up by the olfactory cells in the roof of the nasal cavity. In other words, flavour relates to your sense of smell, not taste.

An easy way to distinguish between taste and flavour is to crush a fresh bay leaf between your fingers. Sniff deeply – it should smell herbal – the familiar flavour of a béchamel sauce. Now take a tiny bite and chew it – your mouth will be filled with a horrible bitter taste. It is the bay leaf's aroma that flavours the sauce, not the taste.

It is impossible to cook well without having a sound understanding of the five tastes; every dish we make is based upon the interplay between them. Imagine how excruciatingly dull it must be to eat a peach without being able to taste its sweet-sour juice or mildly bitter skin. Then consider how its taste changes and intensifies if sprinkled with sugar and mixed with sour-bitter redcurrants.

Carefully matched, each taste adds depth to another. Sourness, for example, introduces excitement and stimulates the appetite. Bitterness adds complexity and, when combined with sweetness, satiates the appetite. Sweetness induces a sense of pleasure, as does umami. The latter also enhances sweetness and increases salivation. Salt, used in moderation, stimulates the eater, but used in excess dulls the palate and the appetite. Overly strong or mismatched tastes are unappetizing, even repulsive – for example, bitter and sour with no moderating sweetness.

The texture and temperature of your food will also alter your perception of taste. Bite a raw stick of rhubarb dipped into sugar and you'll sense the intensely sweet crunchy sugar before the rhubarb's tart juice bursts out, whereas if you eat a spoonful of rhubarb jelly, its sweet and sour tastes flood your mouth at the same time. Tepid food has the most taste. Coldness reduces your sensitivity to sour and sweet but increases your perception of salt. I explore this in greater depth in the chapter on temperature (p.150).

No matter how long you've been cooking, it's worth consciously rediscovering taste. Start with everyday ingredients, such as bread or milk. Analyze what tastes you are sensing: bread is surprisingly sweet, but also salty. A sourdough will be mildly acidic.

If you find it difficult to distinguish between tastes and flavours, draw yourself back to the idea that tastes can only be sweet, sour, bitter, salty and umami. Thus, the Rhubarb and Rose Water Jelly (p.106) may have the flavour of roses, but it tastes sweet and sour.

Some people find it hard to initially differentiate between certain tastes, such as bitter and sour. However, if you give them a slice of sour lemon to suck and then get them to nibble the lemon's bitter skin, they will quickly learn the difference, albeit the hard way.

Other people, so called super-tasters, can be hyper-sensitive to the different tastes, in particular bitterness, which they can find repellent. This is because they have more taste buds in their mouths. Using bitterness as a test, it's been estimated that around 25 percent of the population are super-tasters and another 25–30 percent are 'non-tasters', or those who perceive minimal bitterness. The remaining 45–50 percent are in the middle.

Each category of taste can range from mild to strong; for example, acidity spans from mildly sour French butter to intensely sharp vinegar. Most ingredients have several tastes and you have to decide which to enhance and which to negate.

One of the fascinating aspects of cooking is that, although we are born with an innate recognition of the five different tastes, our perception of taste changes with time. Babies love sweet tastes because they signify energy-rich nutrients. As we grow our tastes change. Most small children hate bitter and sour foods because they are a natural warning of potentially harmful ingredients. However, as we age we develop a liking for both bitter and sour tastes, starting in childhood with chocolate and lemon squash.

Neither does our taste remain the same in adulthood – we can shape it by changing our exposure. For example, radically reduce your salt intake and you will become super-sensitive to the subtlest tastes. Tomatoes will taste surprisingly savoury and steamed rice very sweet. The same principle applies to sweetness.

In recent years, scientists have started to explore whether we possess other tastes. How do we respond to astringency in tannin-rich foods? Can we taste different metals? Work by Zoe Laughlin and Mark Miodownik implies that the more readily a metal oxidizes, the more likely it is to taste metallic when plated on to a spoon. At the moment, there is no evidence that these are technically tastes. Some metals appear to alter your perception of taste, making certain foods seem more bitter or sweeter. There has also been inconclusive research into whether we have a sixth taste for fatty acids coined 'oleogustus'. Since fatty acids are not water-soluble, most attribute our sensitivity to them to their physical texture, so I've included them in the chapter on texture (p.98).

Taste Notes

'The most experienced artists, cannot be sure of their work, without Tasting; they must be incessantly Tasting … that the least fault may be perceived in an instant.'

THE COOK'S ORACLE by Apicius, 1817

Cooking is often seen as an intuitive art, but in truth it is founded on practical knowledge. Recognizing both good and bad tastes within ingredients is essential, but it's equally important to learn how best to moderate and balance those tastes. To that end, I've written a simple guide to the five tastes below, before dividing the recipes into the common ways you can alter the taste of food. These recipes naturally fall into six categories: marinating, blending, layering, dressing, saucing and accompanying.

Sweet

If you consciously taste everything you consume, you will discover that sweetness is widespread, albeit in varying degrees from mild (oats and cream) to ultra-sweet (scallops, peas and honey). It occurs naturally in any calorific ingredient, including foods that are predominantly tart, bitter or umami, such as redcurrants, cabbage and Parmesan. The skill of the cook lies in recognizing its presence and utilizing it to best effect. Too much sweetness will kill your appetite, especially when combined with umami, bitterness or salt. In moderation, umami increases your perception of sweetness, but too much can make food taste cloying. Sourness has the opposite effect, by making sweet ingredients taste fresher. Curiously, the more sweetness we consume, the less sweetness we can taste. Cut back and you will discover myriad unsuspected tastes.

Taste test
Do you feel more or less hungry after eating a little bitter-sweet dark chocolate, compared to some sweet-sour orange segments at the end of a meal?

Sour

Sourness is an under-utilized taste. It stimulates our desire to eat, by making ingredients taste more exciting. It's found in all acidic foods, from yogurt, sorrel and cherries to tamarind and wine, but varies greatly in its intensity: vinegar and lime juice being at the opposite end of the scale to a mild crème fraîche or sourdough bread. Any extreme taste is unpalatable – so, in the case of primarily sour ingredients, it's necessary to either reduce their acidity by dilution (for example, olive oil dilutes vinegar in a vinaigrette), and/or negate it by sweetening (such as by adding sugar to a blackcurrant compote). Your perception of sourness can be increased by a hint of salt or bitterness. This is particularly delicious in starters and main courses. A subtle use of sourness can introduce lightness to a recipe and underline the other tastes.

Taste test
Try sweet ripe melon with and without a small squeeze of lime juice. Does the lime make it taste more intensely sweet and tempting?

Taste test
Eat a little sourdough bread with and without a drizzle of bitter extra-virgin olive oil. Which is more interesting?

Bitter

A taste for bitterness is acquired with age, and bitterness can be used to add an intriguing edge to dishes. It acts as a warning against eating substances that affect your bodily functions; caffeine, nicotine and strychnine, for example, are all bitter. If bitterness is the dominant taste of an ingredient, such as in tea, coffee and cocoa, it has to be diluted or sweetened in some way. Salting can extract the bitter juices from some ingredients, such as gourds and older varieties of aubergine (eggplant) and cucumber, while blanching in boiling water dilutes the bitter chemicals in foods such as watercress, spring greens (collards), cabbages and citrus pith. Conversely, you can intensify bitterness in food by drying ingredients such as orange zest. Bitterness will add a deeper, more complex taste to a dish, such as caramelized sugar syrup on sliced oranges. It also appears to lessen the appetite, especially when combined with sweetness.

Taste test
Try not adding extra salt to your food – for example, in the Greek Salad (p.210). You'll discover a whole new world of taste.

Salt

You can detect the tiniest amount of salt (sodium chloride) in food. In moderation, it will excite your appetite – imagine potato crisps with and without salt. There are naturally salty foods, such as oysters, mussels, clams, seaweed and samphire, but most are man-made. Originally, many were developed for preservation, for example: bacon, cheese, salted anchovies, miso paste and kimchee. As a result of this salted maturation, they also have a strong umami taste. A little bitterness and/or sourness highlights saltiness, but it can also increase sweetness, and sweetness can lessen your perception of salt. As over-salting is unpleasant, some salted ingredients need careful handling. Soaking, rinsing, blanching or dilution will reduce saltiness.

Taste test
Compare the taste of some lightly seasoned butter-dressed tagliatelle with and without some freshly grated umami-tasting Parmesan.

Umami

Although Kikunae Ikeda first recognized umami (*umai* is Japanese for delicious) as a distinct savoury taste, in Tokyo in 1907, it was not until 2000 that scientists began to prove that we had specialized umami taste receptors in our mouths. These are sensitive to foods that contain high levels of free glutamate (a common amino acid) and can be found in matured, cured, dried and fermented foods, such as Parma ham, dried shiitake mushrooms, kombu (dried kelp), fish sauce and smoked salmon. It is also present in many fresh foods, such as tomatoes, peas, asparagus and scallops. It has a distinctive, easily recognizable savoury taste that makes you salivate and want to eat more, perhaps because it heightens your sensitivity to salty and sweet tastes. It may also lessen your perception of sour and bitter tastes. It's important to use umami in moderation, as it can dominate more subtle tastes.

Marination

Marinades are primarily used to tenderize or preserve food, but they're also an interesting way to change the taste of an ingredient. They can be wet or dry and are usually variations of salt, sweet and sour ingredients. Salt and sugar are widely used, while acidic ingredients vary according to local culture, ranging from citrus juice and yogurt to wine and vinegar.

Any aged protein-rich foods, such as salted fish, beef and ham, will develop an umami taste with time.

Many salty seasonings – for example, naturally fermented soy sauce, miso paste and fish sauce – also taste strongly of umami, so it's important to use them cautiously in any marinade. Some, such as kombu (dried kelp) have such high levels of glutamates that they must be used very lightly to prevent them from overpowering an ingredient. Kombu contains some 2,240 mg per 100 g of glutamates, compared to 1,200 mg per 100 g in Parmesan cheese.

Few cooks want to create a bitter marinade, as it could imbue the primary ingredient with an unpleasant taste, but greater depth and interest can be added to a marinade by including bitter notes, such as cold-pressed oils, beer, citrus zest and bitters. Western marinades commonly use wine and olive oil to tenderize meat, for example, in Boeuf Bourguignon or venison casserole.

Lamb Shish Kebabs

Serves 4

Acidic ingredients are widely used in marinades to tenderize protein, but their sourness also cuts through the heavy umami taste of meat. Shish kebabs belong to an ancient school of cooking that spans Islamic cuisine – the meat is grilled over a barbecue and can be marinated for up to 12 hours in either a lemon juice or yogurt marinade. You can also eat these with Saffron Rice (p.218).

1 medium onion, roughly grated

2 lemons, juiced

6 tbsp extra-virgin olive oil

1 tsp ground cinnamon

1 tsp ground ginger

2 tsp ground cumin

900 g/2 lb lean lamb leg steak

1½ medium red onions, cut into 2-cm/¾-inch dice

salt and freshly ground black pepper

To serve

350 g/12 oz ripe tomatoes, diced

½ cucumber, peeled and diced

1 small red onion, diced

½ lemon, juiced

200 g/7 oz/1 scant cup natural Greek yogurt

3–4 tbsp cold water

4 large pitta breads or 8 Chapattis (p.142), warmed

In a medium-sized bowl, mix together the grated onion, lemon juice, 4 tbsp of the extra-virgin olive oil, cinnamon, ginger and cumin.

Remove any sinews and fat (the latter is optional) from the lamb, before cutting into 2-cm/¾-inch cubes. Mix into the marinade and season with some black pepper. Cover and chill for a minimum of 2 hours, and up to 12 hours.

Thread alternate pieces of meat and red onion onto 6 x 25-cm/10-inch flat-edged skewers and place on a plate.

Mix the diced tomatoes, cucumber and onion in a small bowl. Season with the lemon juice and some salt and freshly ground black pepper. Place the yogurt in a separate bowl, season with salt and thin with the cold water.

Ideally the lamb should be cooked over glowing white-hot charcoal, otherwise preheat a grill (broiler) to high.

Once hot, season the lamb with salt, coat with the remaining 2 tbsp olive oil and place on the barbecue or under the grill. Cook the lamb for 7–10 minutes, turning regularly, until the meat is golden brown on the outside and just pink inside, or cooked to your taste.

Slide the lamb from their skewers and divide between 4 plates. Place the salad, yogurt and warm pitta bread or chapattis on the table, and let everyone wrap their own mix in the warm bread.

Light dry salting transforms the salmon's taste

Salted Salmon with Tarragon Butter

Serves 6

Fish and meat in European cooking are traditionally salted to help preserve them – for example, smoked salmon or duck confit. In countries such as China and Japan, salting is also used to change the texture of food and, equally importantly, to remove fishy or meaty odours, partly by extracting blood and bitter juices.

Dry salting, such as here, is used for oily fish such as mackerel, herring and salmon. The longer any ingredient is salted, the more liquid is extracted and the saltier the ingredient will taste. The art is to allow just enough salt to develop the umami tastes, but not so much that all the tastes are submerged beneath the salt. The tarragon butter adds a tempting rich texture and depth of flavour.

6 x 175 g/6 oz salmon fillets with skin

3 tsp fine sea salt

2–3 tbsp extra-virgin olive oil

For the tarragon butter

1 tbsp finely chopped tarragon leaves

1 lemon, finely grated, plus 1 tsp juice

55 g/2 oz/scant 4 tbsp unsalted butter, softened

salt and freshly ground black pepper

Note

Compare the melted texture of this compound tarragon butter with the whisked tarragon butter emulsion on p.166.

Place a plate or tray large enough to hold the fish on the work surface. Evenly sprinkle the surface of the plate/tray with half the salt. Lay the fillets skin-side down on the plate/tray, then sprinkle the remaining salt over the fish. Chill for 40 minutes.

Make the tarragon butter by beating together the chopped tarragon, lemon zest and juice and butter in a small bowl. Very lightly season to taste, as the fish is already salty. Spoon the butter onto some greaseproof (wax) paper to roughly form a sausage shape – roll up the paper and gently roll it under your fingers until it forms a smooth cylinder. Chill until needed.

Preheat 2 non-stick frying pans (skillets) over a medium-high heat. Once hot, add 1–1½ tbsp olive oil to each pan, then add 3 salmon fillets, flesh-side down, to each pan. Fry briskly for 3 minutes, or until seared and golden, then turn and cook for 3–4 minutes, or until the skin is crisp and the salmon is just cooked through. Plate the salmon, topping each fillet with a round slice of tarragon butter. Serve immediately.

Grilled Sea Bass with Kombu

Serves 4

The Japanese have refined the art of infusing food with umami by briefly marinating food with kombu (dried kelp), *Laminaria longicruris*. Kombu is rich in glutamic acid, which imbues ingredients with an intense savoury, umami taste, which makes this fish taste deliciously sweet and moreish.

4 x 15-cm/6-inch dried kombu

1 tbsp sake

4 x 450 g/1 lb line-caught or farmed sea bass, filleted

2 tbsp extra-virgin olive oil

1 lemon, quartered

Place the dried kombu on a large plate and gently rub all over with the sake. Leave to soften for 10 minutes.

Cut 3 angled slashes into the skin of each sea bass fillet. Place a piece of softened kombu onto the flesh of the first fillet and sandwich the second fillet, flesh-side down, on top of the kombu. Repeat with the remaining fillets. Set aside for 20 minutes and no longer.

Preheat a cast-iron griddle pan over a medium-high heat for 5 minutes. Discard the kombu and gently rub the fish with the olive oil. It needs no further seasoning. Grill flesh-side down for 3–4 minutes, or until seared with golden marks, then flip over and cook for a further 3 minutes or until cooked through. Serve with the lemon quarters.

Note
Chemicals that have an umami taste include glutamate (found in kombu) and certain synergistic umami nucleotides, such as inosinate (found in bonito flakes). Interestingly, combinations of these different umami chemicals don't just add to each other, they amplify each other, for example in Dashi (p.72).

Sweet Orange Soy Duck

Serves 6

Sugar, like salt, was often added to salt marinades to help preserve food, such as with bacon or gravadlax, changing their texture and enhancing their umami taste in the process. This gorgeous marinade is also a good example of a complex-tasting marinade where bitter-sweet brown sugar is combined with salty-umami soy sauce and bitter sesame oil and citrus zest to create a tempting and satisfying dish.

This duck is gorgeous served chilled with the Sesame Soy Spinach (p.50) and a finely sliced sweet-sour cucumber salad made by lightly salting the 2 cucumbers, then seasoning with 4 tbsp caster (granulated) sugar and 6 tbsp rice wine vinegar.

85 g/3 oz/7 tbsp light brown muscovado sugar

55 g/2 oz/¼ cup coarse sea salt

2 tsp ground star anise

¾ tbsp finely chopped peeled fresh ginger

1 garlic clove, finely chopped

finely grated zest of 2 oranges

1 Thai chilli, finely chopped

3½ tbsp naturally brewed soy sauce

3½ tbsp toasted sesame oil

6 boneless duck breasts, each about 175 g/6 oz

Mix the sugar, salt, star anise, ginger, garlic, orange zest, chilli, soy sauce and sesame oil in a china dish.

Trim the duck breasts of sinews and score the skin into diamonds. Thoroughly coat the duck in the marinade, cover and place in the refrigerator. Marinate for about 18 hours, turning halfway through to ensure that the duck breasts are thoroughly coated in the marinade.

Preheat the oven to 200°C fan/220°C/425°F/gas mark 7.

Place the duck breasts skin-side down in a cold non-stick frying pan (skillet) and set over a medium heat. Cook for about 6 minutes, or until the skin turns golden brown and releases lots of fat. Turn over and fry for 30 seconds, then place in a non-stick roasting pan and roast in the hot oven for 15 minutes or until just pink.

Remove from the oven and set aside to cool, then chill, covered, until needed. To serve, finely slice and plate each breast, accompanied by the sesame spinach and cucumber salad.

Note

Sweet marinade ingredients, such as mirin, honey or sugar, can be used to introduce bitter-tasting caramelized flavours to the finished cooked dish, such as in the Sticky Asian Beef Kebabs (p.92).

Cardamom Jalebis

Makes 25 jalebis

- -

Sweet marinades are commonly used to create a sticky moist texture in a relatively dry or crisp sweet dish, such as a Sticky Spiced Lemon Gin Cake (p.75) or Turkish konafa. Such syrups can be sweet, or sweet and sour, or sweet and bitter. They are often flavoured with herbs, spices, flower waters and/or citrus zest.

Traditionally, in northern India, the jalebi batter is lightly fermented overnight to imbue it with a hint of sourness, before it's deep fried and macerated in a sugar syrup, which is sometimes flavoured with distilled rose water. This delicious modern version uses self-raising flour in place of the natural ferment – which results in a very light jalebi. This new method comes from the wonderful food writer Roopa Gulati, who – in true Indian style – was given it by her friend's mother.

You will need a squeezy bottle with a medium nozzle to make this dish.

For the syrup
400 g/14 oz/2 cups granulated
    sugar
½ tsp ground green cardamom
    seeds
1 tsp lemon juice

For the jalebis
corn oil, for deep frying
a large pinch of saffron threads
3 tbsp natural yogurt
250 g/9 oz/scant 2 cups
    self-raising flour
1 rounded tbsp gram (chickpea)
    flour
275 ml/10 fl oz/scant 1¼ cups
    cold water

Begin by making the syrup. Put the sugar and 500 ml/18 fl oz/2 cups and 2 tbsp water in a wide saucepan, set over a low heat and stir occasionally until the sugar has dissolved. Add the cardamom seeds and simmer for 3 minutes until you have a sticky syrup. Add the lemon juice and set aside.

Clip a jam thermometer onto the side of a wide, deep, heavy-based saucepan. Add a 5-cm/2-inch depth of oil to the pan. Don't try to cook these in a deep-fat fryer – they will stick to the basket. Place a wire cake rack over a drip tray and set a large plate by the sugar syrup.

Crumble the saffron into a small bowl. Add 1 tsp boiling water, stir until dissolved, then mix in the yogurt. Sift the self-raising flour into a mixing bowl and mix in the gram flour, followed by the saffron yogurt. Rinse the yogurt bowl with some of the cold water, tip into the flour and, using a wooden spoon, gradually stir in sufficient water to form a thick smooth batter – the consistency of drop scones. Spoon a test amount into a squeezy bottle with a medium nozzle. If the batter is too thin, you will need to beat a little more flour into the batter, if it is too thick, mix in some more water.

Heat the oil to 130–140°C/265–275°F. Once hot, squeeze a spiral ring into the oil – starting with the centre and spiralling out to the size of a small pineapple ring. Repeat until you have about 4 jalebis frying in your pan. They will sit on the bottom and then rise up in the fat. Fry for 3–4 minutes, flipping over halfway through. Don't let the oil get too hot. Once the jablebis are pale gold and crisp, remove to the cooling rack to drain for a few seconds.

Reheat the syrup so that it is warm. Take off the heat and add the jalebis. Turn to coat on each side and, once they've absorbed enough syrup, transfer to the clean plate. Continue until the batter is finished. They are best eaten on the day of making.

Combination

There is something magical about combining different tastes to create one bold exciting taste. It has to be sufficiently alluring to keep your interest, regardless of whether it is a refreshing glass of sweet-sour pear shrub or a wintery dish of umami-bitter-sweet cauliflower cheese soufflé.

An essential part of understanding how taste works lies in your awareness of how you sense taste as you eat. At a basic level, recipes can be divided into single-textured and multi-textured dishes. The taste remains constant throughout eating the former types of dishes, whereas each mouthful reveals a different combination of tastes in the latter types of recipes, such as in the Mango and Passion Fruit Salad (p.37).

As can be discovered in the chapter on texture (p.98) single-textured foods are surprisingly diverse, ranging from liquid and puréed items, such as drinks, soups, fools, ice creams and sorbets, to more airy concoctions, such as mousses, soufflés, breads and sponges. In reality, different tastes and textures may slip in – for example, the Cauliflower Cheese Soufflé (p.28) will turn golden on top, creating a slightly different-tasting caramelized crust.

Pear and Rosemary Shrub

Makes 700 ml/1¼ pints/3 cups

Shrubs divide imbibers – I find their vinegary back notes delicious, but my husband finds them too acidic. For me, they are a classic example of a refreshing sweet and sour drink. Drinks can be any combination of taste, ranging from bitter dry martinis and salty-sour lassis that pique the appetite, to bitter-sweet negronis that close the appetite.

400 g/14 oz quartered and cored ripe pears (prepared weight)

400 g/14 oz/2 cups granulated sugar

2 tsp fine sea salt

4 sprigs rosemary

300 ml/10 fl oz/1¼ cups cider or white wine vinegar

To serve
ice

sparkling mineral or soda water

Cut the pears into 1-cm/ ½-inch chunks and place in a china bowl or crock with the sugar and salt. Mix well and cover. Leave the mixture at room temperature for 3 days, stirring twice a day.

After 3 days, lightly bruise the rosemary sprigs and add to the pears, along with the vinegar. Mix well, cover and refrigerate for 2 weeks.

Strain the mixture into a jug (pitcher) and transfer it to a sterilized bottle (see below) that has a screw top lid or cork. It will keep chilled for up to 6 months, if you can resist drinking it.

To serve, place lots of ice in a highball glass, add 3 tbsp of the shrub and sparkling water to taste.

To sterilize jars, bottles and lids
Wash the jars or bottles in hot soapy water, rinse in very hot water, and then place in a cool oven to dry out, 130°C fan/150°C/300°F/gas mark 2. Place screw-top lids in a small pan of boiling water. Boil the lids for 10 minutes, remove and leave to dry on a clean cloth. Alternatively, wash jars or bottles and their lids in the dishwasher, then leave to dry with the dishwasher door partly open.

Note
Do the soda bubbles make this drink taste more exciting? Try some with still water and see how your perception of its taste and flavour changes.

Persian Sour Lentil Soup

Serves 6

Soups often taste umami and sweet, with a hint of salt, largely because many are made with umami stock and predominantly sweet, starchy or umami-tasting ingredients such as roots, pulses and legumes. This makes them both satisfying and filling. However, if you add a touch of sourness, such soups will become irresistible, as can be discovered with this popular Middle Eastern soup. It is slightly textured which adds further interest.

3 tbsp cold-pressed sunflower oil

1 large onion, finely diced

1 fat garlic clove, roughly chopped

2 celery stalks, finely diced

1 large carrot, peeled and finely diced

2 tsp ground cumin

2 tsp ground turmeric

340 g/12 oz/1⅔ cups yellow moong (mung) dal, washed

1.4 litres/48 fl oz/6 cups good-quality Chicken Stock (p.47)

up to 300 ml/10 fl oz/1¼ cups boiling water

freshly squeezed juice of 1 lemon, or to taste

a handful of parsley leaves, roughly chopped (optional)

salt and freshly ground black pepper

Set a large pan over a medium-low heat. Add the oil, followed by the diced onion, garlic, celery and carrot. Fry gently for 10 minutes, stirring occasionally, until the vegetables are soft. Mix in the cumin and turmeric, and cook for 2 minutes.

Check the lentils for any stones and wash thoroughly. Add to the softened vegetables, along with the chicken stock. Bring to the boil, then reduce the heat and simmer for 30 minutes, until the lentils are meltingly soft and disintegrating into a pulp.

Partially blend the soup so that it retains some of its texture. A hand-held stick blender is the easiest way to do this. Season to taste and add enough boiling water to thin the soup to taste. Reheat the soup when ready, add the lemon juice to taste and finish with parsley, if wished.

Sourness adds excitement to umami-rich soups

Cauliflower Cheese Soufflé

Serves 6 as a starter

It's become fashionable to serve bitter, umami-tasting starters and main dishes that satiate the eater. This is a delicious example. Note how the tastes develop as the soufflé cools. Blanching reduces the cauliflower's bitterness and the umami cheese sauce enhances its sweetness.

40 g/1½ oz/3 tbsp unsalted butter, plus extra for greasing

1½ tbsp freshly grated Parmesan, for dusting

1 small cauliflower, cut into florets

2 bay leaves

425 ml/15 fl oz/1¾ cups full-fat (whole) milk

40 g/1½ oz/generous ¼ cup plain (all-purpose) flour

70 g/2½ oz mature Cheddar cheese, finely grated

3 medium egg yolks

¼ tsp English mustard powder

a pinch of cayenne pepper

a large pinch of freshly grated nutmeg

4 medium egg whites

salt and freshly ground black pepper

Preheat the oven to 180°C fan/200°C/400°F/gas mark 6. Butter 6 x 250-ml/9-fl oz/1-cup soufflé dishes. Dust with Parmesan and set on a baking sheet.

Add the cauliflower florets and 1 bay leaf to a pan of unsalted boiling water. Cook briskly for 8 minutes, or until the cauliflower is tender. Drain, discard the bay leaf and measure out 225 g/8 oz cooked cauliflower. Pat dry with paper towels and crush into a granular mush with a potato masher.

Put the milk and second bay leaf in a small pan. Bring to the boil over a medium heat, then set aside. Melt the butter in a separate saucepan over a low heat. Using a wooden spoon, stir in the flour and cook for 2 minutes to make the roux. Remove the bay leaf from the milk and, bit by bit, add the hot milk to the roux, stirring all the time to make a smooth sauce. Simmer gently, stirring occasionally, for 5 minutes. Remove from the heat and mix in 55 g/2 oz/generous ½ cup of the grated Cheddar, followed by the mashed cauliflower.

Place the egg yolks in a large bowl and mix in the mustard powder, cayenne pepper, nutmeg, and salt and pepper to taste. Gradually beat the warm cauliflower mixture into the egg yolks.

Put the egg whites in a large, clean, dry bowl. Whisk until they form soft peaks. Using a flat metal spoon, fold a dollop of whisked egg white into the cauliflower sauce before gently folding in the remaining egg whites. Divide the mixture between the prepared soufflé dishes. If necessary, level their tops before sprinkling with the remaining Cheddar.

Place the baking sheet in the centre of the hot oven and bake for 15–20 minutes for a soft set soufflé and 20–25 minutes for a firm set.

Jasmine Tea Chocolate Truffles

Makes 32 truffles

Taste can be released in myriad ways. Here, the bitter-sweet taste of chocolate slowly melts in your mouth as you bite into a truffle, which in turn allows a greater release of airborne flavour compounds, including the subtle scent of jasmine tea.

2 tbsp loose-leaf jasmine tea

200 ml/7 fl oz/generous ¾ cup double (heavy) cream

300 g/10½ oz good-quality dark chocolate, such as Valrhona Caraibe

cocoa powder (unsweetened), for coating

Place the tea leaves and cream in a small saucepan. Set over a low heat and slowly bring to the boil. Turn off the heat, cover and leave to infuse for 20 minutes.

Find a large bowl that will fit snugly over a saucepan. Fill the pan one-third full with water that has just boiled, making sure it doesn't touch the base of the bowl. Finely chop the chocolate and place in the bowl. Leave the chocolate to melt.

Bring the cream back to the boil, then strain the mixture through a sieve into the melted chocolate, pressing as much cream as possible through the mesh. Stir until the chocolate has melted and the cream is incorporated.

Remove the bowl to a work surface and leave it to cool to room temperature. Then, beat the mixture with an electric whisk for 10 minutes. As you whisk, it will become thick, shiny and paler in colour. Leave to set for 1½–2 hours. If your kitchen is very warm, briefly chill in the refrigerator.

Set a small bowl of cocoa powder beside you and, working over a dinner plate, liberally dust your hands with cocoa powder. Take 1 tsp of the mixture and roll it into a truffle-sized ball between the palms of your hands. Once shaped, lightly roll the truffle in the bowl of cocoa powder until it is barely dusted, then place on a small clean plate. Recoat your hands in cocoa powder and repeat the process until you've finished the mixture. You'll need to wash and cool your hands regularly, to prevent them from becoming sticky.

Chill the truffles in the refrigerator for 1 hour, or until firm.

Note
Any truffle coating changes the mouth feel and taste slightly – compare with and without the bitter cocoa powder.

Layering

The majority of dishes that we eat contain different textures, from a morning bowl of muesli (p.199) to a late-night curry. From the cook's perspective, every new texture that is added to a recipe introduces a different layer of taste to the final dish, depending on how easy the different elements are to chew. This allows you to introduce spikes of complementary tastes into a single dish.

Some textures, for example, leathery ones, will slowly release their flavour, while others, such as liquids, will instantly hit you with their uniform taste. Thus, if you take a sip of miso soup (p.64) you will first taste the umami broth before detecting other subtle umami notes from the salty nori fragments or sweet tofu pieces. The same principle applies to other textured foods, such as beef stew (p.128). Initially it tastes of umami, but if you add carrots, you will get sweet bursts of interest. Create a more complex texture, such as by topping the stew with buttery puff pastry (p.126) and your mouth will be zinging with excitement.

Tomato and Courgette Risotto

Serves 4

The basis of any risotto is a soft-textured mixture of naturally sweet rice, umami-tasting stock and a hint of salt. The cook then layers different tastes by adding different ingredients, in this case a fusion of sweet, sour, umami-tasting tomatoes and acidic wine, highlighted by the chunks of mildly bitter, fried courgettes (zucchini).

5 tbsp extra-virgin olive oil

1 medium onion, finely diced

1 litre/35 fl oz/generous 4 cups good-quality Chicken Stock (p.47)

450 g/1 lb ripe tomatoes

350 g/12 oz/1¾ cups Carnaroli or Arborio rice

1 sprig rosemary

150 ml/5 fl oz/⅔ cup dry white wine

350 g/12 oz small courgettes (zucchini), trimmed

4 tbsp freshly grated Parmesan, plus extra for serving

salt and freshly ground black pepper

Note

Tomatoes contain all five tastes. They have high levels of umami, especially in the jelly-like pulp around their seeds, as cited by Michelin-starred chef Heston Blumenthal in his scientific paper with D.S. Mottram in 2007.

Set a wide saucepan over a medium-low heat. Add 3 tbsp of the olive oil and, once hot, add the diced onion and fry gently for 10 minutes, or until soft and golden. Pour the stock into a separate saucepan and bring up to simmering point.

Place the tomatoes in a bowl, cover with boiling water and lightly cut the skin of each tomato. After 2 minutes, drain and peel the tomatoes. Set a sieve over a small bowl. Quarter the tomatoes and place the seeds in the sieve. Strain the juice from the seeds into the bowl and discard the seeds. Roughly dice the tomato flesh and add to the juice.

Once the onion is soft, mix in the tomato flesh and juice and cook briskly for about 8 minutes, or until it forms a thick paste. Season to taste. Add the rice and rosemary sprig and keep stirring for 2 minutes, then mix in the wine.

Once the wine is absorbed, stir in a ladleful of hot stock. This should simmer briskly. Stir regularly, adding another ladleful of stock as each becomes absorbed. After 18–20 minutes the rice should be tender and cooked but still a little sloppy. Remove from the heat.

Cut the courgettes into pretty quarter-moon chunks. Set a non-stick frying pan (skillet) over a high heat. Add the remaining 2 tbsp olive oil and, once hot, add the courgettes. Stir-fry briskly for 1 minute, season to taste and mix into the rice, followed by the grated Parmesan. Season to taste and serve with a little extra Parmesan.

Onion, Bacon and Soured Cream Tart

Makes 6 slices

Any form of tart or pie creates another level of taste. In this recipe, the crumbling pastry melts in your mouth, releasing the creamy baked custard in different proportions with each bite. Within the custard, you can play with different tastes and textures, ranging from sweet sautéed onions to pieces of bitter-sweet asparagus. Here, the soured-cream custard makes the salty umami notes of chewy bacon and sweet caramelized onions taste intensely moreish.

For the shortcrust pastry

225 g/8 oz/1½ cup plain (all-purpose) flour, plus extra for dusting

115 g/4 oz/½ cup cold unsalted butter, diced

3 tbsp cold water

For the filling

200 g/7 oz smoked back bacon, trimmed of fat

3–4 tbsp extra-virgin olive oil

3 medium onions, finely diced

1 medium egg

1 medium egg yolk

200 ml/7 fl oz/generous ¾ cup soured cream

30 g/1 oz Comte cheese, roughly grated

salt and freshly ground black pepper

Note

Compare this recipe with one using 'sweet'-tasting double (heavy) cream. Another option is to replace the bacon with 250 g/ 9 oz sliced bitter-tasting asparagus (fried with the onions for 10 minutes).

To make the shortcrust pastry, place the flour, a pinch of salt and the butter in a food processor. Process in short bursts until the mixture forms fine crumbs. Tip the crumbs into a bowl and mix in 3 tbsp cold water with a fork or enough water to form a rough dough.

Lightly knead the dough and roll out the pastry on a lightly floured surface and use it to line a 20-cm/8-inch flan or quiche dish (tart pan). Prick the base of the pastry, line with baking parchment and fill with baking beans. Chill for 30 minutes.

Preheat the oven to 180°C fan/200°C/400°F/gas mark 6.

Bake the pastry case in the hot oven for 15 minutes, then remove the paper and beans and return to the oven for a further 5 minutes.

Meanwhile, cut the trimmed bacon into medium-sized dice. Place a non-stick frying pan (skillet) over a medium heat. Add the oil and, once hot, add the diced bacon and fry briskly until lightly coloured. Reduce the heat to medium-low, mix in the onions and continue to fry for 15 minutes, or until the onions are soft and golden. Season lightly and spoon into the pastry case.

Beat together the egg, egg yolk and soured cream. Season and pour into the pastry case, mixing it with a fork into the onion/bacon mixture. Sprinkle with the cheese and bake for 25 minutes, or until golden and set.

Serve the tart warm or cold.

Combining different textures increases your perception of taste

Miso Caramel Cake

Serves 12

It is becoming increasingly fashionable to introduce umami and salty elements to bitter-sweet dishes. Here, sweet sponge acts as a foil to the luscious bitter-sweet caramel icing (frosting) – which slowly reveals its salty umami notes.

This recipe makes a little extra miso caramel sauce – but it's so good, you'll find yourself spooning it over pancakes, and vanilla ice cream with sliced bananas!

For the miso caramel sauce

250 g/9 oz/1¼ cups caster (granulated) sugar

4 tbsp cold water

2 tbsp golden syrup

150 ml/5 fl oz/⅔ cup double (heavy) cream

70 g/2½ oz/5 tbsp unsalted butter, diced

1 tsp lemon juice

4 tbsp shiro white miso paste

For the sponge

1 tsp cold-pressed sunflower oil, for greasing

225 g/8 oz/1 cup unsalted butter, softened

225 g/8 oz/1 generous cup caster (granulated) sugar

¼ tsp vanilla extract

4 medium eggs

225 g/8 oz/1¾ cups self-raising flour, sifted

For the miso caramel icing

250 g/9 oz/1 cup miso caramel sauce (see left)

280 g/10 oz/1 cup plus 4 tbsp unsalted butter, softened

70g/2½ oz/¾ cup icing (confectioners') sugar, sifted

Begin with the miso caramel sauce. Put the sugar, water and golden syrup into a medium heavy-based saucepan and set over a low heat. Don't stir – just give it a swirl now and then. Once the sugar has melted you can increase the heat to medium and boil vigorously until the syrup turns golden brown. Keep swirling and allow it to darken to a rich dark brown. As soon as it darkens and starts to smoke, remove from the heat and whisk in the cream, followed by the diced butter and lemon juice. Pour into a bowl and leave until tepid, then beat in the miso paste – don't worry if this seems a little salty, it will be diluted in the icing. Set aside.

Preheat the oven to 160°C fan/180°C/350°F/gas mark 4. Lightly oil 2 x 20-cm/8-inch sandwich cake pans and line the base of each with baking parchment.

Continued on p.36

Layering sweet tastes with complementary sweet umami salty notes

To make the sponge, beat the softened butter and sugar together in a large bowl, using a wooden spoon or electric whisk, until pale and fluffy. Add the vanilla extract, followed by one egg at a time, beating them in well. If the mixture starts to curdle, beat in 2 tbsp of the flour. Once all the eggs have been beaten or whisked into the mixture, gently fold in the remaining flour in 3 batches with a flat metal spoon. Divide the mixture between the 2 cake pans and smooth level before placing in the oven.

Bake for 25 minutes or until the cakes are well risen, golden brown and spring back when lightly pressed with a fingertip.

Place on a wire rack to cool for 5 minutes. Then, using a knife, gently loosen the sides of each cake from its pan. Turn out, peel off the baking paper, and leave to cool.

You need an electric beater to make the icing. Place 250 g/9 oz/1 cup miso caramel sauce with the softened butter in a bowl and beat until fluffy. Set the beater at a low speed and add the icing sugar.

Once the sponge cakes are cold, spread some of the butter icing on one of the cakes. Sandwich the other cake on top, baked-side up. Spread more butter icing on the top before gently packing and spreading the remaining icing round the sides of the cake. Chill for 1 hour to set the buttercream.

Mango and Passion Fruit Salad

Serves 4

This addictive pudding is an example of how you can pique the appetite by layering a restricted number of tastes. Here, the shape, size and texture of each ingredient will influence your perception of the different sweet and sour tastes within the dish.

Those of an experimental bent can make two versions of this pudding. A simpler version is made solely with 4 passion fruit and 5 mangos. The acidity of the passion fruit enhances the sweet-tasting mango. The version below adds further layers of sweet-sour fruit, thereby increasing the complexity of both texture and taste.

2 large passion fruit

2 ripe mangos

400 g/14 oz/3½ cups small strawberries, hulled and halved

225 g/8 oz/2 scant cups raspberries

15 g/½ oz/4 tsp caster (granulated) sugar, or to taste (optional)

Halve the passion fruit and scrape the seeds into a large mixing bowl. Peel the mangos and cut the flesh away from each mango's stone, so that you have four segments. Slice each segment into evenly sized chunks about the same size as the raspberries.

Mix into the passion fruit with the strawberries and raspberries. Taste the mixture – it should be sweet enough, but if not, mix in some caster sugar to taste. Serve at room temperature.

Note
Try adding bitter notes to a sweet-sour fruit salad, for example, add bitter, sweet-sour pomegranate seeds to sweet-sour orange slices.

Dressing

An exciting way to uniformly alter the taste of a dish is to coat all the ingredients in a dressing, such as for a salad or a bowl of noodles. A dressing can be as simple as a bitter olive oil mixed into a salad of juicy camone tomatoes, or lime juice tossed into a sweet melon salad.

Consider the predominant taste or tastes of your salad ingredients and then which tastes would work best with them and what you want your eaters to experience. A salty, umami, sour and sweet Thai dressing based on fish sauce, lime juice, sugar and chilli (p.136), for example, wakes up the palate and works well with bitter, umami and sweet ingredients alike; whereas a creamy bitter, mildly acidic mayonnaise (p.44) induces a feeling of contented repletion and tastes best with salty, umami and sweet foods. You can test this out by mixing together some shredded green cabbage, carrots, celery and spring onions (scallions), and then dressing half the salad in the Thai dressing and half in the mayonnaise.

Coating is usually achieved either by some form of fat emulsion, as in oil, egg yolks, cream, yogurt or coconut cream, or by a sweet stickiness, such as honey, sugar or mirin. I have given some very simple examples here, but you'll find more in the index under 'dressings'.

Mustard Vinaigrette with Mixed Salad Greens

Serves 2

This is my favourite vinaigrette recipe – a classic bitter-tart emulsion with just a hint of sweetness to temper the bitterness of the mustard. It tastes best with bitter ingredients, such as salad leaves, chicory (endive), asparagus and avocado.

For the dressing

½ small shallot, finely chopped

¾ tsp smooth Dijon mustard

¼ tsp caster (granulated) sugar

1 tbsp white wine vinegar

1 tbsp extra-virgin olive oil

1 tbsp cold-pressed sunflower oil

salt and freshly ground black pepper

For the salad

1 plump cos (romaine) lettuce

55 g/2 oz mixed bitter salad leaves, such as mustard leaves and rocket (arugula)

1 ripe avocado (optional)

Place the diced shallot, mustard, caster sugar and seasoning to taste in a salad bowl. Using the back of a spoon, blend together, then whisk in the vinegar, followed by the two oils. Adjust the seasoning to taste.

Wash and dry the salad leaves. Rip or slice the cos lettuce and place in the salad bowl with the mixed leaves. If adding the avocado, quarter, stone and peel before cutting into easy-to-eat slices. Add to the salad and toss thoroughly. Check the seasoning and serve immediately.

Oriental Dressing for Chilled Noodles
with Prawns

Serves 2

- -

There are myriad different types of dressing for both noodles and pasta. This is a Westernized version of a Japanese dressing that combines umami, salt and sweetness to create an utterly delicious summer dish.

For the dressing

2 tbsp sake

2 tbsp naturally brewed soy sauce

2 tbsp mirin

1 tsp wasabi paste

6 spring onions (scallions), trimmed and finely sliced into rings

For the noodles

200 g/7 oz semi-wholewheat udon noodles

200 g/7 oz peeled raw king prawns (jumbo shrimp)

2 tbsp cold-pressed sunflower oil

½ lime, juiced

1 ripe avocado, quartered, stoned and peeled

shichimi (seven spice mixture), to taste (optional)

Put the sake, soy sauce and mirin in a small saucepan. Set over a low heat and slowly bring up to a simmer, then cook gently for 2 minutes. Chill the pan in a bowl of iced water while you prepare the other ingredients.

Bring a large pan of unsalted water to the boil and gradually add the noodles, taking care that the water never stops boiling. Stir occasionally and cook according to the packet instructions until al dente. This is usually 5–7 minutes. Tip into a colander and rinse thoroughly, before tipping into a bowl of iced water. Swirl around to chill thoroughly and drain.

Make a small incision down the length of the back of each prawn and remove the dark digestive thread. Rinse clean and pat dry.

Set a non-stick frying pan (skillet) over a high heat. Add the sunflower oil and, once hot, fry the prawns, turning regularly, for 3 minutes or until pink and cooked through. Tip into a colander and rinse the fat off under cold running water. Pat dry with paper towels, place in a bowl and season with the lime juice.

When you are ready to serve, whisk the wasabi paste into the cooled dressing, followed by the finely sliced spring onions. Mix in the noodles. Slice each avocado quarter into triangles (rather than lengthwise) and gently toss through the dressed noodles before dividing them between two bowls. Slip the prawns in amongst the noodles and, if you like a little spice, sprinkle each bowl with some shichimi before serving immediately.

Dressings uniformly season your chosen ingredients with their taste

Lavender Lemon Syrup for Nectarine Salad

Serves 4

Sweet dressings work well with all fruits. They are also a useful way to carry flavour (smell), which in turn helps the cook convey seasonality from dreamy flower-filled summer days to spice-scented winter nights. I often make this recipe with peaches, but it's also good with apricots and cherries.

100 g/3½ oz/½ cup granulated sugar

5 sprigs lavender flowers

1 lemon, finely pared and juiced

10 ripe nectarines or peaches

Place the sugar, 150 ml/5 fl oz/⅔ cup water, lavender sprigs and lemon rind in a small non-corrosive saucepan. Dissolve the sugar over a low heat, then simmer for 10 minutes. Remove from the heat and add the lemon juice.

I love the subtle bitter notes from nectarine (or peach) skin, but if you don't like the texture, you can peel the fruit before you begin. Quarter and stone the peaches before cutting into segments.

If wished, strain the warm syrup over the fruit. Serve at room temperature or chilled.

Saucing

Whereas dressings uniformly coat ingredients, saucing is dependent on the eater dipping their food into the sauce. In other words, each bite will vary in taste, depending on how and what is dunked into the accompanying sauce. This allows the cook to serve a punchy sauce with a dominant taste that will enhance the other element – for example, a piquant Béarnaise sauce makes poached salmon taste sweeter, just as bananas taste sweetly alluring when dipped into a vanilla custard. You can adapt the Basil Custard (p.174) by replacing the basil leaves with 1 split vanilla pod to test this. The tarragon butter sauce (p.166) meanwhile will work in place of a Béarnaise sauce.

As you might expect, sauces can be dominated by any one of the five tastes. I have chosen three classic examples to illustrate the point here, but obviously you could write an entire book on sauces and dips.

Mayonnaise

Serves 6

A simple way to add a subtle bitter note with a hint of acidity to certain dishes is to accompany them with mayonnaise, made partly with some extra-virgin olive oil – add too much and the mayonnaise can taste overly bitter. This recipe tastes particularly good with cold roast chicken, salmon, prawns (shrimp) and new potatoes. See also The Most Delicious Chicken Sandwich (p. 177).

2 medium egg yolks

1 tsp English mustard powder

1 tbsp lemon juice

2 tbsp white wine vinegar

200 ml/7 fl oz/generous ¾ cup groundnut (peanut) oil

100 ml/3½ fl oz/7 tbsp extra-virgin olive oil

salt and freshly ground black pepper

Place the egg yolks, mustard powder, lemon juice, vinegar, and salt and pepper to taste in a small food processor. Process until the egg yolks are pale, then slowly add the groundnut oil, a few drops at a time. As the mixture emulsifies, increase the flow of groundnut oil to a trickle. Once it has finished, continue with the olive oil until it is finished and you have a thick mayonnaise. Season to taste and transfer to a bowl. Cover and chill until needed.

Tomato Ketchup

Makes 620 g/1lb 6 oz/2½ cups minimum

Tomato ketchup is the perfect example of how a sauce can act as a taste stimulant to other foods, as it contains all five tastes with high levels of umami, sweetness and sourness. If you don't believe me, try eating British Chips (p.164) with and without this ketchup.

The only problem with home-made ketchup is that it's impossible to go back to store-bought. Luckily, this recipe will keep unopened for up to a year. Once opened, store in the refrigerator. The amount this recipe makes varies according to how much fibre and water your tomatoes contain.

3 kg/6 lb 8 oz ripe tomatoes

1½ tsp celery salt

200 g/7 oz/1¾ cups onions, diced

1 outer stick celery, diced

2 garlic cloves, roughly diced

1 bay leaf

1 tsp ground mace

10 g/⅓ oz/1 heaped tbsp black peppercorns

15 g/½ oz/2 tbsp peeled fresh ginger, crushed

3 cloves

5 g/¼ oz/1½ tsp allspice berries

1 dried Ancho chilli, about 10 g/⅓ oz (optional)

200 g/7 oz/1 cup granulated sugar

250 ml/9 fl oz/1 cup white wine vinegar

Slice the tomatoes thickly and, as you slice, place them in a large mixing bowl, sprinkling each layer with a little celery salt. Cover and leave for 12 hours or overnight.

Tip the mixture along with all the liquid into a large non-corrosive saucepan. Add the onions, celery, garlic and bay leaf. Place the spices and whole dried Ancho chilli on a square of muslin (cheesecloth), tie them up into a bundle and tuck into the tomatoes. Cover the pan and bring to the boil, then uncover and simmer over a medium-low heat for at least 3½ hours or until the mixture forms a thick mush and has a good tomato flavour. Remove the spice bag to a plate to cool. Discard the bay leaf.

Push the cooked tomatoes through a sieve into a large clean non-corrosive saucepan. Add the sugar and vinegar and set over a high heat. Stir occasionally with a wooden spoon until the sugar is dissolved, then bring up to a gentle boil, half cover and leave to reduce for 30 minutes–1 hour. You will need to stir regularly towards the end to prevent it from catching, but be careful – it spits! As soon as it becomes thick and jammy it's ready

Sterilize your jars and lids (see p.25).

Using a clean jam (canning) funnel, pour the hot ketchup into the warm jars or bottles, so that it comes up to just under 2.5 cm/1 inch from the top. Seal with the lids, label and store in a cool dark cupboard.

Chicken Jus

Serves 4

This is really chicken gravy, but as Dan Jurafsky points out in his entertaining book *The Language of Food*, the insertion of foreign words on a menu conveys refinement to the aspirational eater as they are mainly found on menus in expensive restaurants. Whatever you choose to call this sauce, it acts as an umami-enhancer to other dishes, as it is made from a reduction of roasted chicken stock with a hint of acidity from the white wine. The emulsion of butter enables the sauce to coat both the accompanying food and the inside of your mouth.

1 litre/35 fl oz/generous 4 cups good-quality Chicken Stock (see opposite)

200 ml/7 fl oz/generous ¾ cup dry white wine

55 g/2 oz/3½ tbsp cold unsalted butter, diced

fine sea salt

Remove any fat that has set on top of your stock. Pour the stock into a saucepan and boil vigorously until it has reduced by four fifths (you need about 200 ml/7 fl oz/generous ¾ cup). Add the wine and continue to boil until it has reduced again to about 200 ml/7 fl oz/generous ¾ cup or until it has a rich, intense taste. This will take 30–50 minutes, depending on the width of your saucepan. You can prepare this stage in advance and chill the reduction until needed.

The sauce must be finished at the last moment as the butter will split if you return it to the boil. If you're nervous, you can finish it and keep it warm in a thermos flask. Otherwise, when you are ready to serve, bring the reduced liquid to simmering point, reduce the heat to very low and gradually whisk small cubes of chilled butter into the hot but not bubbling liquid. Taste and add salt if necessary.

Chicken Stock

Makes 2.5 litres/4½ pints/11 cups

As every cook knows, a good stock is essential to creating good food. This is because all stocks, including vegetable stocks, imbue dishes with umami. The level of umami depends on the type of stock you make, browned bones, for example, produce a stronger, sweeter umami taste.

Chinese and Thai chefs blanch their stock bones at least once by bringing them up to the boil in cold water, before draining and starting afresh in cold water with few vegetables and flavourings. This removes any bitter blood tastes and potentially any rank meat flavours. The resulting broth has a lighter umami taste than this recipe.

1.3 kg/3 lb good-quality chicken

3 tbsp cold-pressed sunflower oil

2 onions, peeled and halved

2 garlic cloves, peeled

½ celeriac, peeled and cut into large chunks

3 large carrots, peeled

3 outer sticks celery

2 leeks, trimmed and washed, white and light green part only

1 bay leaf

a few parsley stalks

3 black peppercorns

You need a large (about 7 litre/12¼ pint/8 quart) stainless-steel saucepan (stockpan) for this recipe.

Remove the legs from the chicken and cut each leg in half at the joint. Remove the breasts. Remove the wings from the breasts and cut the wings in half at the joint. The breasts can be refrigerated or frozen for another recipe. Slice off and discard the parson's nose from the carcass. Cut the carcass in half by going in under the ribs and snapping the spine in two.

Set your saucepan over a medium-high heat. Add the oil and, once hot, start adding the chicken pieces. Fry until they are golden brown.

Continue by adding the onions, garlic and celeriac. Cut each carrot, celery and leek into 3 or 4 pieces. Add each vegetable as you go, stirring them into the browned chicken. Colour lightly, then add cold water to the top of the saucepan.

Turn the heat to high and skim off the melted fat as it floats up to the surface. As the water heats up, more and more fat will appear along with some scum. Skim regularly, until the stock comes up to the boil. This will take between 10–20 minutes.

As soon as it starts to boil, reduce the heat to a trembling simmer and add the bay leaf, parsley and peppercorns.

Simmer gently for 3 hours, or until it tastes good. If the liquid boils briskly, it will turn cloudy.

Strain the stock through a fine sieve into a large bowl. Ladle it into clean containers suitable for the freezer. Once cool, cover and chill in the refrigerator, before freezing.

Accompanying

It is a peculiar fact that many cooks pay little attention to how the taste of an accompaniment will alter their perception of the other dishes. Bread is a good example. Plain White Bread (p.52), which is naturally sweet with just a hint of salt, will introduce a delicate sweet foil to any food, from an intense sweet-sour-umami tomato soup to an umami-salty Smoked Salmon Pâté (p.182). However, the salty bitterness found in an olive focaccia will make the same soup taste twice as exciting but make the pâté taste odd.

Thus, it is worth analyzing the taste of each primary dish in a meal before planning your accompaniments. Remember that complicated combinations are not necessarily better. Consider how the taste of Turkish coffee is transformed from delicious to sublime by the simple act of eating a sticky date as an after-dinner accompaniment.

It's also worth noting that our sensitivity to any taste is reduced over a period of exposure. In other words, if you eat a sweet-umami starter, for example, squash and Parmesan soup, followed by a sweet-umami main course, such as roast lamb, gravy, peas and potatoes, and finish with the Miso Caramel Cake (p.34) your enjoyment of the bitter-sweet-umami cake would be less than if you had had more varied tastes throughout the meal.

Sorrel Salad

Serves 4

Certain recipes, such as fried fish or grilled veal, benefit from a tart side dish to cut their richness and enhance their natural sweetness. Sorrel salad makes a perfect tart accompaniment during the spring and summer months.

a generous handful of young sorrel leaves

3 soft round lettuces

3 sprigs tarragon, roughly chopped

½ bunch chives, snipped

1 tbsp white wine vinegar

3 tbsp extra-virgin olive oil

salt and freshly ground black pepper

Wash and dry the sorrel leaves. Strip away their stems by folding each leaf together (glossy side in) and pulling the stem down towards its tip and then away from the leaf, so that you are left with two pieces of stalkless leaf. Rip these into slightly smaller pieces and place in your salad bowl.

Twist out the hearts of the lettuces – the outer leaves can be used for soup. Separate the heart leaves before washing and drying them. Mix them into the sorrel leaves, then mix in the tarragon and snipped chives.

In a small bowl, whisk together the vinegar with the olive oil. Season to taste. Once you are ready to serve, pour the dressing over the salad leaves and lightly toss before serving.

Sesame Soy Spinach

Serves 4

Bitter side dishes are an acquired taste. To my mind, vegetables such as spinach and all forms of brassicas taste lovely with lamb, beef, duck, chicken and white fish. However, some people are highly sensitive to bitter tastes and don't enjoy the complex play of taste between salty, savoury and bitter, so the bitterness in this salad is reduced by blanching, and moderated by the dressing.

800 g/1 lb 2 oz baby leaf spinach

2 tbsp white sesame seeds

1 plump garlic clove

2 tbsp naturally brewed soy sauce

2 tbsp mirin

2 tbsp toasted sesame oil

Wash your spinach leaves in cold water. Drain and, if the leaves are large as opposed to tender baby spinach, strip away their stems by folding together each spinach leaf and pulling the stem down towards its tip and away from the leaf, so that you're left with two pieces of stalkless leaf.

Bring a large pan of water to the boil, add half the spinach and cook for 30 seconds. Then, as soon as the spinach has wilted, transfer the spinach to a colander in the sink and cool under cold running water. Return the saucepan of water to the boil, add the remaining spinach and repeat the process.

Take a handful of blanched spinach leaves at a time, and squeeze out as much water as you can, then roughly reshape the leaves. Set aside until needed.

Dry roast the sesame seeds in a small frying pan (skillet) over a low heat. Keep moving them around the pan until they turn pale gold and release a nutty aroma. Tip into a mortar, add the garlic and roughly grind for 1 minute to release the flavour from the seeds. Scrape into a mixing bowl and stir in the soy sauce, mirin and sesame oil.

Mix the spinach into the dressing and serve within an hour of making, either at room temperature or chilled. Try serving this with the Sweet Orange Soy Duck (p.21) or the Honey Chilli Chicken in Lettuce Leaves (p.214).

Side dishes can introduce tastes that contrast with other dishes

Plain White Bread x 2

Makes a 900 g/2 lb loaf

These two variations of a recipe are adapted from Andrew Whitley's wonderful book *Bread Matters* – a must-read for all keen bakers. The first version makes a sweet white bread, while the second introduces subtle sour notes. Both loaves make fantastic toast.

1 tsp active dried yeast

425 ml/15 fl oz/1¾ cups tepid water

600 g/1 lb 5 oz/4¼ cups strong white stone-ground flour (bread flour), plus extra for dusting

1 tsp fine sea salt

1 tsp cold-pressed sunflower oil, for greasing

Note
Bread books often use different types of yeast, so here is Andrew Whitley's very useful metric yeast ratio: 10 g fresh yeast = 5 g traditional active dried yeast = 3 g fast-action yeast.

For the first version: Place the yeast in a small bowl and add about 150 ml/5 fl oz/⅔ cup of the measured tepid water. Stir slightly and set aside for a few minutes until the yeasty water starts to froth and bubble slightly. If it doesn't, the yeast is dead and not worth using.

Place the flour and salt in a large bowl and mix together. Add the remaining water and the frothy liquid yeast and, using your hands, mix together into a sticky dough. Scrape the mixture onto a dry clean work surface and knead for 10–15 minutes until smooth and elastic. Return to a clean bowl and invert a larger bowl on top to form a draft-free dome. Set aside – the dough needs to double in size, which will take about 2 hours.

Take 170 g/6 oz of the risen dough and place in a small covered bowl in the refrigerator for 24 hours (this will be used for the second version of the loaf).

Oil a 900 g/2 lb bread tin (loaf pan). Lightly flour your work surface and dust your hands with flour. Turn the remaining dough out and shape into a sausage twice as long as the longest side of the bread tin. Using your knuckles, flatten the sausage and fold it in three. Flatten once again to form a rectangle about two-thirds the length of the tin. Starting at the edge furthest from you, fold it over and roll it up firmly but not so tightly it tears. Place the roll in the tin – seam-side down so that it lies along the bottom of the tin. It should only partly fill the tin. Cover the tin with the large bowl again and leave to rise for 30 minutes. It's ready when it has risen by half and the dough springs back when lightly pressed.

Meanwhile, preheat the oven to 200°C fan/ 220°C/425°F/gas mark 7.

Bake the loaf for 10 minutes, then turn the heat down to 180°C fan/200°C/400°F/gas mark 6 and bake for a further 20-30 minutes. It is cooked when golden and crusty all over. If it looks pale underneath – return to the oven and cook for another 5 minutes or so. Otherwise, place on a wire rack until cold.

For the second version: The next day, measure out 350 ml/12 fl oz/1½ cups tepid water, add about 150 ml/5 fl oz/⅔ cup to 1 tsp dried active yeast and, once the yeast has dissolved, mix it into 500 g/1 lb 2 oz/generous 3½ cups strong white flour (bread flour) mixed with 1 tsp salt. Turn out and knead for 5 minutes, then add the 170 g/6 oz reserved dough and continue to knead for 10 minutes before following the recipe from the first rising stage, as before.

Flavour

Flavour Recipes

Anticipation
the scent of food shapes expectation

Infusion
the simplest way to extract flavour

Blending
every time you cook, you blend flavours

Transformation
changing flavour through temperature

Final additions
add ephemeral notes at the end

Flavour

'His heart astir he pushed in the door of the Burton restaurant. Stink gripped his trembling breath: pungent meatjuice, slop of greens. See the animals feed.'

ULYSSES by James Joyce, 1922

In cooking, one man's bad is another man's good. James Joyce goes on to describe in Ulysses how 'the animals', or rather the men that Leopold Bloom sees in the restaurant, are 'scoffing up stew-gravy with sopping sippets of bread', ramming down cabbage and almost licking their plates in a repulsive maelstrom of greed. Bloom smells the food, senses its flavour and has a visceral reaction. Flavour links us closely to our emotions via our memories of different smells.

Every cook needs to understand what makes something bad as well as good. Crucially, you need to trust in your own senses; just because someone says something is good, doesn't make it so. Currently, there is a fashion for combining unlikely flavours in recipes. It stems from the latest theories of food pairing, where flavours as incongruous as coffee and asparagus are matched together in the belief that because they share certain chemical flavour components, they must taste good together. This is not always the case.

Flavour is not the easiest word to define. It's often mistaken for taste – but, as discussed in the previous chapter, the act of tasting is limited to your sensitivity to water-soluble compounds that are sweet, salty, sour, bitter and umami.

Flavour relates to your sense of smell and is restricted to your sensitivity to airborne compounds that are released from your food during eating. These airborne compounds are detected by the olfactory receptor cells in the roof of your nasal cavity.

As Gordon Shepherd explains in his book *Neurogastronomy* (2012), we sense flavour in our mouths 'not by sniffing in, which we usually associate with smelling something like an aroma, but by breathing out, when we send little puffs of smell from our food and drink out the back of our mouths and backward up through our nasal passages as we chew and swallow.' And just as everything we eat contains different tastes, so everything we consume has myriad flavours.

This simple meaning is often lost in the food world, where it has become popular to regard flavour as a mixture of smell, taste, texture, memory and emotion. It's true that these all influence your perception of flavour, but as a cook it's important to start with the basics.

Naturally, the texture of the food will affect how these airborne compounds are released. A chewy toffee will continue to release its buttery caramel notes every time you exhale. However, were you to eat a bag of toffees, you would find that your enjoyment of their honeyed notes waned with familiarity. This is because repeated stimulation leads to a desensitization of a smell. Conversely, this means that you are highly sensitive to any new flavour that is introduced during the course of eating, especially if it's unfamiliar. This is one of the reasons why the Eastern tradition of serving a succession of small dishes is far more appetizing than eating a single large plate of food.

Unlike taste, you are not born with an innate recognition of smells. Instead you have to learn them through experience. We instinctively sniff an unfamiliar food. If it smells bad, we may refuse to eat it. Durian fruit is a classic example – it's said to smell of stale vomit, but if aversion is overcome eaters claim that it has a strangely addictive flavour, reminiscent of cream cheese, onion sauce and brown sherry.

Over time, you build up layer upon layer of experiences around each odour. These are linked directly to an area in the brain that handles emotion and memory. Thus, if you love chocolate, you will feel good whenever you catch a whiff of melted chocolate. The opposite happens with bad associations. I still cannot abide the reek of spam, as I was forced to eat spam fritters at school; as a result I cannot stomach any similarly flavoured food, such as mortadella. In other words, the discernment of flavour is highly subjective and emotional.

The pervasive smells of your environment also influence how you flavour your food. In rural north India, for example, the evening air is fragrant with sizzling ghee, spices and the aromatic smoke from dried cow-dung fires. Local dishes, such as rice and dal, are infused with smoky flavourings, such as tar-like black cardamoms and heavy-scented cloves, which resonate with the smell of everyday life. The same is true everywhere. Thus, the scent of sea spray, heather, rain and peat smoke in the Outer Hebrides can be discovered in the local Islay malt whisky, hot-smoked salmon, oatcakes and tea-soaked fruit cake.

You can transform how you cook by developing your sensitivity to flavour in food, in much the same way as wine enthusiasts learn to categorize different fragrances in their drink. Since there are literally thousands of different flavours, begin by dividing them into broad groups. As you start to categorize, you'll find that almost every ingredient has a complex range of flavours, each of which can lead you into other flavour categories.

It helps to start with familiar foods. Begin by identifying their different aromas and highlight their dominant notes. This enables you to draw out the best aspect of any ingredient. An apple, for instance, has a predominantly fresh fruity flavour, but it can also contain floral, spicy, sappy, nutty or herbal tones. In other words, depending on the type of recipe you want to make, rose water could be added to highlight its floral nature, or sorrel its verdant flavour.

Flavour can also be used to counteract any negative notes in a dish – for example, Chinese cooks use ginger and spring onions (scallions) to suppress rank odours in meat and fish recipes.

Finally, it's important to consider the flavour structure of your recipe. In perfumery, scents are designed to have top, middle (heart) and bottom notes. The top notes are fresh and light and quickly fade. The heart notes form the body or structure of the fragrance, and the bottom notes are heavy and linger after the others have vanished. In other words, when creating a dish, look to first impressions, and then try to devise the release of exquisite middle notes as the food is eaten, before ensuring that the final lingering flavours are delicious. You don't want sulphurous garlic or metallic sweet pepper flavour repeating on someone hours later.

Flavour Notes

'The secret of cooking is the release of fragrance and the art of imparting it.'

HONEY FROM A WEED
by Patience Gray, 1986

Since it's impossible to categorize the thousands of different flavours that exist in this short space, I've outlined a series of flavour groups, which I've found helpful in my own cooking. Use these as a starting point to create your own categories. I've included some of the emotions that are commonly associated with them, but obviously these are highly subjective. The accompanying flavour tests are meant to provoke your perception of smell and the recipe section is designed to explore the different ways flavour can be added and released in food.

Ozone – Sulphur

Ozone is the ephemeral scent of the sea, such as can be momentarily experienced when slipping an oyster into your mouth or lifting the lid of a bowl of piping hot Miso Soup (p.64). It's commonly found in marine-related foods, such as prawns (shrimp), seaweed and samphire and consequently carries a sense of wildness, freedom and happiness. Ozone-flavoured food often tastes strongly of umami and salt. Citrus, herbal, smoky and creamy flavours can work well with ozone notes.

Take care, however, as strong ozone notes can be quite close to sulphurous smells. Sulphur notes are found in eggs, asafoetida, alliums and brassicas and can provoke revulsion in the eater, so most cooks try to negate or mask it in their food – for example, by adding a bay leaf to boiling cauliflower.

Flavour test
Challenge yourself by comparing the ozone whiff of moules marinière with the sulphurous odour of a freshly peeled hard-boiled egg.

Earthy – Fungi

The next time you dig some soil or disturb damp fallen leaves, inhale deeply. You will smell two similar flavour groups: musty, earthy aromas and mouldy, dank fungi scents. Both are surprisingly widespread in food and must be used in moderation, as over-use can provoke repulsion. Earthy flavours can be detected in many starchy ingredients, including grains, roots and pulses (e.g. oats, potatoes and lentils) and, perhaps because of this, they can also induce a sense of comfort. Verdant, herbal, citrus and dairy flavours work well with them.

Fungi flavours can be found in mushrooms, truffles, beer, yeast-based doughs, umami-tasting cheeses and air-dried meats such as salami. They are often associated with bitter tastes and can imbue a dish with a delicious wild edginess, but need a light hand and sensitive pairing with dairy, citrus, herbal, verdant and caramel flavours.

Flavour test
If possible, sniff the earth that sticks to a freshly dug up potato and then compare it to the smell of a freshly baked potato.

Fruity – Spicy

Fruity can hardly describe the enormous range of flavours in this group. They range from tropical resinous mangos and flowery mangosteen to intense wine-like blackcurrants and aniseed pears. Cooking and drying fruit creates deeper aromas and freezing reduces their flavour. Many fruity scents induce pleasure in the eater, no doubt in part because of their association with delicious sweet, sour and or bitter tastes.

The breadth of spicy flavours is immense, but it is important to understand that some, such as chillies, ginger, cloves, black, Sichuan and sansho peppers and various types of mustard also act as chemical irritants. These will be explored in greater depth in Temperature (p.150). Spicy flavourings are added to create excitement or to subtly enhance other flavours. Many dried spices need to be cooked to soften their flavour.

Flavour test
Compare the fruity flavours of two tomatoes, both eaten at room temperature – one roasted and the other raw.

Floral – Citrus

Floral notes instantly conjure up a sense of time and place from the first spring cherry blossoms in Japan to summery elderflowers in England. They are often associated with sweetness, although many flowers taste bitter. Always analyze the undertones of your floral flavours and, depending on what you want to evoke, draw out the citrus, herbal, verdant, peppery, fruity or nutty notes to enhance them.

Citrus notes add excitement to food. Their aroma is often classified as a top note in perfumery. They are instantly perceived, but fade quickly, so are best added towards the end of cooking. They can be found in all forms of citrus zest and juice as well as lemongrass, lime leaves and herbs such as lemon balm and lemon verbena.

Flavour test
Make the Pork and Spinach Meatball mix (p.160), omitting the lemon zest. Fry a tiny patty, then add the lemon zest to the mix, fry another patty and compare their flavour.

Herbal – Verdant

Crush a medicinal sage leaf or stroll through a patch of peppery fennel and it's easy to identify herbal flavours. They cover a gamut of flavours including fleeting citrus tones of lemon thyme and lingering musky notes of pelargoniums. Some hint at temperature with cooling mints and fiery nasturtiums. Creamy, buttery, citrus, floral, spicy and/or fruity notes work well with them all. Most are best infused or added relatively late to the cooking process. Drying changes their flavour, often introducing musty, hay-like tones.

Verdant flavours are closely associated with herbal flavours. Parsley, sorrel and watercress, for example, evoke strong verdant notes reminiscent of rain-soaked grass, despite the fact that they are also herbal. Verdant ingredients are usually bitter and some, such as spinach or greens, require blanching to bring out their green flavour. Others, such as sorrel, can also taste sour.

Flavour test
Drizzle some fresh feta with some peppery olive oil, then sprinkle some with dried thyme and some with fresh thyme and compare their flavours.

Creamy – Buttery

Creamy and buttery flavours tend to be associated with pleasure, partly because they are based on fat-textured dairy ingredients (see p.123). They can be found in anything that contains dairy products, such as milk, cream, yogurt, butter and cheese, thus creamy drinks, soft cheeses, sauces, syllabubs, home-made pastry and cakes all contain creamy or buttery notes.

Their fatty texture ensures that they linger in your mouth. As a result, a little goes a long way, so depending on your recipe, it is important to lighten and/or deepen their tone with complementary flavours. Flowery, verdant, herbal and citrus notes add lightness, and smoky, toasty, nutty, cheesy and spicy flavours suggest depth.

Flavour test
Choose a good-quality soft fresh goat's cheese and try to identify its different flavours, such as herbal, peppery or citrus, then experiment by seasoning the cheese with an ingredient dominant in one of the flavours, such as thyme, marjoram, black pepper, olive oil or lemon zest.

Toasty – Nutty

Some flavours are fundamentally linked to bitter tastes. By default, toasty flavours are the result of food being browned through heat, which automatically creates bitterness and interesting new flavours. In sugar this generates caramelization. In coffee and chocolate beans, bread, dark beer and roasted meat it releases more complex, savoury notes through what is called the Maillard reaction (named after the French physician who first described it in 1910). Toasty flavours can generate a sense of excitement, which comes with developing a taste for bitter foods in adolescence from late-night toast-fests to beer.

Nutty flavours can range from delicate, milky, fresh walnuts to browned butter. They often share toasty characteristics and complement each other in dishes. Buttery, creamy, citrus and some fruity flavours play well with both.

Flavour test
Compare the flavour of a blanched hazelnut with that of a shelled unblanched hazelnut, and with that of a roasted hazelnut (see p.85).

Smoky – Woody

Used lightly, smoky flavours can introduce an intriguing complexity to recipes, especially as many smoked foods, such as smoked trout and bacon are rich in umami. However, take care, as smokiness is the culinary equivalent of mid-notes in perfumery and can overwhelm a dish. A little Lapsang Souchong, Islay malt whisky or smoked paprika goes a long way. Fresh citrus and herbal notes lighten smoky flavours, especially when they have been created by barbecuing. Earthy, fungi, fruity, spicy, dairy and toasty flavours add depth.

Woody notes often underlie other flavours including smoky, spicy, nutty, fruity herbal and tobacco flavours. They add warmth and depth and can be described by wood type. Whisky, sherry and oak-aged wines contain woody notes, as do dried mushrooms, some wood-stemmed herbs, such as rosemary and sage, and certain spices, such as cinnamon, coriander and cumin, and spice mixes such as dukkah.

Flavour test
Cut a slice of Picnic Fruit Cake (p.203) and compare your reactions to accompanying it with English breakfast tea versus smoky Lapsang Souchong tea.

Anticipation

When questioned, Britons list warm bread, fried bacon, freshly cut grass, coffee, baking cake, sea air and roast meat as some of their favourite smells. I would add fried onions, crushed mint, warm summer rain, melted chocolate and marmalade toast to the list. They are all smells that make people feel good for the simple reason that they are associated with positive memories.

As Gordon Shepherd explains in his fascinating book *Neurogastronomy* (2012), 'sniffing in a smell gives rise to a spatial pattern of activity in the brain. These patterns function as images of smell, with different images for different smells, much as different faces form different images in our visual system.' Further associations mean that on visualizing the image of baked bread you immediately conceptualize eating the bread – its taste, flavour and texture – from the feel of bread in your hand to the lingering aroma left in your mouth after the final swallow.

Everything you smell alters your mood and your perception of food. In Japan, for example, restaurants have a pleasant fresh smell. There is rarely a hint of cooking odours. Instead, the diner is introduced to an appetizing fragrance only when he or she lifts the lid of a soup bowl and inhales a waft of steam. You can test this by eating food outside, provided, of course that the air smells sweet. Sip a drink with some slightly bruised mint (see opposite) tickling your nose and see if your pleasure is amplified by your increased perception of its minty aroma.

Few choose to invite guests into a home filled with what are deemed unpleasant smells, such as stale, fried, fishy or cabbage-like odours. However, a careful mix of freshness and a subtle waft of a natural feel-good aroma, such as coffee or freshly baked bread, will make people feel happy.

Mint Julep

Serves 1

Lifting a drink to your mouth is the most focussed way of receiving an anticipatory smell. This recipe (photographed on p.133) requires serious preparation, as the master of cocktails David A. Embury advises in his brilliant book *The Fine Art of Mixing Drinks* (1958). It is not a drink to be hurried, but you will be rewarded by the heady scent of bourbon and mint as you sip it ice-cold on a hot day. Multiply the proportions according to the number of glasses you are making (1 tbsp = 15 ml/½ fl oz).

lots of tiny top mint sprigs

1 tbsp sugar syrup (see below)

Angostura bitters

6 tbsp Woodford Reserve bourbon

crushed ice

Note

For the sugar syrup, follow mixologist Dale Degroff's method of filling a jam jar half with caster (granulated) sugar and half with water. Seal and shake vigorously for about 1 minute or until the sugar dissolves. Leave for 5 minutes or until the mixture starts to clear, then shake again. It is now ready for use. Keep chilled.

Chill a highball (or silver julep) glass in the freezer. Wash the mint. Snip off the mint tips and gently dry on paper towels. Large leaves, old leaves and mint stems are too bitter for this recipe.

For each drink, place the sugar syrup, 12 young mint tips and 2 or 3 dashes of Angostura bitters in a bar glass. Lightly bruise the mint with a muddler as you blend the ingredients by stirring and pressing gently for several minutes. Do not crush the leaves as this releases bitter-tasting juices.

Add the bourbon and stir thoroughly to mix.

Using a cloth to prevent your hands from sticking to the icy cold glass, strain most of the bourbon mixture into your glass, then fill two thirds of the glass with the ice, removing any larger lumps as you do so. Use a long bar spoon to churn the mixture through the ice. Add more ice and top with the remaining bourbon mixture so that it comes close to the rim. Churn again until the glass starts to frost. Insert a long, eco-friendly straw into the glass and decorate with mint sprigs. Serve immediately.

Miso Soup

Serves 4

Traditionally miso soup is served in a lacquer bowl with a tight-fitting lacquer lid. The diner releases the soup's smoky ozone scent as they lift the lid and are expected to inhale the scent of the soup in an appreciative manner before contemplating the beauty of their bowl. Such rituals prepare the eater to fully savour the flavours of their soup.

2 large shiitake mushroom caps, finely sliced

2 spring onions (scallions), trimmed and finely sliced

55 g/2 oz/½ cup tofu, cut into 1-cm/½-inch cubes

About ½ dried nori sheet, snipped into 1-cm/½-inch squares (to obtain about 1 tbsp)

4 tbsp aka red miso paste

850 ml/29 fl oz/3½ cups Dashi (see p.72)

Begin by preparing the garnishes. Finely slice the shiitake mushroom caps and spring onions and set aside. Dice the tofu into small cubes and set aside. Snip enough small squares of nori to fill 1 tbsp.

Place the miso paste in a small mixing bowl. Gently heat the dashi until tepid in a medium saucepan. Then, using a wooden spoon, add a few spoonfuls of dashi at a time to the miso paste, stirring constantly until it forms a smooth thin mixture.

Meanwhile, heat the remaining dashi until it simmers. Gradually stir the tepid liquid miso into the barely simmering dashi to create a smooth soup.

Add the shiitake mushrooms, spring onions, tofu and nori to the barely simmering soup. Do not let it boil or the flavour will change. After 2 minutes or as soon as the added ingredients are warm, ladle the soup into individual bowls, distributing the ingredients equally between each bowl.

Pide with Nigella Seeds

Makes 2 medium-sized breads

In Turkey and Morocco, the fragrance of freshly baked pide, pitta and semolina bread hangs in the morning air, tempting everyone to start their midday meal. This recipe comes from Ghillie Basan's lovely book *Mezze: Small Plates to Share.*

250 ml/9 fl oz/1 cup lukewarm water

1 tsp active dried yeast

450 g/1 lb/3¼ cups strong white (bread) flour

1 tsp fine sea salt

2 tbsp extra-virgin olive oil, plus extra for greasing

2 tbsp natural Greek yogurt

1 small egg, beaten

1 tbsp nigella seeds

Place half the water in a small bowl. Sprinkle over the yeast, stir slightly and set aside for a few minutes until it starts to froth and bubble.

Sift the flour and salt into a large bowl. Add the yeasty water, rinse the yeast bowl with the remaining water and, using your hands, mix into the flour with the olive oil and yogurt. You want a slightly sticky dough, so add more water if needed.

Tip out onto a clean work surface and knead for 10 minutes, until the dough feels smooth and plump. Return the dough to a clean bowl, cover and set aside until it has doubled in size – about 2 hours.

Preheat the oven to 200°C fan/220°C/425°F/gas mark 7. Lightly oil 2 baking sheets.

Turn the dough out, knead briefly and divide into two pieces. Flatten the first into a circle using the heel of your hand, then using your fingers stretch it from the middle, creating a thick lip at the edges. Indent the dough with your finger tips and place on a baking sheet. Repeat the process with the second piece of dough.

Brush both pides with some beaten egg and scatter with the nigella seeds. Bake in the hot oven for 10 minutes, then reduce the heat to 180°C fan/200°C/400°F/gas mark 6 and continue to bake for 10 minutes, or until the bread is golden and crisp. Serve warm, ripped into pieces.

Apricot and Raspberry Sponge Pudding

Serves 4

The sugary scent of the freshly baked buttery almond sponge is a wonderful way to fill your home with appetizing smells, especially as the hints of fruit bubbling underneath conjure up childhood memories of warm jam and cake.

500 g/1 lb 2 oz apricots, halved and stoned

140 g/5 oz/scant ¾ cup caster (granulated) sugar, plus ½ tbsp for sprinkling

350 g/12 oz/2½ cups raspberries

85 g/3 oz/6 tbsp unsalted butter, softened

85 g/3 oz/⅔ cup self-raising flour

55 g/2 oz/½ cup ground almonds

2 medium eggs, beaten

Preheat the oven to 160°C fan/180°C/350°F/gas mark 4.

Mix the halved apricots with 55 g/2 oz/4 tbsp of the caster sugar before gently mixing in the raspberries. Tip into a 1.25-litre/1½-quart deep pie dish.

In a large bowl, beat the butter with the remaining sugar until pale and fluffy. In a separate bowl, mix together the flour and almonds. Beat an egg at a time into the butter mixture, followed by half of the flour mixture. Repeat until all the ingredients are used up. Roughly spoon the mixture over the fruit. Don't worry if there are a few holes. Immediately place in the centre of the hot oven.

Bake for 50 minutes, or until the almond topping is golden and risen. The underside will be gooey with fruit juice. Remove from the oven and sprinkle with the extra caster sugar. Serve hot, warm or at room temperature.

Jammy, buttery, sugary scents evoke happy memories

Infusion

One of the simplest ways to extract flavour is by infusion. All liquids can be infused, from oil and wine to water and cream. Milk is infused with a vanilla pod, for example, before the pod is removed and the sauce thickened to make custard (p.174).

Infusion is a method that is widely used in cooking, as it allows the cook the freedom to instil flavour with or without the texture of the flavouring. The cream in the Chocolate Truffles (p.29), for example, is infused with jasmine tea before being strained into the melted chocolate. This imbues the truffles with a subtle floral fragrance without the irritation of finding bitter tea leaves within a luscious chocolate, whereas the rich cream sauce for the Truffle Taglierini (p.73) is flecked with fine shavings of black truffle, which subtly punctuate every mouthful with irresistible fungi notes.

Ingredients quickly release their flavour in hot and warm liquids, but it's also worth experimenting with much slower cold infusions, such as the Rich Chocolate Nori Ice Cream (p.74). In either case, the longer you leave your ingredients in their liquid, the greater the change in both flavour and taste. Dried bonito flakes, for example, can only be infused for a brief time in Dashi (Japanese stock, p.72) before they start imparting unpleasant fishy odours.

The skill of any cook lies in mentally matching different flavour categories within a recipe to create a more intense emotional reaction to their food, such as with the summery infusion of lavender into the Nectarine Salad (p.42).

Infusion can extract exquisite flavours

Charred Leek Salad with Thyme Oil

Serves 4

It can be hard to retain fresh herbal flavours when macerating, however this method works really well and will retain its fragrance for several days if chilled.

The dominant flavours in this recipe (photographed on p.69) are the lingering smoky, green allium notes of the charred leeks. I wanted to create a fresh-tasting early autumn dish, so I've chosen lighter herbal, citrus and dairy notes, in the form of the lemon thyme oil and feta, to lift the dish. If you wanted to create a wintery dish, you could draw on the smoky woody notes of the leeks instead, by adding toasted nuts or smoky bacon in place of the feta.

For the thyme oil
2 bunches lemon thyme
100 ml/3½ fl oz/generous ⅓ cup cold-pressed sunflower oil
finely grated zest of 2 lemons, plus 1 tbsp lemon juice
salt and freshly ground black pepper

For the salad
700 g/1 lb 9 oz medium-thin leeks
2 tbsp cold-pressed sunflower oil
2 heads Treviso or red chicory (endive), separated
115 g/4 oz brined cured feta, drained

Note
To add more autumnal notes, replace the lemony feta cheese with 2 handfuls of trimmed chanterelles that have been fried briskly in a little sunflower oil.

The day before you need the oil, wash the thyme and strip the leaves, discarding their stems as you do so. Drop the leaves into a small saucepan of boiling water. Cook for 4 minutes, drain the leaves into a sieve, then plunge the sieve into a bowl of iced water. Once the thyme leaves are cold, drain and squeeze dry. Place in a small container with the sunflower oil and lemon zest. Finely chop with a hand-held stick blender. Cover and chill for 24 hours.

After 24 hours push the mixture through a fine sieve. Season the aromatic green oil with salt and pepper. This will keep for 1 week covered in the refrigerator. When you're ready to dress the salad, whisk in the lemon juice.

For the salad, trim the leeks, cut away their dark green leaves and remove several layers of their tough outer leaves. Wash thoroughly and pat dry. Cut each leek into 4 equal lengths.

Set a cast-iron griddle pan over a medium-high heat. Once hot, lightly coat the leeks in the sunflower oil. Season lightly and place on the griddle pan – slipping the leek chunks in between the ridges so that the entire side of each leek turns golden brown. Griddle for about 10 minutes, turning regularly until tender and al dente in the centre. The outer leaves will look lightly charred, while the inner section will turn bright green.

Transfer the leeks to a large mixing bowl. Toss in 4 tbsp of the lemon thyme oil dressing. Leave for a few minutes to cool a little, then mix in the Treviso or red chicory and season lightly. Divide between 4 plates. Crumble the feta over each salad, drizzle with a little more lemon thyme oil and serve.

Dashi

Serves 4

Timing is everything in the making of dashi; left too long or infused at the wrong temperature and the broth tastes harsh. There are many versions of this Japanese stock, including pure kombu infusions, and kombu and dried shiitake combinations, but in this classic version the kombu is slowly infused in cold water and the bonito flakes are added to warm water.

40 g/1½ oz kombu (dried kelp)

1 litre/35 fl oz/generous 4 cups cold soft mineral water, plus 4 tbsp

30 g/1 oz/2½ cups dried bonito flakes (hana-katsuo)

Wipe the kombu lightly with a clean damp cloth. Place in a china bowl and add the cold soft mineral water. Hard water can impair the flavour of dashi. Cover the bowl and leave at room temperature overnight or for at least 8 hours.

Remove the kombu and pour the water into a medium stainless-steel saucepan.

Make sure you have the 4 tbsp cold mineral water and a muslin (cheesecloth)-lined sieve set over a large bowl ready.

Set the kombu-infused water over a high heat and bring to a full boil. Add the cold mineral water to reduce the temperature quickly and add the bonito flakes. Bring to a full boil, then remove from the heat immediately. **Do not let the bonito flakes boil for more than a few seconds**, otherwise they will make the broth taste bitter and overly fishy. The flakes will take 30 seconds–1 minute to start settling on the bottom of the pan. Immediately skim any foam from the surface of the stock, then quickly strain through the lined sieve. The stock is now ready to be used in Miso Soup (p.64).

Note
Dashi has an intense savoury taste because the inosinate in the dried bonito flakes, combined with the glutamate in the kombu, has a synergistic effect that amplifies our perception of umami.

Truffle Taglierini

Serves 2

Is it the taste, the flavour or the texture of this sensual recipe that fills the eater with delight? In reality it's all three – the velvety texture of the cream stimulates you as much as the intense umami taste of the reduced chicken stock, and the fallen-leaf, fungi notes of black truffle. For maximum truffle aroma, I used the exquisitely scented *Tuber melanosporum vittadini*, otherwise known as the Périgord truffle.

650 ml/23 fl oz/2¾ cups good-quality Chicken Stock (p.47)

250 ml/9 fl oz/1 cup dry Champagne or white wine

250 ml/9 fl oz/1 cup double (heavy) cream

1 tbsp raw black truffle shavings, or to taste

125 g/4½ oz egg taglierini pasta (no. 105)

salt and freshly ground black pepper

Allow yourself time to make the sauce. Pour the stock into a medium-small saucepan and set over a high heat. Boil vigorously for 20–25 minutes, until the stock has reduced down to about 100ml/3½ fl oz/generous ⅓ cup intense-tasting liquid.

Add the Champagne or white wine and continue to boil vigorously for a further 15 minutes, until the liquid has reduced down to about 100 ml/3½ fl oz/generous ⅓ cup. Strain into a small saucepan and add the cream. It can now be set aside until shortly before you need it.

When you are ready to serve, bring a large saucepan of salted water to the boil. At the same time, return the cream to a simmer and cook for 5 minutes, or until the liquid has thickened into a velvety beige sauce. Season to taste.

Clean your black truffle with a dry nail brush. You need about 1 tbsp of either finely sliced or roughly grated truffle – depending on whether you have a truffle slicer or domestic grater to hand. Mix the shaved truffle into the hot sauce and set aside while you cook the pasta.

Add the taglierini to the boiling water and cook for about 3 minutes, or until al dente. Drain into a colander then return to the pasta pan. Mix in the warm pasta sauce, toss thoroughly and plate. The decadent can add a few more shavings of truffle.

Rich Chocolate Nori Ice Cream

Serves 8

The iodine flavour of the nori slowly infuses into the frozen bitter-sweet chocolate custard to create an amazing, sophisticated ice cream. Nori is made from dried laver, *Porphyra umbilicalis* – a small-leaved, red seaweed.

200 g/7 oz/1 cup granulated sugar

5 medium egg yolks

200 g/7 oz good-quality dark chocolate, such as Valrhona Caraibe

250 ml/9 fl oz/1 cup full-fat (whole) milk

250 ml/9 fl oz/1 cup double (heavy) cream

5 g/⅛ oz nori sheets, snipped into grape pip-sized pieces

Place the sugar and 100 ml/3½ fl oz/generous ½ cup water in a small heavy-based saucepan and clip a jam thermometer onto the side of the pan. Set over a medium heat and stir occasionally until the sugar has dissolved, then bring to the boil and boil vigorously, until the mixture reaches 120°C/250°F (hard ball stage). This will take 5–7 minutes.

Meanwhile, using a hand-held electric whisk, beat the egg yolks in a heatproof dish until thick and creamy. As soon as the sugar syrup reaches the correct heat, turn the electric whisk to its highest setting and pour a thin, slow stream of the just-boiled sugar syrup into the egg yolks as you whisk. The egg yolks will gradually expand into a thick, pale, creamy mousse – keep whisking until it is really thick. Set aside.

Break the chocolate into a large bowl. Set it over a large pan of just-boiled water off the heat. Stir occasionally, until the chocolate has melted. You may need to replace the hot water once.

Put the milk and cream into a saucepan. Bring up to just below boiling point – it should be just a little hotter than the chocolate. Bit by bit, stir the hot milk into the chocolate. As it becomes amalgamated, add more milk. Once it is fully blended, pour into a jug and chill in the refrigerator.

Once the chocolate is tepid, mix in the snipped nori and whisk the mixture into the egg mousse. The nori will stick to the whisk, but scrape it off and return it to the mixture. Pour into your ice cream machine and churn according to the manufacturer's instructions. Alternatively, pour into a shallow container, freeze and, after the first hour, beat with a fork every 40 minutes to create a smooth texture. Freeze for 12 hours before serving, to allow the flavour to fully develop.

Sticky Spiced Lemon Gin Cake

Serves 6

Maceration is a useful way to add another layer of flavouring. This delicate-flavoured lemon and almond cake is transformed by saturating it in syrup zinging with exciting citrus, spicy and woody notes from the lemon, black pepper, cloves and cinnamon. As you eat, you will notice an intriguing numbness in your mouth from the irritant chemicals in the black pepper and cloves. Interestingly, piperine in the black pepper makes your mouth hypersensitive to touch, texture and temperature, while eugenol in the cloves induces numbness!

For the cake

175 g/6 oz/¾ cup unsalted butter, softened, plus extra for greasing

175 g/6 oz/generous ¾ cup caster (granulated) sugar

finely grated zest of 1½ lemons

3 large eggs, separated

85 g/3 oz/scant ⅔ cup self-raising flour, sifted

85 ml/3 fl oz/6 tbsp muscat dessert wine

85 g/3 oz/generous ¾ cup ground almonds

For the syrup

finely pared zest of 1 lemon (use a potato peeler), plus the juice of 2 lemons

30 g/1 oz/2½ tbsp granulated sugar

8-cm/3¼-inch cinnamon stick, roughly broken

2 cloves

3 black peppercorns

3 tbsp London dry gin

Preheat the oven to 170°C fan/190°C/375°F/gas mark 5. Lightly butter a 20-cm/8-inch spring-form cake pan and line the base with baking parchment.

In a large bowl, beat together the butter, sugar and finely grated lemon zest until pale and fluffy, then gradually beat in the egg yolks, followed by 2 tbsp of the flour and the dessert wine. Lightly fold in half the almonds, followed by half the remaining flour. Then fold in the remaining almonds and the last of the flour.

Immediately whisk the egg whites in a clean, dry bowl until they form firm peaks. Gently fold them into the cake mix, then spoon the mixture into the cake pan and place in the centre of the hot oven.

Bake for 50 minutes, or until an inserted skewer comes out clean. Remove and turn out onto a cooling rack set over a deep-rimmed plate.

While the cake is baking, make the syrup. Place the lemon peel, granulated sugar, cinnamon, cloves, black peppercorns and 150 ml/5 fl oz/⅔ cup water in a small saucepan set over a low heat. Dissolve the sugar, then simmer gently for 10 minutes. Cover, remove from the heat and leave to infuse for 15 minutes.

As soon as the cake is turned out of its pan, bring the syrup to the boil. Add the lemon juice and gin and strain into a jug (pitcher). Prick the warm cake with a fine skewer and drip-feed the syrup into the cake in small batches. Make sure it's evenly fed and use all the syrup – it's surprising how much a cake will absorb. Serve once cold.

Blending

Every time you cook, you blend flavours – unless you are preparing a single item such as a plain sliced orange. However, as soon as you sprinkle your orange with a little orange-flower water you are mixing flavours and altering your perception of its delicate aroma.

There are two ways to approach blending flavours. The first is to analyze the flavour of your primary ingredient(s). Which accompanying flavours could draw out its good points and which negate its bad notes? Salty, umami-tasting Roast Chicken (p.170), for example, releases caramelized skin and mildly metallic meat flavours. Baste your bird in butter and its toasty caramelized notes will be enhanced by nutty buttery flavours. Stuff its cavity with thyme and lemon, and resinous herbal and citrus flavours will replace its faintly bloody, metallic tones.

The second approach is to conceptualize the feeling that you want to evoke from your food, and then decide which flavourings would best express your emotions. Perhaps you want to create a summery Pea and Sorrel Soup (p.105). You need verdant, fresh flavourings, such as are found in dairy, herbal and citrus groups – for example, yogurt, mint, sorrel and lemon zest. You could even add light, green, peppery notes, such as rocket (arugula), nasturtium leaves or olive oil. Conversely, a wintery pea soup needs heavier, lingering flavourings such as smoked bacon, parsley, cumin and cream.

If you are uncertain of how particular flavours will work together, combine a small amount and, depending on what they are, either eat raw or test-fry a tiny sample. Remember that different textures within a dish will release their flavours at different times. Thus, a complex-textured dish, such as the Spring Chicken Pie (p.80), will alter its flavour depending on which pie ingredients are in your mouth. Other dishes, such as the Lamb Rogan Josh (p.82), are more one-dimensional in that every mouthful is the same meat in the same spiced sauce. New flavours have to be introduced by accompanying dishes.

Red Onion, Ham and Blue Cheese Pizzetti (p.78)

Red Onion, Ham and Blue Cheese Pizzetti x 2

Serves 6

Every part of this umami-tastic dish (photographed on p.77) contains flavour. Faint fungi flavours can be found in many yeast-risen doughs, including pizza dough. They can be enhanced by adding further layers of fungi flavourings such as mushrooms and blue cheese, or negated by adding sweet and/or sour toppings, such as caramelized onions and fennel, or tomatoes and roast (bell) peppers. When developing new flavour combinations, it's worth comparing different mixtures – for example, you could try making half of the pizzetti here without any mushrooms.

For the pizzetti dough
275 ml/9½ fl oz/scant 1¼ cups lukewarm water

2 tsp active dried yeast

400 g/14 oz/scant 3 cups strong white (bread) flour, plus extra for dusting

1 tsp fine sea salt

For the topping
8 tbsp extra-virgin olive oil, plus extra for greasing

500 g/1 lb 2 oz red onions, finely sliced

2 garlic cloves, finely chopped

225 g/8 oz button mushrooms (for 6 pizzetti), or 115 g/4 oz (for 3 pizzetti), trimmed, halved and finely sliced

12 fat black olives, stoned and sliced

200 g/7 oz fine slices of Consorcio Serrano ham (or prosciutto)

200 g/7 oz dolcelatte (or Gorgonzola) cheese, diced

30 g/1 oz/½ cup finely grated Parmesan

Begin by making the pizzetti dough: place half of the lukewarm water in a bowl and mix in the yeast. Place the flour in a large bowl and mix in the salt. As soon as the yeast has dissolved and looks frothy, pour it into the flour. Rinse the yeast bowl with some of the lukewarm water and tip into the flour. Using your hands, mix thoroughly until it forms a soft dough – adding any remaining lukewarm water if necessary.

Knead the dough on a clean work surface for 10 minutes until smooth and elastic. Dust with a little flour if the dough is too sticky. Place in a large clean bowl, cover with clingfilm (plastic wrap) and leave to rise for 2 hours or until doubled in size.

Preheat the oven to 220°C fan/240°C/475°F/ gas mark 9. Oil 3 baking sheets.

Set 2 non-stick frying pans (skillets) over a low heat. Add half the oil, onions and garlic to each and fry gently for 15 minutes, or until soft and golden. (If making half with mushrooms and half without, add 115 g/4 oz sliced mushrooms to one pan.) Otherwise divide the sliced mushrooms equally between the 2 pans and fry briskly for 5 minutes. Tip the mixture into a bowl and add the olives. (For half and half, keep the mushroom mixture in a separate bowl and divide the olives between the bowls.) Lightly season, remembering that the cheese and ham are salty.

Divide the dough into 6 evenly sized lumps and roll each out into an oval pitta-shaped pizzetti, about 20 x 10 cm/8 x 4 inches. Place 2 on each baking sheet. Either top all with the onion and mushroom mixture, or top 3 pizzetti with the onion and mushroom mix, and 3 pizzetti with the onion mix only.

Remove the fat from the ham and rip the meat into strips as you do so. It's easiest to curl the strips of meat onto each pizzetti as you rip them. Dot the pizzetti with the dolcelatte (or Gorgonzola) cheese and sprinkle with the Parmesan.

Bake in the hot oven for 15–20 minutes (the time varies from oven to oven), until the dough is crisp and the cheese melted and golden. Remove, slice and plate. Serve immediately.

Note
Introduce nutty earthy notes by replacing half the strong white (bread) flour with stoneground wholewheat flour; or increase the fungi notes by replacing the button mushrooms with chanterelles, as in the photograph.

Spring Chicken Pie x 2

Serves 4

What flavours express early spring? The first young herbs, the fresh taste of lemon, buttery notes of cream and pastry? Since seasonality is an important aspect of cookery, try to combine flavours and textures that evoke a sense of the moment, such as in this fragrant pie. Traditionally, tender young chickens were only available in the spring. You can compare the flavour of this pie with the wintery version (see note).

This pie also illustrates how you can layer ingredients to create different flavours as you eat.

225 g/8 oz shortcrust pastry (p.32)

4 plump chicken breasts (about 900 g/ 2 lb), skinned

7 tbsp cold-pressed sunflower oil

200 g/7 oz smoked back bacon, trimmed and diced

2 tbsp plain (all-purpose) flour

2 fat leeks, trimmed, halved and sliced

3 large carrots, peeled and sliced into rounds

200 ml/7 fl oz/generous ¾ cup dry white wine

2 strips finely pared lemon zest

2 sprigs of thyme, leaves only

500 ml/17 fl oz/generous 2 cups good-quality Chicken Stock (p.47)

150 ml/5 fl oz/⅔ cup double (heavy) cream

1 small egg, beaten

salt and freshly ground black pepper

Roll out the pastry to fit the top of a 2 litre/ 3½ pint/2 quart pie dish and chill on a plate in the refrigerator. Line the rim of your dish with a strip of pastry, and set aside.

Preheat the oven to 180°C fan/200°C/400°F/ gas mark 6.

Cut the chicken breasts into roughly 2.5-cm/ 1-inch chunks. Set a large non-stick frying pan (skillet) over a medium-high heat. Add 3 tbsp of the oil and fry the bacon briskly. Using a slotted spoon, remove the bacon to a large mixing bowl.

Season the flour and toss the chicken in it. If necessary, add another 2 tbsp oil to the pan and fry the chicken in batches – turning the pieces to seal the meat. As soon as the chicken pieces are flecked gold, transfer to the bowl with the bacon with a slotted spoon.

Add 2 more tbsp oil to the frying pan and reduce the heat to low. Add the sliced leeks and fry for 2 minutes, before adding the carrots. Fry for a further 3 minutes, then mix in the little flour that is left in the chicken's mixing bowl. You need about 1 tbsp. Cook for 1 minute.

Increase the heat to high, then stir in the wine, lemon zest and thyme leaves with a wooden spoon. Boil vigorously until reduced by half. Stir in the stock and boil until reduced by a good half. Add the cream and boil until the sauce has thickened slightly. Season to taste and mix into the chicken and bacon. You can either cool the mixture at this stage or tip it straight into the pie dish.

Lightly brush the pastry rim with some beaten egg. Cover with the pastry lid and, working quickly, seal the edges with a fork. Brush the lid with some beaten egg, prick with a small knife and bake in the centre of the hot oven for 35–40 minutes, or until the pastry is crisp and golden.

Note
To evoke a wintery version of this dish, replace the leeks with 1 large onion and add 1 finely diced garlic clove and 250 g/ 9 oz mushrooms, then add 2 extra tbsp flour to thicken the chicken stock and omit the cream.

Lamb Rogan Josh

Serves 4

Many dried spices need to be cooked to release a more rounded flavour. In this recipe, their flavour is released at the same rate, so the skill of the cook is to find a harmonious blend. The ginger and cardamom, for example, counteract the lamb's meaty odours, while the chilli is added as much for its fruity woody flavour as for its mildly stimulating heat. This recipe is delicious served with Chapattis (p.142) or Saffron Rice (p.218).

1.5 kg/3 lb 5 oz lamb leg, trimmed

5 tbsp cold-pressed sunflower oil

3 onions, finely diced

2 garlic cloves, finely diced

1 tsp peeled, finely chopped fresh ginger

4 cloves

seeds from 8 green cardamoms

¼ tsp black peppercorns

1 tsp paprika (not smoked)

¼ tsp chilli powder

1 tsp ground turmeric

large pinch of saffron strands

fine sea salt

350 ml/12 fl oz/1½ cups boiling water

100 ml/7 fl oz/generous ⅓ cup natural Greek yogurt

Trim the meat, removing any fat or sinews so that you are left with lean tender meat that you cut into 2.5-cm/1-inch cubes. I often use lamb leg steaks, which yield a lot of wastage. Depending on how fatty your lamb is, you will have between 700 g/1 lb 9oz and 900 g/2 lb trimmed meat. The sinewy meat can be browned and used in stock – see method for Chicken Stock (p.47).

Set a heavy-based pan over a medium-low heat. Add the oil and the diced onions and fry for 10 minutes, or until just turning golden brown. Add the garlic and ginger and continue to fry for 4 minutes.

Finely grind the cloves, cardamom seeds and peppercorns in a mortar or small spice grinder. Mix into the golden onions, together with the paprika, chilli powder and turmeric. Fry for 1 minute, then increase the heat to high and stir in the diced meat.

Stir the meat regularly until it is browned all over, then add the saffron, salt and boiling water, so that the meat is covered. Stir and reduce the heat to low. Simmer gently, uncovered, for 75 minutes, or until the lamb is tender.

It can be chilled at this stage, if wished, and reheated when needed. Otherwise, remove from the heat, stir in the yogurt and adjust the seasoning to taste.

Blended spices release a constant rounded flavour

Chilli Prawn Cakes with Ginger Dip

Makes 16

The fresh ginger and spring onions (scallions) in these prawn cakes negate any overtly fishy tones, while the citrus herbal flavours in the dip amplify the prawn cakes' sweet fragrance.

For the dip

3 tbsp naturally brewed soy sauce

3 tbsp mirin

3 tbsp sake

¾ tbsp peeled, finely chopped fresh ginger

½ tsp dried chilli flakes

For the chilli prawn cakes

375 g/13 oz raw peeled prawns (shrimp)

1 garlic clove, finely chopped

¾ tsp peeled, finely chopped fresh ginger

½ Thai chilli, finely chopped

1 tsp Thai fish sauce

½ small egg white

1½ tbsp finely chopped, drained canned water chestnuts

2 spring onions (scallions), trimmed and finely chopped

3 tbsp cold-pressed sunflower oil

To make the dip, put the soy sauce, mirin, sake, ginger and dried chilli flakes into a small saucepan. Simmer gently for 5 minutes, then add 3 tbsp water, transfer to a small pretty serving bowl and set aside.

Clean the prawns by making a small incision down the length of the back of each one. Remove the dark digestive thread. Rinse under cold running water and pat dry on paper towels.

Place the prawns in a food processor with the chopped garlic, ginger, chilli, fish sauce and egg white. Process in short bursts, until the mixture forms a rough paste, then tip into a bowl and beat in the finely chopped water chestnuts and spring onions. Check the seasoning by frying a tiny patty to taste. If necessary, adjust any of the ingredients to taste. Chill, covered, until needed.

When you are ready to serve, set a heavy-based non-stick frying pan (skillet) over a medium heat. Add the oil, then wet your hands and take a walnut-sized spoonful of prawn paste, flatten it into a round patty and add to the pan. Repeat the process until the mixture is finished, but don't overcrowd the frying pan. This should yield about 16 patties. Lower the heat slightly if the prawn cakes are colouring too fast, and cook for 2 minutes on each side or until pink and cooked through. Remove and drain the prawn cakes on paper towels. Serve warm with the dipping sauce.

Spiced Hazelnut Macaroons

Makes 24 small hard macaroons

Toasty nut flavours work well with what are often termed 'warm' flavourings, such as orange, cinnamon, nutmeg and cloves. In this recipe, the spices and orange zest reveal themselves as you bite into the crunchy nutty meringue.

100 g/3½ oz/¾ cup shelled hazelnuts

55 g/2 oz/generous ⅓ cup shelled walnuts

1 tsp cornflour (cornstarch)

2 cloves, finely ground

1 tsp ground cinnamon

½ tsp finely grated nutmeg

1 large egg white

115 g/4 oz/scant ⅔ cup caster (superfine) sugar

finely grated zest of 1 orange

Preheat the oven to 180°C fan/200°C/400°F/ gas mark 6.

Spread the hazelnuts on one small roasting pan and the walnuts on another and toast both in the oven for 10 minutes, or until they smell really nutty. Tip each onto a plate to cool. Once cool, rub between your hands to remove most of their brown skins. Don't worry if the walnuts keep much of their skin.

Once cold, place the nuts in a food processor with the cornflour (cornstarch), ground cloves, cinnamon and finely grated nutmeg. Whiz in short bursts until finely ground – do not over-process or they'll form a paste. Tip into a bowl and set aside.

Preheat the oven to 120°C fan/140°C/275°F/ gas mark 1. Line two baking sheets with baking parchment.

Place the egg white in a clean, dry bowl and whisk until it forms stiff peaks, then gradually whisk in the sugar, adding it bit by bit, until the mixture becomes thick and glossy. Fold the ground spiced nuts and the orange zest into the mixture using a flat metal spoon.

Using a teaspoon, place 12 small round blobs of the nut meringue on each sheet of baking parchment. Place in the oven and cook the biscuits for 30 minutes, or until they are pale and slightly cracked. Remove and leave to cool on the baking sheet. Once cold, store in an airtight tin.

Transformation

For many, cooking is a form of alchemy. The simple act of applying heat to an ingredient can transform it into a completely different type of food, with an entirely different range of flavours. Most cooks take this for granted, but in 2011 Swedish chef Niklas Ekstedt realized that many of the world's top chefs were using less and less heat in their cooking. Many modern culinary techniques, such as sous vide, cook food at very low temperatures and chefs were using warm oils and delicate raw ingredients to complement it. Ekstedt decided to return to the ancient tradition of literally cooking over a wood fire in his eponymous Michelin-starred restaurant.

Wood is extremely variable in its behaviour and depends on the skill of the chef to capture different flavours, depending on its heat and how he or she accesses it. With cooler fires, around 200°C/390°F, wood releases aromatic chemicals that react with the amino acids and sugars in food to change its colour and generate that smoky flavour. At about 300°C/570°F a range of more volatile chemicals are released; these all have distinctive aromas, reminiscent of flavours such as cloves, caramel or peat, which infuse the food.

Out went Ekstedt's baby vegetables and in came robust old carrots and leeks, whose strong flavours were enhanced by being cooked over fire. He started to cook with cast-iron pans, discovering what the Sami people had long known, that seasoned cast-iron pans can imbue food with a deeper flavour – a mixture of fire, treacle and chocolate. Anyone who has roasted chestnuts in hot embers or fried sausages over a campfire will appreciate the depth of flavour wood generates.

Few cooks have access to wood fires and ovens, but it's still worth focussing on how heat can alter the flavour of an ingredient. Barbecued corn-on-the-cob, for instance, takes on a rustic smokiness, and sappy, honeyed purple figs develop intense wine-like flavours if roasted in a domestic oven. Challenge your culinary boundaries and experiment with different forms of heat, to see how you can alter the flavour of an ingredient. Even an aubergine (eggplant) will take on a deep smoky flavour if cooked on an open gas flame.

Moroccan Burnt-Aubergine Salad

Serves 6

The aubergine (eggplant) takes on an intriguing smoky aroma in this recipe, which is enhanced by the paprika and made more earthy by the parsley. This dish is delicious eaten with Pide (p.65), salty black olives and the Labneh (p.95).

4 aubergines (eggplant)

225 g/8 oz tomatoes

4–5 tbsp extra-virgin olive oil

2 garlic cloves, roughly chopped

2 tsp ground cumin

2 tsp smoked paprika

1 tbsp white wine vinegar

a handful of parsley, finely chopped

salt and freshly ground black pepper

Prick the aubergines all over with a fork. If you have a gas hob, place each aubergine, one at a time, over the flame and turn regularly until its skin has blackened and its flesh softened. Otherwise set your grill (broiler) to high and, once hot, place the aubergines under the grill and turn regularly until blackened and soft.

Place the tomatoes in a bowl, cover with boiling water and lightly cut the skin of each tomato. After 2 minutes, drain and peel the tomatoes. Roughly chop and liquidize, either in a food processor or with a hand-held blender. Push through a sieve to remove the seeds.

Heat the oil in a small saucepan, add the garlic and, once it begins to sizzle, add the puréed tomatoes and cumin. Cook briskly until the tomato mixture forms a dark paste that exudes oil, about 8 minutes.

Meanwhile, peel and chop the 'burnt' aubergine. Mix into the cooked tomato with the paprika, and salt and pepper to taste and cook for 5–10 minutes. Remove from the heat, season to taste with the vinegar and mix in the parsley. Serve tepid or cold.

Roast Carrots with Toasted-Cumin Yogurt

Serves 4

- -

Root vegetables deepen their earthy tones when baked. These flavours can be exaggerated by combining them with other earthy seasonings, such as cumin or black pepper. However, root vegetables' natural sweetness combined with earthy flavours can become cloying, so it helps to cut the sweetness with fresh, mildly acidic dairy notes, such as yogurt and feta.

600 g/1 lb 5 oz bunches of baby carrots

4 tbsp extra-virgin olive oil

finely grated zest of 2 lemons, plus 2 tbsp juice

2 bunches of watercress, washed and snipped into sprigs

salt and freshly ground black pepper

For the cumin yogurt

100 g/3½ oz/scant ½ cup natural Greek yogurt

4 tbsp cold water

½ tsp cumin seeds

a pinch of fine sea salt

Preheat the oven to 180°C fan/200°C/400°F/gas mark 6.

Wash the carrots, trimming their roots and a little of their green tops. Peel and, if fat, cut in half lengthwise. Place in a mixing bowl with the olive oil and salt and pepper to taste. Spread out in a single layer on 2 shallow baking sheets.

Roast the carrots for 20 minutes or until tender when pierced with a knife. Tip into a large bowl and mix in the finely grated lemon zest.

Place the yogurt in a bowl with the cold water and a pinch of salt and whisk to form a smooth sauce.

Put the cumin seeds in small dry frying pan (skillet) and set over a high heat. Toast for 2–3 minutes or until the seeds darken and release a heady aroma. Tip into a mortar and grind (or use a small rolling pin on a large plate). Sprinkle over the yogurt.

Once the carrots are tepid, mix in the lemon juice and watercress sprigs. If necessary, adjust the seasoning and divide between 4 appetizer plates. Either drizzle with the cumin yogurt or serve with 4 small bowls of cumin yogurt on the side.

Woody toasted cumin enhances the carrots' earthy notes

Sappy, honeyed figs develop rich wine notes with heat

Basil and Lemon Baked Figs

Serves 4

A fresh fig develops honeyed caramel notes when dried and rich wine-like tones when cooked. Both fresh and dried figs absorb their culinary flavourings when poached or baked so season according to your mood. This recipe draws on the intense herbal verdant flavour of summer that, when combined with the fig, becomes almost floral.

3 sprigs basil

55 g/2 oz/¼ cup caster (granulated) sugar

1 lemon

unsalted butter, for greasing

12 plump black or white figs

To serve
100 ml/3½ oz/generous ⅓ cup crème fraîche

Preheat the oven to 180°C fan/200°C/400°F/gas mark 6.

Put the basil sprigs in a small saucepan with the sugar, 4 finely pared strips of lemon zest and 200 ml/7 fl oz/generous cup water. Place over a medium heat, stirring occasionally until the sugar has dissolved. Bring to the boil, then simmer for 15–20 minutes or until the mixture becomes quite sticky. Remove from the heat and mix in the juice of half a lemon.

Butter a shallow china baking dish that is just large enough to hold the 12 figs or line a baking sheets with liberally buttered baking parchment.

Trim the fig stalks and place in the buttered dish. Strain the warm syrup over the figs and bake in the oven for 25 minutes – taking care to baste them after the first 15 minutes. Serve warm or cold with their fragrant juice and a bowl of crème fraîche.

Sticky Asian Beef Kebabs with Cucumber Dip

Serves 6

When cooked over charcoal, these sticky kebabs (photographed on p.8) develop delicious spicy smoky notes that cling to their caramelized crust. These make a gorgeous starter, but you could serve them as part of a main course.

Dipping sauce

4 tbsp fish sauce (nam pla)

2 tbsp lime juice

2 tsp caster (granulated) sugar

1 Thai chilli, or to taste, finely chopped

1 garlic clove, finely chopped

½ cucumber, peeled and seeded

2 tbsp finely chopped coriander (cilantro) leaves

For the marinade

2 stems lemongrass, finely chopped

1 Thai chilli, finely chopped

1 garlic clove, finely chopped

1 shallot, finely chopped

½ tbsp fish sauce (nam pla)

1 tbsp naturally brewed soy sauce

2 tbsp lime juice

2 tbsp dark muscovado sugar

1 tbsp cold-pressed sunflower oil

For the beef kebabs

450 g/1 lb lean sirloin steak, trimmed weight

1 tbsp cold-pressed sunflower oil

You will need to make the dipping sauce a good 3 hours before it is needed. Mix together the fish sauce, lime juice, sugar, and finely chopped chilli and garlic in a small bowl. Cover and chill for 1 hour. Cut the seeded cucumber into quarters lengthwise, then finely slice and mix into the dipping sauce with the chopped coriander and transfer to a pretty bowl. Chill for at least 2 hours.

Mix together the marinade ingredients in a medium-sized bowl. If necessary, trim the fat off the beef, then cut the meat into 2.5-cm/1-inch cubes and thoroughly coat in the marinade. Cover and chill for 30 minutes.

Soak 8 x 25-cm/10-inch wooden skewers in water for 20 minutes.

Heat a barbecue until the coals are glowing white or preheat an cast-iron griddle pan over a high heat. Divide the beef equally between the wooden skewers and snip off the ends of each skewer. Grill the beef for about 4 minutes, turning regularly. Serve immediately with the cucumber dipping sauce.

Chilli Marmalade

Makes 2.25 kg/5 lb

The Seville orange completely changes its flavour when subjected to heat. Its effervescent citrus notes deepen into a rich, deep-toned flavour, as can be discovered in this unusual marmalade. I've lightened the orange with lemon and added a subtle but addictive zing of chilli. Here the chilli is used more for the tingle-inducing chemical properties of its capsaicin, rather than its fruity fresh flavour. Try this on toast made from the Plain White Bread (p.52) – it's gorgeous!

680 g/1½ lb Seville oranges, washed

4 lemons, washed

2 medium red Thai chillies, or to taste, halved, seeded and finely sliced

1.4 kg/3 lb/7 cups granulated sugar

Put the fruit and 1.7 litres/3 pints/7½ cups water in a large pan. Cover, bring to the boil, then simmer gently for 1½ hours, until the fruit is soft and easily pierced with a knife.

Transfer the fruit to a bowl, leaving the cooking liquid in the pan. Once the fruit is cool enough to handle, slice each in half and, with a dessert spoon, carefully scrape out the pulp, pips and pith into the cooking liquid in the pan. Thoroughly mash up the pulp in the pan. Bring back to the boil and reduce the liquid by half, before straining thorough a sieve into a jam (preserving) pan or large saucepan. Leave the pulp to drip through the sieve to extract as much clear, pectin-rich liquid as possible.

Sterilize your jam jars and lids (see p.25).

Place a small plate in the refrigerator. Finely slice the orange and lemon skins into thin strips and add to the jam pan with the strained fruit water and sliced chillies.

Clip a jam thermometer on to the side of the pan. Return the mixture to the boil. Mix in the sugar and stir regularly until the sugar has completely dissolved, then bring the marmalade up to the boil. Continue to boil vigorously for about 10 minutes, or until it reaches setting point 106°C/220°F. You can also test the setting point by dropping a small blob of hot marmalade onto your chilled saucer. Push the blob gently with your finger, if it wrinkles, setting point has been reached.

If necessary, skim the marmalade. Then, leave to settle for a few minutes before pouring into warm, dry, sterilized jam jars. Cover with paper discs. Seal once cool, label and date. It will keep for years.

Final Additions

There is often a flourish at the end of cooking, when a chef will add a final flavouring just before the dish is whisked out to the table, in much the same way as a barman will squeeze a twist of lemon zest over a dry martini, so that it releases a fine spray of lemon oil just before it is served.

Many last-minute flavourings are ephemeral. A squeeze of sour lime or a grating of nutmeg quickly lose their fragrance, the former only retaining its acidity. Some, such as herbal butters, release their flavour as they are melted on to a dish at the last minute – for instance, the tarragon butter on the Salted Salmon (p.19). Others will retain their independence for a brief period before being absorbed into the general flavour of the dish. A classic example is the tempering of a curry with a spicy seasoning that is fried in ghee before being added at the last minute.

The Michelin-starred Italian chef Massimiliano Alajmo, took this concept one step further in 2008, when he partnered up with the perfumer Lorenzo Dante Ferro to create distillates of natural flavours, such as cardamom, bergamot and ginger. At the last moment, he would spray his dish with his chosen distillate, perhaps seared langoustine with a lemon distillate. No sour lemon juice touched his dish, but his customer would detect the scent of lemons. Such flavourings add to the magic of your final dish, regardless of whether it's a scattering of coriander (cilantro) leaves on a black bean chilli or some coarsely grated orange zest on a pineapple Romanoff (diced pineapple macerated in Cointreau and rum then folded into cream whipped with kirsch).

Labneh with Herbs

Serves 4–6, depending on whether you're serving it with other dishes

The last-minute sprinkling of herbs will transform any dish. Since labneh is often served with other dishes, including crudités such as spring onions (scallions), cucumber and radishes, choose your herbs to draw out the herbal notes in both the cheese and the accompaniments.

Labneh is very easy to make from any type of full-fat (whole) natural yogurt and can be eaten on its own with Pide (p.65) or toasted pitta bread.

500 g/1 lb 2 oz full-fat (whole) natural Greek yogurt (made with sheep's, cow's or goat's milk)

½ tsp fine sea salt, or to taste

To serve

1 tbsp finely chopped celery heart leaves

1 tbsp finely chopped mint leaves

2 tbsp finely chopped chives

freshly ground black pepper

1 tbsp extra-virgin olive oil

Place a colander in a rimmed dish. Rinse and squeeze dry a large clean square of muslin (cheesecloth), letting its sides flop over the rim of the colander.

Tip the yogurt into a bowl and mix in the salt. Spoon the mixture into the muslin and fold the cloth over the top of the yogurt. Leave in the refrigerator for 24 hours. The whey will drain from the yogurt. The longer you leave it, the thicker and firmer the labneh will become.

Transfer to a serving bowl. Mix together the chopped herbs, then season the labneh with some freshly ground black pepper, drizzle with the olive oil and sprinkle with the herbs. Serve immediately.

Sichuan Pepper and Orange Dressed Squid

Serves 4

Sichuan pepper contains sanshools that can numb the lips and make you more sensitive to touch and to cold. Serve this dish quickly to maximize their aromatic flavour. I've presumed that you are using fresh spice in this recipe, but remember that the flavour of Sichuan pepper fades with age.

2 oranges

½ tsp Sichuan pepper

1 tsp runny honey

2 tsp rice or white wine vinegar

2 tbsp naturally brewed soy sauce

3 tbsp extra-virgin olive oil

900 g/2 lb squid, cleaned (see p.144 for method)

1 curly endive heart, trimmed and washed

salt and freshly ground black pepper

Slice both ends off each orange. Stand each fruit upright; slice off their skin and thick white pith, leaving only the flesh. Hold the first orange over a bowl large enough to catch the juice and use a small-serrated knife to cut away each segment so that it drops into the bowl, leaving behind the fibrous casing. Repeat with the remaining orange.

Set a dry frying pan (skillet) over a medium heat. Add the Sichuan pepper and cook for 2 minutes, shaking regularly until the pepper releases its fragrance. Tip into a mortar and roughly grind, before placing in a medium-sized mixing bowl.

Add 1 tbsp orange juice from the segmented oranges to the Sichuan pepper, then mix in the honey, vinegar, soy sauce and 1 tbsp of the olive oil.

Rinse the cleaned squid and cut up the side of each body so that you can open it out as a flat sheet. Using a sharp knife, neatly score a diamond pattern on the inside of each squid and cut into wide strips. If you are cooking the tentacles, carefully scrape off their suckers.

Pat dry the prepared squid and mix in the remaining olive oil. Lightly season with salt and black pepper.

Set a cast-iron griddle pan over a high heat. Once very hot, cook the squid in batches. Thick-fleshed squid will take 3 minutes in total. Thin-fleshed pieces of squid will only take a few seconds to cook. As soon as the squid turns white with golden flecks, remove and mix into the marinade. Leave to cool for about 30 minutes.

Place the curly endive leaves and orange segments in a mixing bowl. Mix in the tepid squid and, if necessary, season. Arrange on 4 small plates and serve immediately as a starter.

Banana Flambé

Serves 2

Many spirits, such as rum and brandy, are highly aromatic. They retain their flavour if added to a cold dish. For example, if you add rum to a banana ice cream mixture it will taste the same as if you sipped it from a glass. However, add the same rum to a hot dish and it will change its flavours and turn slightly harsher. This can be softened by setting it alight, which – as Harold McGee describes in his book *On Food and Cooking* – 'gives a lightly singed flavour to a dish'. You can test it out for supper one night.

4 small or 2 large bananas

30 g/1 oz/2 tbsp unsalted butter

juice of 1 small orange

juice of ½ lemon

1 tbsp caster (granulated) sugar

2 tbsp of white or dark rum

Peel the bananas. If they are large, cut each banana into 2 shorter lengths before halving lengthwise. If small, just halve lengthwise.

Melt the butter in a non-stick frying pan (skillet) over a moderate heat. Add the bananas to the sizzling butter and fry briskly for 2 minutes before turning and frying for another 1 minute.

Add the orange juice, lemon juice and sugar. Cook briskly for 2 minutes or until the sugar has dissolved and the juice has reduced to a light syrup. Have a box of matches to hand, pour in the rum and set alight – standing well back as you do so, to prevent frazzled hair. Give the pan a quick shake, then as soon as the alcohol has burned itself out, spoon the bananas and juice into 2 bowls and serve.

Texture

Texture Recipes

Learning about texture
developing textural awareness

Changing texture
take one ingredient and experiment

Fat sensitivity
fat-like textures can alter perception

Sound
noise influences our appreciation of food

From hand to mouth
how you eat changes your textural experience

Challenging textures
what makes a texture unpleasant?

Texture

'The merit of each dish lies two-thirds in its flavour and one-third in its texture. The latter is an inescapable quality of food, whether good or bad, so it must be controlled.'

CHINESE GASTRONOMY
by Hsiang Ju Lin and Tsuifeng Lin, 1969

How does texture work in cooking? Most cooks, myself included, spend our early adult lives trying to create the textures advocated in recipes. How could I ensure that my pastry was flaky or that my stewed steak was tender? Few of us think about how texture alters our perception of food. I enjoy eating crisp apples and find the gloopy soft nature of porridge comforting, but until recently, I never questioned why.

Yet, in the commercial world, food scientists and chefs have been studying our physical and emotional reactions to different textures in food for some time, in a bid to make ready-made foods more tempting.

Many chefs regard texture as the delivery mechanism for flavour. This sounds very technical, but it's common sense. Different textures in a dish release their tastes and flavours in different ways. Try eating a smooth whipped lemon syllabub – its creamy texture coats your mouth so that you taste the cream, lemon juice and sugar at the same time. This experience remains the same with every spoonful, until it becomes dull. Compare that with eating a crunchy Greek Salad (p.210), which releases its tastes and flavours at different rates. Within seconds, the soft chunks of tomato spurt their savoury juice into your mouth, before the taste changes as you bite on to some peppery crisp onion or an oily, salty black olive. As you chew, your mouth becomes coated in the crumbly feta cheese, changing your perception of the other ingredients. Every mouthful is slightly different and therefore interesting.

Once you start to think about how the texture of food affects you, it's easy to begin playing with different textures. You could, for example, experiment by cutting the vegetables in the Greek salad into larger or smaller pieces to see how it changes your experience. Or, you could add finely grated lemon zest to the syllabub to give tiny bitter lemon spikes of flavour. The human palate is incredibly sensitive; we can detect particles as small as 20 microns (1/50th of a millimetre) within our mouths. That is why some melted chocolate has a grainy texture – the cocoa nibs haven't been ground to the undetectable 17 microns necessary for a silky finish.

In the same way, the creamy custard of a crème brûlée becomes more tempting when its crunchy caramelized sugar topping breaks into bitter-sweet fragments that punctuate the thick cream. Compare your perception of a crème brûlée with a similarly flavoured but slippery textured crème caramel.

We're very sensitive to the viscosity of food and to different fat textures. As Edmund Rolls explains in the *Journal of Texture Studies*, 'texture in the mouth is an important indicator of whether fat is present in a food, which is important not only as a high-value energy source, but also as a potential source of essential fatty acids.'

Soon you will find yourself analyzing everything that you eat. How does it feel in your mouth? How are the tastes and flavours being released? How could it be improved? What noise does it make as you eat it?

Scientists believe that the sound we hear eating food is integral to our experience of texture and flavour. Thus, biting into a carrot stick that crunches is more pleasurable than one that does not. Conversely, many people hate squeaky food, such as lightly cooked green beans. You don't need to be an expert to consider whether such elements add or detract to your enjoyment of a dish.

We may all chew in the same way, but our preferences for different textures are shaped by our culture. According to Malcolm Bourne of Cornell University, Americans relish crispy, creamy and chewy textures. In British cooking, many textures, such as stringy, gritty, mealy and lumpy, are considered unpleasant. The Chinese, however, have learned to appreciate myriad unusual textures, from rubbery goose intestines to bouncy fish balls, in their search for culinary perfection.

The skill of a Chinese chef lies in seeking to improve on nature without obvious artifice. Duck skin is naturally soft and greasy, but in Peking Duck it is transformed into a crisp, dry and fragrant delicacy. Over the centuries, Chinese gourmands have sought out interesting-textured foods that have no intrinsic taste or flavour, such as edible bird's nest or shark's fin. As Hsiang Ju Lin and Tsuifeng Lin explain in *Chinese Gastronomy*, 'the cook was confronted with the problem of creating flavours for things which had no flavour in themselves. In Chinese cooking at its most sophisticated, substances with texture but no flavour were wedded to stocks of great flavour but no substance.'

Japanese chefs also have a wide appreciation of different textures in their food, that range from brittle deep-fried fish bones to flaccid simmered beef tendon. Many such textures are challenging to Westerners, but with time you can grow to love them.

Much pleasure can be found in gently expanding the range of textured foods that you eat. The soft, chewy, almost slimy texture of Indian Lemon and Ginger Pickle (p.149), for example, is wonderful – especially when nibbled while eating a luscious soft pea and paneer curry with chapattis (see pp.140–43).

Coincidentally, this exemplifies the importance of how you eat food. Eating with your fingers is much more sensual than eating with a knife and fork. Scooping the curry into a ripped piece of chapatti with your fingers instantly tells you how soft the peas are and whether the chapatti is tender or tough. An easy test is to eat a chip (p.164) with a fork and then with your fingers. The latter is far more enjoyable as your fingertips quickly detect the crisp, fluffy or soggy nature of the said chip.

The utensils we use to eat, also influence our perception of texture. A wooden spoon, for example, feels rough and warm, compared to the cold smooth feeling of a metal spoon. You can test this out by eating some porridge (p.138) with both types of spoon. The porridge feels heavier and more clumpy on the wooden spoon and creamier with a more delicate texture on a stainless steel or silver spoon.

Your choice of cutlery will also change how you eat. Chopsticks, for example, restrict you to taking small pieces of food, whereas how you use your fork will modify the mix and texture of food in a very different way. No matter which utensil you use, it's surprising how eating in a more measured way can heighten your enjoyment.

Texture Notes

If you haven't consciously thought about texture in your food, take a moment whenever you eat to think about how it feels in your mouth. As with taste, I've outlined some of the broad categories of texture below, with easy tests to help conceptualize them. The recipes that follow are designed to develop textural awareness, including how noisy food and fatty-textured ingredients can be used in cooking.

Liquid

The fluidity of a liquid can vary from the water-like lightness of a clear broth to the thick viscosity of a puréed vegetable soup or the molten interior of a chocolate pudding. It is a highly sensual texture – there are few actions as satisfying as the quenching of thirst, and the cook can play on this association by combining refreshing tastes and delicate flavours in drinks, soups, syrups, jellies and ices. Thin flavoursome liquids in soups (p.64) and fruit salads (p.42) can be used to contrast with the texture of a few choice morsels. The thicker the liquid, the less defined the contrast with other ingredients, such as in minestrone or blueberry compote. Liquid textures often appear in meals as an accompaniment in the form of an intense-tasting sauce – ranging in texture from a thin dip to a thickened sauce that clings to its accompaniment.

Texture test
Make a thick home-made soup, such as Spiced Sweetcorn Soup (p.213) – thin some of it and compare how the thick and thin versions of the soup taste and feel in your mouth.

Jellied

Textures often merge into one another and the most fragile jellied textures can melt into liquid regardless of whether they're a wobbly plum jelly (jello) or the set juices within a pork pie. However, there are many other jellied textures, including unctuous, gelatinous-textured meat, such as pulled pork; crunchy cloud ear fungus (p.136); slippery tapioca (p.147 and p.183); or dense agar-agar set sweets. Some even verge on the chewy, such as marshmallows (p.112) or Turkish delight. In all cases, care is required when matching jelly-like textures with other foods. Complementary soft ingredients are needed when a jelly is going to turn to liquid in the mouth, such as lychees in a lemongrass jelly, and denser-textured ingredients are needed when the dominant food retains its consistency, such as pulled pork within a soft bun.

Texture Test
Make a home-made jelly (p.106 or p.211), but before mixing in the gelatine, set aside a little of the liquid. Once the jelly has set, compare the taste and feel of the flavoured liquid to the set jelly.

Soft

There are myriad different textures that could be described as soft. They range from the fluffy lightness of whipped cream to the chewy softness of a pancake. Many soft-textured dishes induce a sense of comfort in the eater, perhaps because they are a direct throwback to childhood foods, such as egg and cress sandwiches or apple snow. It might also be because many soft foods contain fat. As mentioned on p.123, we have fat-sensitive receptors in our mouths – these heighten our sensitivity to any form of fat and provoke pleasure when we consume fat, in much the same way as when we eat something sweet. Soft foods work well with different-textured ingredients as these can make them more exciting to eat – for example, a creamy spinach tart with crisp, friable pastry.

Texture test
Compare eating some soft Smoked Salmon Pâté (p.182) spread on a slice of soft bread and crisp toast.

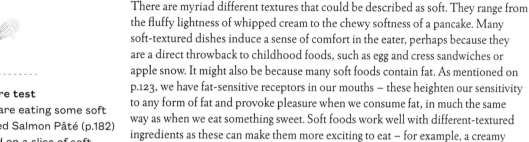

Chewy

As with all textures, chewiness can be good or bad depending on the context. In a toffee, for example, chewiness is wonderful, as it slowly releases its delicious caramel buttery flavours, but the chewiness of a garlic-buttered snail is unbearable for someone who dislikes eating molluscs. Chewy ingredients can be used to prolong or highlight flavours in a dish. A chewy pizza base (p.78), for example, allows the eater to enjoy the different tastes and textures of its topping, while chunky strips of candied orange peel in rough-cut marmalade underline the bitter-sweet orange taste of the marmalade jelly. However, tastes and flavours change with prolonged mastication, so it's wise to consider the final taste and texture on any dish when introducing a chewy element.

Texture test
Make a simple burger with good chopped beef, salt and pepper and grill alongside a sirloin steak. Compare the flavour and texture of the two.

Hard

For the purposes of this book, I'm including crunchy, crisp and brittle textures within this category. At first glance, hardness might seem an unpromising texture in cooking. However, in moderation, hard-textured elements can add excitement by introducing textural contrast and flavours that are released at different rates into a dish. Among the most commonly used hard-textured foods are nuts and crunchy vegetables such as raw carrots, and celery. Brittle-textured foods, such as vegetable crisps, filo pastry and caramel, can add a surprising lightness to a dish, while crackling textures, such as bacon fat, pork crackling and Melba toast, are often used as a textural contrast in richly flavoured dishes.

Texture test
Leave a celery heart in your refrigerator until it turns bendy, and then eat a stem alongside a fresh crisp stem of celery.

Learning About
Texture

Appreciating texture is the most sensual aspect of eating. It allows you to experience food in a fresh way and can change how you cook. Anyone who has run their finger around a mixing bowl after making chocolate cake, will know that there is a quiet moment of bliss as the mixture slowly dissolves and releases its intense chocolate aroma and bitter-sweet taste in the mouth. Somehow, the baked cake never quite recaptures that melting velvety sensation.

The first step towards appreciation is to consciously focus on different textures. Bizarrely, the English language has remarkably few words to describe the texture of food, but you need to conceptualize every texture you create from the 'flocculent' flesh (loose woolly masses) of a baked Bramley apple to the 'coriaceous' (leathery) nature of dried apple slices in a home-made muesli mix.

Since cooking is best learned through practical experience, this section illustrates some of the textures listed in the notes in this chapter, starting with 'liquid' pea soup and finishing with 'hard' breadsticks. If you want to cook in textural order, make the marshmallows after you've eaten the Rhubarb and Rose Water Jelly (p.106). Experiment with each recipe to see how you react to different textures and make a note of what you most enjoy and why so that you can then go on to develop new recipes.

Pea and Sorrel Soup

Serves 8

Puréed soups can be thick or thin. The thicker the soup, the more it coats the mouth, but if a thin soup contains some form of fat, such as cream, it will cling to the mouth and create a sense of pleasure as it releases a single blast of taste.

Other textures should be added with care to puréed soups. Crunchy croûtons were traditionally added to create small spongy soup-filled sops. Chewy textures in thick soups, such as bacon, can be challenging, but soft-textured foods, such as mushy white beans in a white bean soup can be very satisfying.

Thin emulsified soups can have delicate-, soft- or crisp-textured ingredients, including herb leaves, tiny pieces of cucumber or tomato. Only add a small amount, otherwise they can become an annoyance within the mouth.

3 tbsp extra-virgin olive oil

2 large bunches of spring onions (scallions), trimmed and roughly sliced

2 garlic cloves, roughly chopped

1 litre/35 fl oz/generous 4 cups boiling water

1 kg/2 lb 4 oz shelled peas or frozen petits pois

a handful of mint leaves

175 g/6 oz sorrel, washed

150 ml/5 fl oz/⅔ cup natural yogurt (if serving cold)

150 ml/5 fl oz/⅔ cup crème fraîche (if serving hot)

salt and freshly ground black pepper

For the garnish

125 ml/4 fl oz/½ cup natural Greek yogurt

4 tbsp snipped chives

3 tbsp finely shredded small mint leaves

3 tbsp finely shredded sorrel

Set a large saucepan over a medium heat. Add the olive oil, followed by the spring onions and garlic. Fry gently for 8 minutes or until soft. Add the water and bring to the boil, then add the peas and mint leaves. Return to the boil, then cover and simmer gently for 20 minutes, or until the peas are very soft.

Meanwhile, strip the sorrel leaves from their stems by folding together each leaf and pulling the stem down towards the leaf tip. Discard the stems, roughly chop the leaves and mix into the cooked peas. Simmer for 2 minutes, then remove from the heat and liquidize to a smooth purée in a food processor or with a hand-held blender. For a very smooth texture, pass the soup through a sieve.

If serving chilled, set aside until tepid, then whisk in the yogurt, cover and chill. If serving hot, add the crème fraîche (not the yogurt) and reheat. The soup will thicken as it cools, so you may wish to thin it with water if serving chilled.

Season at the temperature of serving. Divide the soup between 8 soup bowls. Add a swirl of Greek yogurt to each bowl. Mix together the chopped herbs for the garnish and sprinkle over the soup.

Rhubarb and Rose Water Jelly x 2

Serves 6

Wobbly jellies (jello) melt into an intense-tasting liquid in the mouth. As a result, you get a pure burst of taste and flavour, such as in this sweet and sour rhubarb jelly that is flavoured with distilled rose water. Compare how this jelly tastes with and without runny double (heavy) cream.

There are two types of gelatine commonly available: leaf and powdered. It will state on the label whether they're extracted from beef or pork. In Britain, powdered gelatine is usually sold in 11.7g/just under ½ oz sachets, and this weight will set 570 ml/20 fl oz/scant 2½ cups liquid.

1.2 kg/2 lb 10 oz forced rhubarb, washed

340 g/12 oz/scant 1¾ cups granulated sugar

200 ml/7 fl oz/generous ¾ cup cold water

1½ tbsp distilled rose water, or to taste

juice of 1 lemon

30 g/1 oz leaf gelatine

200 ml/7 fl oz/generous ¾ cup boiling water

Note

Compare your perception of taste by making a bubbly-textured version: chill the liquid jelly until it's just set, then whisk vigorously until it forms a frothy pink blancmange-like mass. Spoon into a pretty bowl and chill for 2 hours or until set.

Trim the rhubarb discarding the tops and bottoms. Cut each stem into 2.5-cm/1-inch chunks and place in a non-reactive saucepan with the sugar and cold water. Cover and bring to the boil, then reduce the heat and simmer for 10 minutes or until the rhubarb is very soft.

Set 2 fine sieves over two deep bowls and divide the sloppy rhubarb between the sieves. Leave to drip for about 2 hours – don't force any juice through the sieves or the jelly will be cloudy.

Pour the strained juice into a measuring jug. There should be about 850 ml/29 fl oz/generous 3½ cups. Add the rose water and lemon juice to taste.

Meanwhile, place the leaf gelatine in a bowl and cover with cold water. Leave for 5 minutes, then pour off the cold water and add the boiling water. Stir until the gelatine has dissolved. Mix in some rhubarb juice to cool the liquid, then mix all together and strain into your chosen serving bowl. Don't cover or you will get condensation splashes in the jelly. Place in the top of the refrigerator and chill overnight until set.

The remaining rhubarb makes a lovely breakfast dish if mixed to taste with natural Greek yogurt. You can add raspberries and/or a sprinkling of rolled (old-fashioned) oats.

Wobbly jelly quickly melts in the mouth

Pancakes Three Ways

Serves 4 (makes 12 small crêpes)

The soft, easily torn texture of thin pancakes makes a good sop for other textures, whether it be the crunchy sweet and sour contrast of caster (granulated) sugar and lemon juice, a limpid blueberry sauce, or a luscious melted chocolate sauce. Use this pancake recipe to gradually test all three.

115 g/4 oz/generous ¾ cup plain (all-purpose) flour

a pinch of fine sea salt

1 medium egg, lightly beaten

175 ml/6 fl oz/¾ cup full-fat (whole) milk

1 tbsp cold-pressed sunflower oil, plus extra for frying

1 tbsp calvados (optional, but very good)

caster (granulated) sugar, for sprinkling (optional)

2 lemons, each cut into 8 wedges, pips removed (optional)

Sift the flour and salt into a bowl and make a well in the centre. Pour the beaten egg into the well. Mix together the milk and 60 ml/2 fl oz/4 tbsp water and slowly add to the egg, beating with a wooden spoon. Gradually incorporate the flour from the sides of the bowl. Beat until smooth, then strain into a jug. Stir in the sunflower oil and the calvados.

Traditionally, you're supposed to let a batter rest for 30 minutes – it's supposed to produce more tender pancakes, but I've never noticed the difference.

Heat a small 15-cm/6-inch heavy-based frying pan (skillet) and rub with a thick wedge of oil-soaked paper towel. When the pan is very hot and well-greased, pour in about 2 tbsp batter and rotate the pan so that it is evenly coated in a thin layer. As soon as the batter begins to set and forms small bubbles, loosen the edges with a greased palette knife and flip over. Cook for another 1 minute or so, then slip the pancake on to a warm plate and cover with a clean cloth.

Grease the pan once more and repeat the process until all the batter has been used. If you add too much batter to the pan, simply pour it back into the jug.

To serve: As soon as the pancakes are cooked, serve with lots of sugar and lemon wedges, or accompany with either the blueberry and black pepper sauce or the chocolate sauce (see opposite).

Blueberry and black pepper sauce (optional)

1½ tsp arrowroot

3 tbsp cold water

3 strips finely pared lemon zest

juice of ½ lemon

55 g/2 oz/5 tbsp caster (granulated) sugar

1 bay leaf

300 g/10½ oz/2¼ cups blueberries, washed

a pinch of freshly ground black pepper

Chocolate sauce (optional)

170 g/6 oz good-quality dark chocolate pieces

115 g/4 oz/generous ½ cup caster (granulated)

For blueberry and black pepper sauce: The black pepper here heightens your sensitivity to the soft viscous blueberry sauce (see p.75). Mix the arrowroot with the cold water in a small bowl. Tip into a small non-corrosive saucepan and add the lemon zest, lemon juice, caster sugar, bay leaf and blueberries. Set over a low heat, cover and stir occasionally until the blueberries start to release their juice. Simmer for 3 minutes or until the blueberries are just cooked and the sauce has thickened into a glossy compote. Season with the freshly ground black pepper and serve warm or hot.

For chocolate sauce: Place the dark chocolate pieces in a small saucepan with 285 ml/9½ fl oz/ scant 1¼ cups water. Melt over a low heat, stirring occasionally, until smooth. Add the caster sugar and stir until dissolved, then simmer for 20 minutes, stirring occasionally, until it forms a rich sauce.

Prawn and Pork Pot Stickers

Makes 20 dumplings

It's much more exciting to have several different textures in your mouth at one time; pot stickers encase a soft chewy dumpling filling in a slippery, partially caramelized wrapper. It is then dunked into a salty-sour-umami-tasting dip.

For the filling

85 g/3 oz peeled raw king prawns (jumbo shrimp)

175 g/6 oz minced (ground) pork

3 spring onions (scallions), trimmed and finely chopped

2 tsp peeled and finely chopped fresh ginger root

1 tbsp Chinese rice wine or sake

1 tbsp naturally brewed soy sauce

1 tsp caster (granulated) sugar

For the wrappers

115 g/4 oz/generous ¾ cup plain (all-purpose) flour, plus extra for dusting

a pinch of fine sea salt

125 ml/4 fl oz/½ cup freshly boiled water

For cooking

4 tbsp groundnut (peanut) oil

300 ml/10 fl oz/1¼ cups hot water

For the dip

2 tbsp naturally brewed soy sauce

3 tbsp rice vinegar

3 spring onions (scallions), trimmed and finely chopped

To clean the prawns, make a small incision down the length of the back of each prawn and remove the dark digestive thread. Rinse under the cold tap and pat dry before roughly chopping. Place in a bowl, add the minced pork, spring onions, ginger, rice wine, soy sauce and sugar, then mix thoroughly. Chill, covered, for 30 minutes.

Next make the wrappers: Sift the flour and salt into the bowl and make a well in the centre. Add the freshly boiled water to the flour, beating vigorously with the handle of a wooden spoon until it forms a stiff but pliable dough. Turn out and knead until smooth. Wrap in clingfilm (plastic wrap) and rest for 30 minutes.

Roll the dough into a sausage about 2.5-cm/ 1-inch in diameter. Cut the sausage into 20 discs and cover with a clean cloth.

Liberally dust your work surface and a large plate with flour. Take a disc of dough, lightly flour and flatten it in the palm of your hand before rolling it out into a thin 6-cm/2½-inch diameter disc – simply roll once, move the disc a quarter clockwise, roll again and repeat 3 further times. Lightly flour and lay on a plate. Continue with the remaining discs.

Place 1 heaped tsp of the filling in the centre of the first disc. Fold into a semi-circle, and firmly pinch the edges together in small pleats, so that the dumpling is tightly sealed. Place on the floured plate, cover with a clean cloth and repeat the process with the remaining dumplings. Chill until needed.

Set two 25-cm/10-inch diameter non-stick frying pans (skillets) over a medium heat. You will need 2 lids to place over these. Add 2 tbsp of the groundnut oil to each pan. Once hot, sit 10 dumplings in each pan and fry for about 3 minutes, or until the base of each dumpling is golden brown.

Add half the hot water down the side of each pan. Cover both pans and increase the heat to high. Cook for about 5 minutes or until almost all the water has evaporated. Remove the lid and continue to cook for about 7 minutes, or until all the water has evaporated. Using a palette knife, flip the dumplings over so that their browned sides are uppermost – or, if feeling brave, invert them on to a plate.

Meanwhile, make the dipping sauce by mixing together the soy sauce, vinegar and chopped spring onions. Place in small dipping bowls and serve with the piping-hot pot stickers.

Lime and Rose Marshmallows

Makes 600 g/1 lb 5 oz marshmallows

Jellied textures can develop into velvety, fluffy, billowing, soft and chewy variants depending on the cook (see bubbly version of Rhubarb Jelly on p.106). The viscous texture of egg whites, for example, can be whipped up into aerated froth, with or without sugar, and captured in mousses, soft-baked meringues and marshmallows. All release their tastes and flavours slowly.

cold-pressed sunflower oil, for greasing

3 tbsp icing sugar (confectioners' sugar)

3 tbsp cornflour (cornstarch)

30 g/1 oz leaf gelatine

50 ml/2 fl oz/3½ tbsp boiling water

500 g/1 lb 2 oz/2½ cups granulated sugar

250 ml/9 fl oz/1 cup cold water

2 medium egg whites

2 tsp distilled rose water

finely grated zest of 2 limes

Lightly oil a 20 x 30 cm/8 x 12 inch Swiss roll tin (jelly roll pan). Sift the icing sugar and cornflour together into a large mixing bowl. Mix well before liberally dusting the greased pan with 2 tbsp of the mixture.

Cover the gelatine in cold water and soak for 5 minutes. Drain and squeeze out the excess water. Add the boiling water and stir until it has dissolved.

Put the granulated sugar and measured cold water in a saucepan. Clip a jam thermometer onto the pan. Set over a low heat and stir occasionally until the sugar has dissolved, then bring to the boil.

Put the egg whites in a mixing bowl. Once the sugar syrup is near to hard ball (120°C/250°F on the thermometer), whisk the egg white with an electric whisk until it forms soft peaks.

As soon as the syrup reaches hard ball, pour it into the melted gelatine, taking care as it will bubble up. Stir to mix, then pour a slow, steady stream of the hot gelatine syrup into the whisked egg whites while whisking at full speed. Continue to whisk at full speed for about 10 minutes or until the egg white billows up into a thick, glossy fluff that holds a faint trail.

Finally, whisk in the rose water and lime zest and spoon into the prepared tin. Leave in a cool place for 2 hours until set. Do not chill.

Once the mixture has set, liberally dust a large chopping board with some of the icing sugar mixture. Oil a knife and keep well dusted with icing sugar mixture. Gently turn out the marshmallow mixture. Cut into squares with the dusted knife. Toss the squares in the bowl of icing sugar mixture. It is now ready to pack and/or serve.

Stir-fried Crispy Beef

Serves 4

Taste and flavour gradually change the longer any food is chewed. As a result, it's important to control chewy textures and, if necessary, add contrasting and more easily bitten textures to a dish, to release fresh tastes and flavours as you masticate. In this recipe, the Sichuan pepper imbues the chewy beef with an intriguing tingling sensation, while the orange zest adds a bitter note and the sauce introduces tempting sweet-sour notes. The easiest ways to create chewy textures are to remove excess liquid from ingredients by salting, sugaring, drying or frying them.

2 strips of finely pared bitter (Seville) or sweet orange peel

1 tsp Sichuan pepper

1 tsp cornflour (cornstarch)

pinch of fine sea salt

350 g/12 oz lean beef, such as rump or topside

2⅔ tbsp cold-pressed sunflower oil

2 large carrots, peeled

corn oil, for deep frying

1 tbsp peeled and finely chopped fresh ginger

2 garlic cloves, finely grated

1 tsp dried chilli flakes

1 red (bell) pepper, quartered, seeded and finely sliced

6 tbsp caster (granulated) sugar

4½ tbsp rice vinegar

3 tbsp naturally brewed soy sauce

4 spring onions (scallions), trimmed and finely sliced

Put the orange peel on a small baking sheet. Place in the oven and turn it to 130°C fan/150°C/300°F/gas mark 2. Bake for 30 minutes, until dry.

Put the Sichuan pepper in a small dry frying pan (skillet) over a medium heat. Once it smells fragrant, place in a spice grinder with the dried orange peel and grind to a powder. Tip into a large bowl. Mix in the cornflour and salt.

Cut the beef into long thin matchsticks, mix into the spiced cornflour and marinate for 20 minutes. Then mix in 2 tsp of the sunflower oil and separate the beef strands.

Cut the carrots into sticks roughly the same size as the beef. Heat the corn oil in a deep-fat fryer to 190°C/375°F. Add the carrots in batches and deep fry for 2 minutes, or until they are golden with a slightly dry texture. Remove and drain on paper towels. Increase the temperature to 200°C/400°F. Carefully add some of the beef and cook for 30 seconds, until firm. Remove and drain on paper towels. Once the oil returns to 200°C/400°F, repeat the process until all the beef is cooked.

When ready to serve, heat 2 tbsp sunflower oil in a non-stick frying pan. Add the ginger, stir-fry for a few seconds, then add the garlic, chilli flakes and sliced red pepper. Cook for 30 seconds, then add the sugar, vinegar and soy sauce. Once hot, mix in the beef, carrots and spring onions. Heat through and serve immediately with steamed rice.

Crunchy-Munchy Cauliflower Salad

Serves 4

Crunchy textures belong on the soft side of hard and can be used to add an element of excitement to a dish. They are often combined with crisp or softer textures, as in this salad where the cauliflower contrasts with the crisp cucumber, softer tomatoes and the chewy spring onions (scallions). Raw button mushrooms are added at the last moment to introduce a surprisingly moreish, nutty-flavoured, spongy texture.

1 small garlic clove, finely chopped

1 tsp smooth Dijon mustard

2 tbsp white wine vinegar

6 tbsp extra-virgin olive oil

1 small cauliflower, cut into small florets

½ cucumber, peeled and cut into medium-sized dice

300 g/10½ oz flavoursome tomatoes, cut into medium-sized dice

6 spring onions (scallions), trimmed and cut into chunks

115 g/4 oz button mushrooms, trimmed and diced

salt and freshly ground black pepper

Mix together the garlic, mustard and salt and pepper to taste in a salad bowl. Whisk in the vinegar, followed by the extra-virgin olive oil.

As with all salads, it's important to make sure all your washed ingredients are dry, otherwise their water destroys both the texture and taste of the dressing. Add the cauliflower florets to the bowl. Toss the cucumber and tomatoes into the cauliflower florets with the spring onions. Adjust the seasoning if necessary. Add the diced mushrooms just before serving.

Parmesan Breadsticks

Makes 28 breadsticks

The sharp snap of breaking a breadstick (photographed on p.133) is part of the pleasure of eating hard food.

55 g/2 oz/scant ¼ cup unsalted butter

200 ml/7 fl oz/generous ¾ cup full-fat (whole) milk

1 tsp active dried yeast

175 g/6 oz/scant 1½ cups Italian '00' flour

200 g/7 oz/scant 1½ cups strong white (bread) flour, plus extra for dusting

6 tbsp finely grated Parmesan

½ tsp cayenne pepper

1 tsp fine sea salt

Melt the butter in a small saucepan over a low heat. As soon as it has melted, add the milk and, once tepid, tip into a small bowl. Mix in the yeast.

In a large bowl, mix together the flours, Parmesan, cayenne pepper and salt. Once the yeast has dissolved, pour into the flour bowl and mix thoroughly with your hands until it forms a dough. If it is very stiff, add 2 tbsp water.

Turn out the dough onto a clean surface, knead for 2 minutes, then stretch it into a rectangle about 2.5-cm/1-inch thick. Using your fingers held vertically above the dough, push lots of dimples into its surface to create air pockets. Fold the top third over the dough and lightly indent again, then cover with the bottom third and dimple again. Give the dough a quarter turn and repeat the process – stretching it out, dimpling and folding. Cover with a damp tea towel and leave for 40 minutes.

Repeat this process (stretch and give it a quarter turn, twice). Leave for another 40 minutes.

Preheat the oven to 210°C fan/230°C/450°F/gas mark 8.

Cut the dough in half lengthways, then on a floured surface roll out the first half into a rectangle about 5-mm/¼-inch thick. Using a ruler, slice 1-cm/½-inch thick strips across the width (not length) of the dough. Then, on a clean surface, roll the first strip with your fingertips, starting at the centre and moving outwards so that you gently stretch the dough into 30 cm/12 inch lengths. Lightly flatten each end with your thumb. Place on one of 2 non-stick baking sheets. Repeat until finished. Leave to rest for 10 minutes.

Put them in the oven and turn it down to 180°C fan/ 200°C/400°F/gas mark 6. Bake for 15 minutes or until golden. Turn off heat. Leave in oven for 30 minutes or until crisp. Cool on a wire rack. Store in an airtight container for up to 1 week.

Changing Texture

Much of cookery is focussed on controlling texture. The aim is always to create a harmonious dish, and every cuisine has its tried and tested methods to achieve the desired texture.

However, a useful culinary exercise is to consider how an ingredient might change in taste and flavour if it were subjected to different texture categories, ranging from liquid to brittle. A tomato, for example, can be raw or cooked; it can be liquefied, jellified or frozen as a savoury ice; it can be made into a thin purée or cooked as thick as jam with sugar (à la Marcel Boulestin); its skinned, seeded flesh can be salted or sugared to make it firmer; it can be halved and lightly seared to make it succulent, or roasted until it melts; you can make paper-thin, brittle, dried tomato slices or a luscious, soft, chopped tomato salsa. The possibilities are endless.

Even the way an ingredient is cut will alter your perception of texture. A finely sliced tomato takes on a silken, melt-in-the-mouth texture when cut with a superb Japanese knife, and a detectably rougher mouth feel if cut with a fine German-made chef's knife.

A natural step is to then think about what other ingredients might be added to enhance your chosen texture. Crisp Florence fennel, for example, complements chicory (Belgian endive). Combine both and they can be turned into a refreshing sweet crunchy salad (see opposite) with the addition of juicy sweet sour grapefruit segments; or metamorphosed into a comforting, gooey, bitter-sweet, umami-tasting gratin (p.118) with double (heavy) cream and Parmesan cheese.

You can develop this concept further by focussing on a particular type of textured food. A classic example might be baked custard. What other textures might enhance it? Compare your experience of eating a Crème Caramel (p.120) with a Bread and Butter Pudding (p.122).

Fennel, Pink Grapefruit and Chicory Salad

Serves 4

Varying textures within a salad will make you much more sensitive to its different tastes and flavours. Here, the juicy soft grapefruit segments are used to accentuate the sweet taste and aniseed flavour of the crisp fennel and the bitter sweet notes of the chicory (Belgian endive) to create a more exciting dish. If you want to make the fennel chewy rather than crisp, leave it to macerate for an hour before mixing.

3 pink grapefruit

3 tbsp extra-virgin olive oil

2 large Florence fennel, trimmed

1 heaped tbsp roughly chopped tarragon

4 chicory (Belgian endives), trimmed

salt and freshly ground black pepper

Slice both ends off each grapefruit. Standing each fruit upright, slice down and round the sides of each fruit to remove the skin and thick white pith, leaving only the flesh. Holding the first grapefruit over a bowl to catch the juice, use a small-serrated knife to cut away each segment so that they drop into the bowl, leaving behind the fibrous casing. Squeeze any excess juice from the casing into the bowl. Repeat with the remaining grapefruit.

Measure out 6 tbsp grapefruit juice in a large bowl. Add the olive oil and season to taste.

Top, tail and halve the fennel. Remove and discard the tough outer layer. Finely slice each half into fine fans. Mix into the grapefruit dressing with the tarragon. If you want a softer-textured fennel – leave to macerate for 1 hour at this stage and add the tarragon later, when you mix the salad.

To serve: cut the chicory in half lengthwise, remove any damaged outer leaves, then finely slice each half into fans and mix into the fennel. Add the grapefruit segments to the chicory – you can treat their excess juice as a cook's perk. Adjust the seasoning of the salad to taste, and serve.

Gratin of Fennel and Chicory

Serves 4

The same two crisp ingredients of fennel and chicory (Belgian endive) that are used in the salad on the previous page are transformed here to create a yielding, rich dish. As they soften, their taste becomes mellow and sweet. The cream and butter enhance their sweetness and create a gooey, comforting texture. The crunchy Parmesan topping is added for textural contrast and, crucially, to give a moreish, umami bite to this intrinsically bitter-sweet dish.

The texture, taste and flavour of this dish changes as it cools and the cream and cheese solidify. Texturally, it is at its best hot, but its flavour is perfect when warm.

2 fat Florence fennel, trimmed

2 fat chicory (Belgian endives), trimmed

30 g/1 oz/2 tbsp unsalted butter

3 tbsp soft white breadcrumbs

3 tbsp finely grated Parmesan

200 ml/7 fl oz/generous ¾ cup double (heavy) cream

salt and freshly ground black pepper

Heat the oven to 180°C fan/200°C/400°F/gas mark 6.

Discard any tough outer layers from the fennel, slice in half lengthways and cut into very thick fans. Add the fennel to a saucepan of boiling unsalted water, cover, and return to the boil. Cook for about 8 minutes in total, or until the fennel is tender when pierced with a knife. Drain thoroughly.

Cut the chicory into quarters or sixths lengthwise – they need to be thick and chunky. Melt the butter in a large frying pan (skillet) over a medium-low heat. Add the chicory and fry for 4 minutes, turning regularly, until they are lightly browned on all sides and beginning to soften.

Arrange alternate wedges of the buttery chicory and blanched fennel in a single layer in a shallow, 23 x 23 cm/9 x 9 inch gratin dish. Lightly season.

Mix together the breadcrumbs and Parmesan, then sprinkle evenly over the vegetables, before pouring the cream on top.

Bake immediately (otherwise the chicory will discolour) in the hot oven for about 40 minutes, or until the vegetables are meltingly soft when tested with a small knife and the cheesy crumbs are crisp and golden.

Meltingly soft textures convey comfort

Saffron and Cinnamon Crème Caramel

Serves 6

The perfect crème caramel should have a smooth, almost slippery texture. This is achieved by gently baking a custard made with full-fat (whole) milk and eggs. The more fat the custard contains, as in double (heavy) cream or egg yolks, the more dense and rich its texture will become. You can, of course, infuse it with any flavour you choose, or you can add other textures, such as bread, to alter your perception of the taste and flavour. Compare this pudding with the Bread and Butter Pudding (p.122).

For the custard

a small pinch of saffron threads

85 g/3 oz/7 tbsp caster (granulated) sugar

500 ml/18 fl oz/scant 2¼ cups full-fat (whole) milk

8-cm/3¼-inch cinnamon stick, roughly broken

2 whole medium eggs

4 medium egg yolks

For the caramel

115 g/4 oz/scant ⅔ cup granulated sugar

4 tbsp cold water

Place the saffron in a bowl with a pinch of the caster sugar and roughly grind it, using the back of a teaspoon. Tip into a saucepan and add the milk, cinnamon pieces and remaining caster sugar. Slowly bring to the boil, stirring occasionally, until the sugar has dissolved. Remove from the heat and leave to infuse for 20 minutes.

Place six 150 ml/5 fl oz/⅔ cup soufflé dishes in a deep roasting pan. Add boiling water to the pan to warm the dishes. Then put the granulated sugar for the caramel into a heavy-based saucepan with the cold water. Set over a low heat and stir regularly until the sugar has dissolved. Increase the heat and boil rapidly until the sugar turns a rich brown – it will continue to darken after you remove it from the heat. Quickly divide the caramel between the 6 dishes – turning each dish to ensure that its base is evenly coated in caramel. Discard the hot water from the roasting pan and set the dishes aside to cool.

Using a wooden spoon, beat the eggs and the egg yolks together, then stir in the tepid saffron milk. Strain the mixture through a sieve into a jug (pitcher). Leave to rest for 1 hour in the refrigerator (this removes any bubbles and froth).

Preheat the oven to 130°C fan/150°C/300°F/gas mark 2.

Put several layers of paper towels on the base of the roasting pan. Arrange the soufflé dishes on top and fill the dishes with the custard. Add enough hot (not boiling) water to come three-quarters of the way up the side of the dishes and very carefully place in the centre of the oven. Loosely cover the top of the pots with some foil to stop them forming a skin. Bake for about 40 minutes. The custards are cooked when they wobble slightly if you give them a slight shake; if they ripple, they need a little longer.

Remove from the oven and gently lift each pot from the water. Leave to cool. Once cold, cover with clingfilm (plastic wrap) and chill for a minimum of 2 hours.

To serve, gently press the sides of the baked custard with your finger to release them from the dish or run a small knife around the edge of each. Place a shallow, lipped plate over each dish and invert with a sharp motion – the custard should slip out with its caramel sauce intact.

Saffron and Cinnamon Bread and Butter Pudding

Serves 6

- -

You can use different ingredients to alter the texture of a baked custard pudding. Here, the bread introduces a soft airy interior that makes you hold the custard longer in your mouth, while the crisp topping creates more defined toasted notes. The sultanas introduce chewy nuggets of fruity sweetness.

a generous pinch of saffron threads

115 g/4 oz/scant ⅔ cup granulated sugar, plus 1 tbsp for sprinkling

425 ml/15 fl oz/generous 1¾ cups full-fat (whole) milk

425 ml/15 fl oz/ generous 1¾ cups double (heavy) cream

10-cm/4-inch cinnamon stick, roughly broken

55 g/2 oz/scant ¼ cup unsalted butter, softened, plus extra for greasing

9 medium-thick slices good white bread (p.52)

85 g/3 oz/⅔ cup sultanas (golden raisins)

30 g/1 oz/3½ tbsp chopped mixed candied peel

2 medium eggs

3 medium egg yolks

½ tsp distilled rose water

Place the saffron in a bowl with a pinch of the sugar and roughly grind it, using the back of a teaspoon. Tip into a saucepan and add the milk, cream, cinnamon pieces and remaining sugar. Slowly bring to the boil, stirring occasionally, until the sugar has dissolved. Remove from the heat and leave to infuse for 20 minutes.

Generously butter a 30 x 23 cm/12 x 9 inch oval, shallow, oven-proof dish. Liberally butter the sliced bread, then cut off their crusts and slice into quarters. Arrange half of the bread in the buttered dish, buttered-side up, and sprinkle on the sultanas and candied peel. Cover with the remaining buttered bread, buttered-side up.

In a large jug (pitcher), beat together the eggs and egg yolks. Stir in the saffron milk and add the distilled rose water. Strain the custard through a sieve on to the bread in the dish. Lightly cover and chill for 30 minutes so that the custard has time to soak into the bread.

Preheat the oven to 140°C fan/160°C/325°F/gas mark 3.

Sprinkle the top of the pudding with 1 tbsp granulated sugar. Place in a large roasting pan and add enough just-boiled water to come halfway up the sides of the dish. Bake for 1 hour or until the custard is set and the pudding is flecked gold. Serve hot, warm or at room temperature.

Fat Sensitivity

Scientists are still in the early stages of understanding how we detect and interpret fat in our food. They've discovered that our mouths are very sensitive to viscosity and to fatty textures, ranging from fat-rich ingredients such as cream and chocolate, to chemically completely different substances that have a similar texture, such as mineral oil or silicone oil.

Perhaps not surprisingly, our enjoyment of fat-like textures is moderated by a sophisticated combination of taste, flavour and mouth feel, which is shaped by our cultural background. Offer the average Briton a nutty slice of good Cheddar cheese and the chances are they will thoroughly enjoy eating it. Proffer the same cheese to someone in China and, according to food writer Fuchsia Dunlop, the chances are that they will wrinkle their nose in disgust. The reason is simple – its odorous fatty texture lines the mouth and imparts a lingering pungent aroma, that many Chinese interpret as off-dairy and therefore repugnant.

Crucially, fat-like textures change your perception of a dish by coating the mouth. Thus, if you want to create a dish whose taste and flavours quickly fade, you should minimize the fat content. Conversely, if you want to ensure that the tastes and flavours last longer in the mouth, you should incorporate some form of fat, remembering that fat, too, has its own tastes and flavours. An easy test is to toss some diced cucumber, radishes and apples in salt, pepper and lemon juice (an Indian salad), remove half and then mix a little olive oil into the remaining salad. Compare the taste and flavour of the two salads.

It's worth heightening your awareness of fatty foods. This allows you to draw on a much wider repertoire of oleaginous (oily) rich textures to enhance your cooking, ranging from avocados, egg yolks and coconut, to myriad oils, pulverized nuts, seeds, dairy products and meat fats.

Crab and Avocado Tostadas

Serves 4

Fatty textures are used in three separate ways in this delicious starter. The fried tortillas develop a rich, maize flavour and exquisite brittle texture that contrasts with the creamy puréed avocado. The olive oil in the topping captures the crab's ozone citrus notes and imbues it with a richer texture. Interestingly, if you add too much avocado purée – its velvety texture becomes too dominant and detracts from the dish. Balance is everything.

corn oil, for deep frying

12 x 10-cm/4-inch soft white corn tortillas

200 g/7 oz white crab meat

2 limes

1 Thai chilli, or to taste, finely chopped

1 tbsp extra-virgin olive oil

2 ripe avocados, quartered, stoned and peeled

115 g/4 oz flavoursome tomatoes, peeled

a handful of coriander (cilantro) leaves

salt and freshly ground black pepper

To make the tostadas, heat some oil in a deep-fat fryer to 180°C/350°F. Add a single layer of tortillas and fry for about 2 minutes, or until pale but crisp – they continue to cook a little as they cool. Remove to a plate lined with plenty of paper towels and pat dry. Repeat the process until all are cooked. Set aside.

Pick through the crab meat and remove any tiny pieces of shell. Gently squeeze out any excess moisture and place the meat in a bowl. Finely grate and juice 1 lime and mix the zest and juice into the crab meat. Add half of the finely chopped Thai chilli, or to taste, followed by the olive oil. Season very lightly.

Purée the avocados with the juice of the second lime and the remaining finely chopped chilli. Season to taste.

Peel the tomatoes by placing in a bowl, covering with boiling water and giving each tomato a tiny cut to split the skin. Leave for 2 minutes, then drain and peel. Halve the tomatoes and cut into small dice. Set aside.

When you are ready to serve, spread a spoonful of avocado purée over each tostada, top with a spoonful of crab meat, add a little tomato and scatter with coriander leaves. Serve with paper napkins.

Light fatty textures give pleasure if carefully combined

Pear Syllabub

Serves 6

Fluffy whisked cream is commonly incorporated into recipes to add lightness. It feels fragile on the tongue, yet the cloying richness of the cream conveys depth and quickly satiates the eater. Whipped cream is often used as a carrier of taste and flavour, such as sweetened raspberries in a cream cake or passion fruit purée on a pavlova. In this recipe, the texture of the whisked cream is diluted by the velvety pear purée, while the lemon zest adds fine texture.

4 tbsp Poire William eau de vie (pear liqueur)

2 tbsp calvados

115 g/4 oz/generous ½ cup caster (granulated) sugar

1 lemon, finely grated and juiced

3 ripe pears (about 700 g/1 lb 9 oz)

300 ml/10 fl oz/1¼ cups double (heavy) cream

freshly grated nutmeg, to taste

Place the Poire William eau de vie, calvados, sugar, lemon zest and half the lemon juice in a large mixing bowl. Leave to macerate while you prepare the pears.

Meanwhile, put the remaining lemon juice in a small non-corrosive saucepan. Peel, quarter and core the pears. Cut into chunks and mix into the lemon juice in the saucepan. Cover and set over a medium-low heat, stirring regularly, and cook for about 15 minutes, or until the pears have released their juice and become meltingly soft. Liquidize into a smooth purée in a food processor or using a hand-held blender, transfer to a bowl and cool.

Once the puréed pears are cold, add the cream to the lemon juice in the large bowl. Whisk until it forms soft floppy peaks, then fold in the pear purée using a flat metal spoon. Spoon into wine glasses or small glass bowls and sprinkle with freshly grated nutmeg when you serve the syllabub.

Caramelized Onion and Beef Stew

Serves 6

As Harold McGee states in his book *Food & Cooking,* 'it's largely the contents of the fat tissue that give beef, lamb, pork and chicken their distinctive flavours.' Depending on the animal, this can be marbled throughout its flesh, particularly in the cheaper cuts, such as feather steak. Slow cooking gently releases the fat to create a meltingly tender dish. In this recipe, butter and oil are added to create a rich onion sauce. This stew can be simmered, covered, on a low heat on the stove top if necessary.

5 tbsp extra-virgin olive oil

200 g/7 oz smoked back bacon, trimmed of fat and diced

100 g/3½ oz/7 tbsp unsalted butter

600 g/1 lb 5 oz onions, finely sliced

2 garlic cloves, finely sliced

1.5 kg/3 lb 5 oz beef feather steak

3 tbsp plain (all-purpose) flour

3 strips finely pared lemon zest

2 cloves

1 bay leaf

a few sprigs of thyme

a few sprigs of parsley

4 large carrots, peeled and thickly sliced into rounds

½ celeriac, peeled and diced

salt and freshly ground black pepper

Preheat the oven to 120°C fan/140°C/275°F/gas mark 1.

Set a large oven-proof saucepan (with a lid), or a cast-iron casserole dish, over a low heat. Once hot, add the oil and fry the bacon until it is lightly coloured. Add 70 g/2½ oz/5 tbsp of the butter and, once melted, mix in the onions and garlic and fry gently for 12 minutes or until soft.

Meanwhile, trim any fat and sinew from the beef by cutting along the muscle and thicker fat seams. Cut the trimmed meat into 2-cm/¾-inch pieces. Season the flour with salt and freshly ground black pepper, then toss the meat in the seasoned flour.

Increase the heat under the pan to high and mix the beef into the onions. Keep stirring until the beef is well browned, then add the lemon peel, cloves, bay leaf, thyme and parsley. Season to taste, cover tightly, and transfer to the oven. Cook for 1 hour.

Set a frying pan (skillet) over a medium heat, melt the remaining butter and add the carrot and celeriac. Cook briskly until lightly coloured. Stir the vegetables and butter into the meat. Bake for another 1 hour, or until the meat is meltingly tender and the onions have dissolved into a thick rich sauce.

Remove the lemon zest and herbs and either serve the stew or leave to cool. Cover and chill or freeze once tepid. Reheat when needed or turn into a Rich Beef Pie (p.128).

Rich Beef Pie

Serves 6

Half the fun of playing with texture is to experiment by adding further layers of texture. The Caramelized Onion and Beef Stew (p.127) has a rich beefy flavour and luscious texture, but add another type of fatty texture, namely puff pastry and you will create an even deeper, more intensely satisfying dish. The buttery pastry dissolves in your mouth as you chew an ever-changing mixture of soft meat, carrots and pastry. This pastry can be made in advance and frozen, but if in a rush, use 375 g/13 oz ready-made all-butter puff pastry.

1 x Caramelised Onion and Beef Stew (p.127), cold

For the puff pastry

225 g/8 oz/1¾ cups plain (all-purpose) flour, plus extra for dusting

a pinch of fine sea salt

225 g/8 oz/1 cup cold unsalted butter, diced

125 ml/4 fl oz/½ cup cold water

1 small egg, beaten

To make the pastry: place the flour and salt in a food processor with 30 g/1 oz/2 tbsp of the cold butter. Process until it forms fine crumbs. Tip into a bowl and mix in enough cold water to form a rough dough. Lightly knead into a ball, wrap in a polythene bag or clingfilm (plastic wrap) and chill for 30 minutes.

Remove the remaining butter from the refrigerator 15 minutes before needed to soften slightly. Place the butter between 2 sheets of baking paper and use a rolling pin to flatten it into a 2.5-cm/1-inch thick rectangle.

On a floured surface, roll the dough into a rectangle that is 3 times the length and about 2.5 cm/1 inch wider than the butter. Place the butter in the centre of the dough and fold over the top and bottom flaps of dough, so that the butter is completely covered. Using the rolling pin, lightly press down on each edge so that the butter is sealed in. Give the dough a quarter-turn clockwise.

Using short, sharp, strokes, roll out the dough so that it returns to its original length (3 times that of the butter) but retains the same thickness. Then, fold in the top and bottom ends, press the edges with the rolling pin and give a further quarter-turn clockwise. If the butter is breaking through the pastry or the pastry is becoming warm, stop and return to the polythene bag or rewrap in clingfilm and chill for 30 minutes. If not, you can repeat the rolling process one more time before chilling the dough. Make a note of which way the dough is facing before chilling, as you will need to continue with the clockwise quarter-turns.

After 30 minutes of chilling, replace the pastry on the floured surface in the position that you left off and continue with a further 2 rolls and quarter-turns. Wrap and chill until needed. The butter should be integrated into the dough.

To make the pie: preheat the oven to 180°C fan/ 200°C/400°F/gas mark 6.

Roll out the pastry to fit the top of a 2 litre/ 3½ pint/2 quart pie dish – using the top of the dish as a template to cut out the pastry, making it 1 cm/½ inch larger to allow for the pie funnel. Line the rim of the pie dish with a strip of pastry and brush with a little beaten egg. Add the cold beef stew filling and slip in a pie funnel. Loosely roll the pastry lid around the rolling pin, lift over the pie dish and unroll to cover. Using a fork, press firmly around the rim so that the pastry lid is glued to the rim. If necessary, trim off the excess pastry using a sharp knife. Prick the pastry lid in 3 places with a small sharp knife and brush with some more beaten egg.

Bake for 35 minutes, or until the pastry is crisp and golden, then serve.

Gooey Chocolate Orange Brownies

Makes 12 brownies

- -

What makes a gooey chocolate brownie so good? Is it solely its bitter-sweet taste and chocolate flavour, or is it also the luscious fatty textures of its butter, egg yolks and cocoa fat?

Clearly, it is all of the above, but you can underline these characteristics by adding bitter-sweet, moisture-retentive ingredients, such as soft brown sugar and grated cooked beetroot (beets) to create an even richer brownie, or chewy elements such as diced prunes. The orange zest adds an exciting, almost unexpected flavour. Compare with the crunchy, Chocolate Tiffin (p.226).

2 medium-sized beetroot (beets), cooked, peeled and roughly grated (see method for cooking instructions)

200 g/7 oz good-quality dark chocolate, chopped

2 large eggs, beaten

1 large egg yolk

225 g/8 oz/generous 1 cup light brown muscovado sugar

finely grated zest of 2 large oranges

55 g/2 oz/⅓ cup roughly diced soft prunes

85 g/3 oz/scant ⅔ cup plain (all-purpose) flour, sifted

a pinch of fine sea salt

140 g/5 oz/10 tbsp unsalted butter, diced

If you need to cook your own beetroot, preheat the oven to 180°C fan/200°C/400°F/gas mark 6. Wash and wrap the roots in foil and bake for about 1 hour. Leave to cool, then peel and weigh out 100 g/ 3½ oz and roughly grate. (The rest can be added to a salad.)

Preheat the oven to 170°C fan/190°C/375°F/ gas mark 5. Line a shallow 18 x 27 cm/7 x 10¾ inch baking pan with baking paper.

Put the chocolate in a large bowl that will neatly fit over a pan of just-boiled water (off the heat). Leave the chocolate to melt – you may need to replace the boiling water once, to allow the chocolate to completely melt.

Break the eggs in a large mixing bowl and roughly beat in the egg yolk, sugar and orange zest. Mix in the grated beetroot and diced prunes. Sift the flour and salt into a separate bowl.

Add the butter to the melted chocolate and stir until it has melted. Remove the bowl from the pan of hot water. The chocolate mixture should be warm not hot. Quickly beat the chocolate mixture into the egg mixture, followed by the flour mixture, and pour into the prepared pan.

Bake for about 20 minutes, or until the mixture has set but is still gooey in the centre. If you insert a skewer, it should have moist crumbs clinging to it. The brownies will continue to cook after they are removed from the oven. Place the pan on a wire rack and leave to cool. When ready to serve, cut into 12 pieces.

Sound

The sound of food is rarely mentioned in cookery books, but most chefs instinctively rely on a subtle change in sizzling or bubbling to tell them when to turn, stir or remove a dish from the heat. It's a skill that can only be learned with experience.

Curiously, many cooks, myself included, pay little attention to the noise that food makes as it is eaten. Yet, our perception of texture is influenced by what we hear as we eat. Imagine how you might feel if you sipped some silent fizzy water, or bit into an apple but heard no crunch. Such noises contribute to our interpretation of the textural structure of food in our mouths.

Our appreciation of gustatory sounds varies according to our cultural background. In Japan, for example, it's considered a sign of appreciation to make slurpy sucking noises as you eat hot pots, noodles and such like. As wine lovers will know, mixing in air as you sup will release more flavour from the broth. In Britain, there is a positive delight in eating crunchy potato crisps. It's been found that if a crisp bag pops open with a small explosion of air, the eater's perception of the crisps' fresh crunchiness is increased and greater pleasure is derived from eating the packet's contents.

Conversely, some people find eating noises very distressing. Many Britons dislike squeaky sounds in their mouths and find the noise of other people slurping repellent. Some people dislike any loud eating sounds, regardless of whether it's someone tucking into popcorn in the cinema or enthusiastically gnawing some barbecued ribs. Try the following recipes to test your friends with crunchy, squeaky and slurpy dishes.

Crunchy Indian Spiced Chickpeas

Makes 2 small bowls

Crunchy salty snacks are much loved around the world. I've chosen spicy chickpeas as, aside from being very moreish, they're an interesting example of how a soft, mealy-textured ingredient can be transformed into a hard crunchy nut.

400-g/14-oz can chickpeas (garbanzo beans), drained and rinsed

¼ tsp ground turmeric

¼ tsp chilli powder

¼ tsp ground cumin

¼ tsp ground coriander

¼ tsp amchoor powder (dried sour mango), optional

1 tsp fine sea salt, or to taste

1 tbsp cold-pressed sunflower oil

½ tsp lemon juice, or to taste

At least 30 minutes before cooking, rinse, drain and pat dry the chickpeas on paper towels. Spread them out in a single layer on a plate.

Preheat the oven to 180°C fan/200°C/400°F/gas mark 6.

Mix together the spices and salt in a small bowl. Place the chickpeas and oil in a separate bowl and mix well, before adding the spice mixture. Toss until completely coated, then tip on to a non-stick baking sheet. Spread the chickpeas into a single layer and bake for 35 minutes, giving the odd shake to move the chickpeas around. I have quite a hot oven, so I take them out at this stage, but you could turn off the oven and leave the chickpeas in the oven for another 15 minutes. The former yields crunchy chickpeas with a floury centre, the latter are very crunchy chickpeas. In either case, leave the chickpeas in their roasting pan but season with the lemon juice. Leave until cold, then serve as needed.

Parmesan Breadsticks (p.115) and Mint Julep (p.63)

Slurpy Prawn Laksa

Serves 4

In order to appreciate the power of sound, you need to eat this laksa in two ways. Begin by eating it western style (as best you may); then, hold the bowl close to your chin, use chopsticks to lift out some of the noodles and suck them up before drawing up some of the hot broth mixed with air direct from the bowl. Which tastes better?

For the laksa paste

2 tsp ground coriander

2 tsp ground cumin

2 tsp ground turmeric

4 banana shallots, peeled and chopped

1–2 Thai chillies, roughly sliced

2.5 cm/1 inch fresh ginger, peeled and roughly chopped

2 fat garlic cloves, roughly chopped

4 stems lemongrass, roughly chopped

100 ml/3½ fl oz/7 tbsp coconut cream

1 tbsp shrimp paste (kapi)

For the soup

24 raw king prawns (jumbo shrimp), shell on

3 tbsp cold-pressed sunflower oil

250 ml/9 fl oz/1 cup coconut cream

1 litre/35 fl oz/generous 4 cups good-quality Chicken Stock (p.47)

6 fresh kaffir lime leaves (optional)

1 tbsp light brown muscovado sugar

1 tbsp Thai fish sauce (nam pla)

2 tbsp naturally brewed soy sauce

6 spring onions (scallions), trimmed and finely sliced

200 g/7 oz dried vermicelli rice noodles

2 large handfuls coriander (cilantro) leaves

2 juicy limes, halved

Note

Compare the texture of this recipe, where the noodles are floating in a creamy coconut broth, with the texture of the Chilled Noodles with Prawns (p.40). The oriental dressing for the latter has no fat, so the mouth feel is much cleaner.

Blend all the ingredients for the laksa paste in a food processor until they form a fine paste. Then, peel the prawns, saving the shells (and heads, if attached).

Set a wide saucepan over a high heat. Add 3 tbsp sunflower oil, followed by the prawn shells (and heads, if removed). Fry briskly for 3 minutes, or until they are pink, then mix in the laksa paste and stir-fry for 2 minutes.

Mix in the coconut cream, chicken stock, kaffir lime leaves, sugar, fish sauce and soy sauce. Bring to the boil and simmer for 30 minutes. Strain and, if not using immediately, chill once cool.

Meanwhile, clean the peeled prawns by running a knife down the length of their backs and removing their digestive threads. Rinse under the cold tap and pat dry. Chill, covered, until needed.

When you are ready to serve, return the broth to boiling point. Add the prawns, simmer gently for 2 minutes, then add the spring onions and cook for another 1 minute or until the prawns are pink through.

At the same time, prepare the noodles by soaking them in a bowl of boiling hot water for 3 minutes or follow the instructions on the packet. Divide the noodles between 4 large, deep soup bowls, pour on the piping-hot soup and sprinkle with the coriander leaves. Serve with the lime halves so that your guests can season their own soup.

Squeaky Thai Salad

Serves 6

This is a classic squeaky salad – I've devised it to make lots of crunchy noises, including the gelatinous, squeaky, dried black Chinese mushrooms, so don't serve it to anyone who is sensitive to such sensations.

30 g/1 oz dried black Chinese mushrooms (cloud ear fungus)

1 small green pointed cabbage, finely sliced

2 carrots, peeled and finely sliced into matchsticks

9 cm/3½ inches peeled mouli, or 1 bunch trimmed radishes, finely sliced into matchsticks

115 g/4 oz/1 cup salted peanuts, roughly chopped

2 tbsp fish sauce (nam pla)

2 tbsp lime juice

1 tbsp caster (granulated) sugar

1 Thai chilli, or to taste, finely sliced

6 fresh kaffir lime leaves, finely shredded, or 12 mint leaves, finely shredded

Wash the dried mushrooms and soak in warm water for 20 minutes. Finely slice their tender wavy caps into thin strips, discarding the tough section at the base of their caps and their tough stalks as you go – there is quite a lot of wastage. Rinse the sliced mushrooms thoroughly, pat dry and place in a large mixing bowl.

Mix the rest of the sliced vegetables and the roughly chopped peanuts into the mushrooms.

Mix together the fish sauce, lime juice, sugar, chilli and kaffir lime leaves or mint. As soon as the sugar has dissolved, pour over the salad, toss and serve.

From Hand
to Mouth

As a cook, it's useful to understand the different ways we can experience the texture of food. It's easy to concentrate on how something feels in your mouth, but in reality your perception of texture begins with your hands. Almost subconsciously, you are constantly detecting and interpreting myriad facts through your fingers, from the suppleness of a mango to the amount of salt and grease on a peanut. Everything contributes to your final experience.

It's worth experimenting with eating the same dish in different ways. Try eating the Mattar Paneer (p.140) with your hands and then with a spoon. Similarly, try eating the Stir-fried Squid (p.144) with chopsticks and then with a fork. You will quickly discover that each utensil draws out different textures and consequently releases the tastes and flavours of a dish in different ways.

You can't but take small mouthfuls with chopsticks. The cook, in turn, must focus on assembling stimulating-tasting, interestingly textured, small pieces of food that work well eaten in quick succession. Everything that is served must be easily bitten or broken, rather than cut.

In contrast, food that is eaten with a knife and fork has to be either bigger, or bound together by another food, such as a sauce or soft-textured vegetable. Try spearing individual peas onto the prongs of a fork – they taste very different to those that are greedily piled on to an upturned fork. Commonly, different ingredients are combined on a fork before reaching the mouth. A piece of roast meat, for example, might be forced on to the fork with some peas, gravy and even a bit of roast potato. They will all be placed in the mouth at the same time. The very act of squashing food onto a fork will change its texture. A canny cook will try to ensure a balance of different textures on the plate that work well eaten from the fork.

Amazingly, even the material of your utensils will change your perception of texture. In their paper, 'The Perception of Materials Through Oral Sensation', Philip Howes et al explain how woods and rough polystyrene are experienced as warm and/or rough in the mouth, while metals are felt as cold and hard. Thus, a metal chopstick or fork could feel incongruous if you're eating a fiery stir-fry, whereas sipping a miso soup from a smooth lacquered bowl is warming. I will explore this aspect of perception further in the last chapter.

Proper Porridge

Serves 2

A good way to test how the material of a utensil can alter your impression of a food texture, is to eat some traditional porridge with a wooden spoon and then with a silver or stainless-steel spoon.

Traditional porridge tastes very different from everyday rolled oats. Whole oats are gently dried in a kiln, then lightly ground to free the kernels (groats) from their outer casing. These are milled into fine, medium or coarse nutty-tasting oats. The latter two can be cooked into a fluffy-textured porridge or used in other dishes, such as haggis. Rolled oats were invented in 1877. The groats are steamed and then rolled flat, which ensures that they cook quickly, but produces a more pappy-textured porridge.

This recipe tastes heavenly with salt, double (heavy) cream and light muscovado sugar. I've used cups in this recipe as it's easiest to make porridge by volume rather than weight. Don't worry if you don't have a cup measure (½ cup is 125 ml/4 fl oz), just use a tea cup.

Different brands of oats absorb different amounts of water depending on how much they've been dried – however, as a general rule, allow 4 times the volume of water to oats. Soft water maximizes their oaty flavour.

½ cup of coarse-ground (steel-cut) oats

2 cups soft spring water

⅛ tsp fine sea salt

light brown muscovado sugar, to taste

organic double (heavy) cream

Place the porridge oats in a heavy-based saucepan with the water. Set over a medium heat and stir until the mixture comes to the boil and starts to thicken. Reduce the heat to low and leave to simmer for 20–30 minutes, giving it the occasional stir. Purists advocate constant stirring, but I find it makes little difference.

Once the porridge has thickened to your taste, add the salt and stir vigorously to loosen the porridge from sticking to the bottom of the pan. Remove from the heat, cover, and leave to sit for 5 minutes.

Serve with muscovado sugar and cream, to taste. Now, take one wooden spoon and either a stainless-steel or a silver spoon – nibble a bit of porridge from the wooden spoon and then try some with the metal spoon.

Porridge feels more dense when eaten from a wooden spoon

Mattar Paneer

Serves 4, if served with other dishes

Eating with your fingers will accentuate your perception of texture. Try eating your first few mouthfuls of this dish (photographed on p.7) with a fork (or spoon) before scooping up the paneer with ripped pieces of chapatti (p.142). Compare the two experiences.

Paneer is very easy to make, but you need to allow it to chill in the refrigerator and firm up before using – about a couple of hours. Don't be put off by the length of this recipe, it's very easy to make and you'll find the paneer is wonderfully light when cooked. You can make the paneer the day before it is needed, if wished.

For the paneer

1 litre/35 fl oz/generous 4 cups Jersey gold top (full cream) milk (not homogenized)

3 rounded tbsp natural yogurt

1 tbsp lemon juice

corn oil, for deep frying

For the mattar paneer

3 tbsp cold-pressed sunflower oil

1 small onion, finely diced

½ tsp peeled and finely diced fresh ginger

scant ¼ tsp chilli powder (or to taste)

1 heaped tsp ground turmeric

1 heaped tsp garam masala

340 g/12 oz tomatoes, peeled and finely chopped

500 g/1 lb 2 oz peas in their pods, shelled (generous 200 g/7 oz shelled weight)

300 ml/10 fl oz/1¼ cups whey (from making the paneer)

fine sea salt

a handful of coriander (cilantro) leaves, roughly sliced

To make the paneer, place the milk in a saucepan and set over a medium heat. Bring to a full boil, stirring occasionally. Remove from the heat and stir in the yogurt and lemon juice. Keep stirring until it has fully separated into lumpy curds.

Set a fine sieve over a large jug (pitcher) and pour in the mixture. Leave the curds to drain for 1 hour, until cool and firmed up. Remove from the sieve, place on a plate, cover and chill. Cover and chill the whey. (Save any whey you don't use – it's delicious added to vegetable and chicken curries in place of water, giving them a creamy, slightly sour taste.)

To make the pea curry (mattar paneer), set a wide pan over a medium-low heat. Once hot, add the oil, followed by the onion and ginger. Fry for 10 minutes, or until soft and golden, then mix in the chilli powder, turmeric and garam masala and fry for 2 minutes.

Meanwhile, put the tomatoes in a bowl, cover with boiling water and lightly cut the skin of each tomato. After 2 minutes, drain, peel and chop the tomatoes.

Stir the tomatoes into the cooked spices and increase the heat to high. Cook briskly until they form a thick purée that releases oil if a spoon is run through it. Add the shelled peas and whey to the tomato mixture. Bring to the boil, then reduce to a simmer and cook gently for 10 minutes, or until the peas are soft. Season to taste.

Shortly before serving, heat the corn oil in a deep-fat fryer to 170°C/340°F. Cut the paneer into 2.5-cm/1-inch chunks and add in batches to the hot oil. Cook for 2 minutes or until they float to the surface and turn golden. Drain on paper towels, then mix into the hot pea curry. Simmer gently for 5 minutes, then remove from the heat and leave to sit for 5 minutes – the paneer chunks will swell as they absorb the juices. Salt to taste and mix in the coriander just before serving.

Chapattis

Makes 10–12 chapattis

A Punjabi cook is judged on the quality of their chapattis (photographed on p.7). It takes practice to make tender chapattis that easily rip so that the eater can scoop up their food. Traditionally, Punjabis eat with their hands and often use this unleavened bread to wrap around their spiced vegetables and dip into their dals, so if the chapatti is too tough or thick, it becomes unwieldy and bulky to eat. The only cutlery that might appear on the table is a spoon.

Chapatti flour can be bought in Asian and Middle Eastern stores, but you can use stoneground wholemeal flour instead.

350 g/12 oz/2⅔ cups brown chapatti (wholemeal) flour, plus extra for dusting

1 tsp fine sea salt

250 ml/9 fl oz/1 cup cold water

1 tbsp ghee (clarified butter)

For the ghee
55 g/2 oz/scant ¼ cup unsalted butter

Mix together the flour and the salt in a medium bowl. Add the water, then turn out onto a lightly floured work surface. Knead for a good 10 minutes – it will be very sticky, but keep kneading by pushing the heel of your hand into the dough and away from yourself, before pulling the dough back on itself and repeating the process. Gradually the dough will become less sticky – be patient and don't add too much flour by sprinkling as it will make the chapattis tough. By the end of the 10 minutes, you should have a soft, springy dough. The longer you knead, the lighter the bread. Return to a clean bowl, cover with a plate and leave to rest for 1½ hours.

To make the ghee: Melt the butter in a small pan over a low heat. Simmer until it throws up a pale yellow froth, then remove from the heat. Line a small sieve with clean, damp muslin (cheesecloth) and set over a small bowl. Strain the butter, leaving the milky dregs in the bottom of the pan. Discard the dregs and froth. This will give you more ghee than you need, but it keeps for several weeks in the refrigerator.

Turn the dough out and knead again. It should be quite soft – if stiff, sprinkle with a little more water and knead it in.

When you are ready to start cooking the chapattis, place a handful of chapatti flour in a shallow bowl and place it close to hand. Break off a ping-pong-ball-sized piece of dough. Roll it into a ball between the palms of your hands. Dust it in the chapatti flour, flatten it into a disc and roll out into a thin round pancake.

Place a tava (an Indian iron hot plate with a long handle) or cast-iron frying pan (skillet) over a medium heat and grease it with a little ghee. Toss the rolled chapatti from one hand to the other to make it slightly thinner and then place on the hot tava or pan. Cook for 30 seconds, until it just starts to look cooked, then flip over so that the chapatti is partially cooked on each side. Flip again and encourage it to rise by pressing the sides of the chapatti with a thick folded clean cloth. It should puff up like a balloon. Within a few minutes the chapatti should be cooked – slow-cooking makes tough chapattis.

Keep warm tucked inside a clean cloth on a plate – you can, if wished, smear warm ghee on one side of each cooked chapatti before slipping it into the cloth. Serve warm with the Mattar Paneer (p.140). They're also good with the Lamb Rogan Josh (p.82), Spiced Okra (p.146) and Lamb Shish Kebabs (p.17).

Stir-fried Squid with Chilli and Black Bean Sauce

Serves 2

This is an ideal Chinese recipe to test out chopsticks versus a fork. It's from *Chinese Cookery Secrets: How to Cook Chinese Restaurant Food at Home* (1993) by Deh-Ta Hsiung, and combines tender pieces of squid with crisp green (bell) pepper and onion, lightly coated in a gorgeous savoury sauce. You should start with the chopsticks, so serve it with a small bowl of rice, so that its easy to eat.

For the squid

1 tbsp peeled and finely grated fresh ginger (prepared to obtain 1 tsp ginger juice – see method)

450 g/1 lb squid

1 tbsp Chinese rice wine (or sake)

For the stir-fry

1 small onion

1 green (bell) pepper, quartered and seeded

2 tbsp groundnut (peanut) oil

1 tsp peeled and finely grated fresh ginger

1 spring onion (scallion), trimmed and cut into short sections

1 green Thai chilli, or to taste, finely sliced

2 tbsp black bean sauce

1 tbsp Chinese rice wine (or sake)

a few drops of toasted sesame oil

Begin by making the ginger juice. Mix 1 tbsp cold water with the grated fresh ginger, then squeeze through muslin (cheesecloth) by twisting the cloth over a bowl to extract the ginger-flavoured juice. The excess juice can be used to season other dishes.

Clean the squid by pulling out and discarding the head and transparent backbone, along with the ink sack. Peel off the thin pink skin, then wash and dry thoroughly. Cut open the squid tube so that it can lie flat, then score the inside of the flesh in a criss-cross pattern so that it forms diamonds. Cut into postage-stamp-sized pieces.

Place 1 tsp of the reserved ginger juice in a bowl with the rice wine and mix in the diced squid. Cover, chill and marinate for 25–30 minutes, then discard the marinade.

Bring a saucepan of unsalted water to the boil. Drop the marinated squid pieces into the boiling water and cook for 25–30 seconds. The squid pieces will curl up and the criss-cross pattern will open out. Remove and drain, then rinse under the cold tap, dry well and keep chilled until needed.

Cut the onion and green (bell) pepper into small triangular pieces. Heat the oil in a preheated wok or frying pan (skillet) until smoking, then add the ginger, spring onion and chilli, followed by the onion and green pepper. Stir-fry for about 1 minute, then add the black bean sauce, stir fry another minute before adding the squid with the wine. Mix well, season with the sesame oil and serve immediately.

Challenging
Textures

A common reason for disliking a particular food is texture. I've never been able to abide the spongy nature of tripe and many Britons hate the dense texture of liver, kidneys and heart. However, a true chef often has to learn how to cook such foods. I overcame my childhood prejudice of liver through discovering how to cook meltingly tender strips, finished with Madeira and rosemary.

As I mentioned in the introduction to this chapter, every culture regards texture in a different way. It's not always easy to try challenging textures, but if you concentrate on the tastes and flavours of the food, you may find that you slowly but surely fall in love with new textures and new foods. It is truly worth trying to expand your textural boundaries. You never know where it might lead. I've included four recipes to test out here, although I could have included many more!

Spiced Okra

Serves 2

Once cut, okra, also known as ladies' fingers, releases a thick gummy liquid, which creates a mucilaginous texture in cooked dishes such as gumbos and soft dry curries. This is delicious eaten with the Lamb Rogan Josh (p.82) and Chapattis (p.142).

3–4 tbsp cold-pressed sunflower oil

1 small onion, finely diced

1 garlic clove, finely diced

350 g/12 oz okra, washed

½ tsp ground turmeric

½ tsp ground garam masala

½ tsp cumin seeds

⅛ tsp chilli powder, or to taste

fine sea salt

Set a large non-stick frying pan (skillet) over a medium-low heat. Add 3 tbsp of the sunflower oil and, once hot, add the onion and garlic and fry gently for 5 minutes or until soft.

Meanwhile, top and tail the okra, then cut each finger into 1 cm/½ inch rounds. Set aside.

Add the turmeric, garam masala, cumin seeds and chilli powder to the pan. Cook for 2 minutes, then increase the heat to medium, and add the sliced okra – if necessary add a further 1 tbsp oil. Salt lightly and stir-fry briskly for 5 minutes. Initially, the okra will release a lot of viscous juice – but this disappears as it cooks. Reduce the heat to low and continue to cook for 3 minutes, stirring occasionally, until the okra is soft. Set aside until needed, then reheat to serve.

Coconut Tapioca with Mango

Serves 4

Tapioca, or 'frog spawn' as it was known in my school, was hated by generations of British children for its slippery texture. It was only years later that I discovered what a sublime ingredient it is when cooked with coconut and served with mango.

330 ml/11 fl oz/scant 1½ cups organic coconut cream

85 g/3 oz/generous ½ cup seed tapioca pearls

¼ tsp fine sea salt

30 g/1 oz/2½ tbsp light muscovado sugar, or to taste

2 ripe mangos, peeled, stoned and finely diced

Combine 500ml/18 fl oz/2 cups water and coconut cream in a medium saucepan. Bring to the boil, then stir in the tapioca and salt. Keep stirring until the mixture starts to simmer, then reduce the heat to low and cook very gently for 25 minutes, stirring regularly.

Remove from the heat and stir in the sugar. Leave until tepid, stirring occasionally. Tip into a pretty bowl, cover and chill until needed. It will thicken as it cools.

To serve: spoon the coconut tapioca into 4 shallow bowls, arrange the diced mango around the tapioca and serve. Alternatively, place the mango at the bottom of each bowl and top with tapioca.

Note
Compare how tastes and flavours linger in your mouth with and without fat, by eating this fat-based coconut tapioca with the water-based Peach and Basil Tapioca (p.183).

Japanese Sweet Potato Fritters

Serves 4

Wander past the vibrant market stalls in Kochi's famous Sunday farmers' market in Shikoku, and you will come across a queue of people buying a mid-morning snack of sweet potato fritters. The region is famous throughout Japan for its ultra-sweet, golden-fleshed sweet potatoes. Their dry mealy chestnut-like texture turns to fluff in the fritter and is the perfect way to tempt those who dislike the dry, floury texture of some vegetables, such as squash and sweet potato.

500 g/1 lb 2 oz large sweet potatoes, peeled and cut into 2–3 cm/¾–1¼ inch pieces

corn oil, for frying

175 g/6 oz/1⅓ cups plain (all-purpose) white flour, sifted

1 tsp baking powder

100 g/3½ oz/scant ½ cup caster (granulated) sugar

2 tsp fine sea salt

1 medium egg, beaten

Note

You can experiment with temperature contrasts by serving these fritters hot with banana ice cream – follow the recipe for Strawberry Ice Cream (p.188), but increase the lemon juice to 1 lemon, substitute 3 medium bananas for the strawberries, and replace the eau de vie with rum.

Place the sweet potato chunks in a large bowl of cold water and leave to soak for 30 minutes.

Heat the oil in a deep-fat fryer to 180°C/350°F. Drain the potatoes and pat dry.

In a large bowl, mix together the flour, baking powder, sugar and salt. Make a well in the centre of the flour and gradually stir in the egg and 150 ml/5 fl oz/⅔ cup water until it forms a smooth, thick batter.

Mix the sweet potato chunks into the batter. Drop a few of the batter-coated sweet potatoes into the oil and fry for 6 minutes, until fluffy and golden brown. You don't want the temperature of the oil to drop below 180°C/350°F. Remove to paper towels and leave to cool while you continue to fry the remaining sweet potato chunks in small batches. Leave for a couple of hours or until cold.

Shortly before serving, reheat the oil to 180°C/350°F. Fry the fritters in batches until golden and crisp. Drain on paper towels and serve hot or warm. The second frying ensures that the fritters are crisp and fluffy when eaten hot.

Indian Lemon and Ginger Pickle

Makes 4 x 340-g/12-oz pickle jars

This gorgeous Punjabi pickle (photographed on p.7) is a very addictive, intensely salty-sour nibble. I have been known to eat some of it within a week of making, to test how it is doing. At this stage, you are aware of the bitter lemon pith and mouth-puckering acidic flesh, while the ginger is so fiery it makes you jump around. After a month, the flavours mellow and the lemon becomes soft and unctuous. The older it becomes, the softer and more slimy its texture. Test at different stages to see how you react. It's especially delicious eaten with the Mattar Paneer (p.140).

1 kg/2 lb 3 oz unwaxed lemons

85 g/3 oz peeled fresh ginger

5 green chillies, or to taste

150 g/5½ oz/cup fine sea salt

½ tsp coarsely ground black pepper

¾ tsp ajwain (carom) seeds, lightly bruised

You can use any size of jar, provided it has an acid-proof screw-top lid – you will need 1 extra jar than the final amount yields (5 jars). Sterilize the jars and lids (see p.25).

Wash and dry the lemons. Depending on whether the lemons are small or medium-sized, slice each lemon lengthwise into quarters or sixths. Remove the pips and cut each length into 2 or 3 chunks (about 2 cm/¾ inch). Place in a large mixing bowl with any juice.

Cut the peeled ginger into matchsticks about 2.5 cm/1 inch long and 3 mm/⅛ inch wide. Add to the lemon chunks. Remove the chilli stalks and slice the chillies lengthwise into thin strips, with the seeds, and add to the lemon.

Mix together the salt, ground black pepper and ajwain seeds, then mix into the lemons with your hands. Spoon into the 5 sterilized jars and seal.

Leave the pickle on a window sill for 2–3 weeks, thoroughly shaking each jar once a day. Gradually, the lemons will collapse until they fill two-thirds or half of each jar. Top them up from one of the jars, making sure that you use a clean metal spoon and that you scrape in the salty juice. You should end up with 4 jars which can be kept in a cupboard.

Gradually the lemons will become soft, almost slimy, as the salty juice thickens. Their flavours mellow and their colour darkens with time. They will easily keep for 1 year, if you can resist eating them.

Temperature

Temperature Recipes

Hot
why eat piping hot food?

Warm
the pleasures of warm food

Tepid
the most visceral of temperatures

Cold
what do we mean by cold?

Frozen
a different world of sensory perception

Temperature

'One of the most important things for the housewife to remember is that hot things should be very hot, and cold very cold or iced. Profit by the classic exclamation of a guest at Disraeli's table on arrival of the ice: "Ah, something really hot at last!"'

LOVELY FOOD by Ruth Lowinsky, 1931

The issue of at what temperature food should be served has long vexed cooks and diners alike. Perhaps because I grew up in a cold, draughty English country house, I was taught that traditional meals should be served piping hot, unless, as Mrs Lowinsky points out, something was supposed to be chilled. Only cheese and fruit could be ambient which, in our case, meant cold anyway. Consequently, I was initially nonplussed by my Indian in-laws' habit of gradually laying their table with hot dishes, so that by the time the family sat down to eat, most of the food had cooled to warm.

However, across the East it's normal to serve warm or tepid dishes. As David Thompson explains in his book *Thai Food*: 'There is little concern if the food becomes cold, or if it is served only warm, as on a traditional stove it was almost impossible for all dishes to be produced hot simultaneously. In the heat of the tropics this is not much of an issue. Moreover, flavour is at its optimum just above room temperature.'

As with all aspects of cookery, it's liberating to free yourself from any cultural preconceptions about the correct approach to serving food. Only then can you truly focus on how your perception of temperature alters your experience of eating. Some dishes are best enjoyed very hot. Japanese Sweet Potato Fritters (p.148), for example, are at their fluffiest and crispest when eaten straight from the fryer, preferably as a snack. Other foods can only be appreciated when frozen. A Plum Water Granita (p.189), for instance, is refreshing because its granular ice crystals release refreshing bursts of sweet-sour plummy flavour as they melt in the mouth.

It helps to start with the basics. Consider how the temperature of every dish you serve is first experienced, as this influences the eater's overall perception of a dish. Is it via the fingertips or the lips? Your fingertips are extremely sensitive to heat and cold, as anyone who has tried to steal a freshly cooked sausage from a barbecue will know, but your lips are even more so. You can test this by conducting a simple experiment next time you're roasting meat. Insert a skewer into the centre of the joint, hold for a few seconds and then tentatively place the skewer on your lower lip. It's amazing how you can detect the subtlest differences in temperature compared to your fingers – if the skewer is cold, the meat is very rare; if warm, medium rare; if hot, well done.

The temperature of a dish will dictate how it is eaten once inside your mouth. Very hot and very cold ingredients can be painful, leading the eater to open their mouth, suck in air and shift the food briskly around to alleviate the pain receptors in their mouth. However, within reason, certain levels of heat or cold can also be pleasurable, such as sipping Glühwein (p.158) at a frosty Christmas market, or sucking an ice lolly on a sultry summer's day.

The same pain receptors in the mouth respond to the burning sensation of capsaicin, the chemical found in chillies. This leads me into the tricky area of chemical irritants and stimulants in food and where to place them in this book. Certain ingredients, such as chilli peppers, black pepper, ginger, nutmeg and the mustard family, naturally contain chemicals that alter your sensations in different ways as you eat. These can range from menthol in peppermint extract, that creates a cool feeling, to tingle-inducing Szechuan pepper and numbing cloves.

The majority of these ingredients are usually categorized as a flavour, but clearly, they are more than that, as not only do they have taste, flavour and (in most cases) texture in their own right, they also alter how we eat, even when used in small amounts. Freshly grated horseradish, for example, can make the nose and eyes stream if applied too freely to a beef sandwich. Some irritants, such as capsaicin, make you salivate more, which changes the texture of the food in your mouth and hastens the release of tastes and flavours.

There is much debate as to why some of these irritant ingredients are so addictive. It might be that the discomfort they provoke in the mouth also promotes the production of endorphins, the body's natural painkillers, which in turn induces a sense of well-being. Or perhaps it's the stimulation of a different oral sensation that heightens our awareness of what we're eating? Whatever the reason, chemical irritants create a more complex, exciting gustatory experience, which is worth exploiting. You can contrast or layer chemical perceptions of heat with unexpected temperatures, for example by adding a spoonful of fiery, iced horseradish cream to a piping-hot tomato soup.

Curiously, very little is known as to how temperature alters our perception of taste and flavour. It's widely believed that tepid food has maximum taste, but this may be because we detect more flavours when food is tepid or warm. As Luca Turin writes in *The Secret of Scent* (2006), 'Cold things have little smell, and one of the attractions of a snowy night is the total blank our nose perceives. Part of the fun with ice cream is the surprise when a huge flavour develops in the warmth of your mouth.'

A fascinating side-note to this is that, when drinks creator Tony Conigliaro and his team at The Drink Factory in London set about the supposedly impossible task of creating a bottled cocktail that tasted of 'snow', they discovered that enoki mushrooms had the perfect snowy aroma.

It is thought that coldness reduces our sensitivity to sweet, bitter and sour tastes, but increases our awareness of salt. In spite of this, research has shown significant variability between people. It's also shown that these rules don't always apply – for example, apparently, sweet-tasting saccharine remains equally sweet chilled or warm. Similarly, while a bitter-tasting iced black coffee tastes less bitter than a hot version, the opposite is true of the bitter-tasting quinine in chilled tonic water. Thus, you should always trust your own senses when seasoning a dish.

Temperature Notes

'We sat in the sleigh and picnicked …
I warmed soup in a little apparatus I have
for such occasions, which helped to take
the chilliness off the sandwiches, this
is the only unpleasant part of a winter
picnic, the clamminess of the provisions
just when you most long for something
very hot.'

**ELIZABETH AND HER GERMAN
GARDEN by Countess von Arnim, 1898**

As a cook, my focus on temperature has in the past been twofold: to create a particular culinary affect and to ensure that my food is safe to eat. After all, ice cream needs to be chilled in order to freeze, and poached salmon can't be left out in a room indefinitely. In this chapter, I've tried to devise notes and recipes that explore how temperature alters our perception of taste, flavour and texture. Such knowledge can be used to create recipes that resonate with our preconceptions of what constitutes cooling, refreshing, warming, comforting and/or exciting dishes.

Hot

Sensitivity on food matters is very subjective and what can seem hot to one person can be warm to another. However, common sense should prevail and hot in this context should be interpreted as being comfortably hot to eat. The hotter a dish is, the less you detect its taste and flavour and the more conscious you become of its texture in relation to burning yourself. Care must be taken with some dishes, such as those that are high in fat or sugar or contain ingredients that cling to the mouth, as they can easily burn the eater if served too hot. French onion soup and banana fritters are two classic examples. Ironically, many such recipes benefit texturally from being served at the hotter end of the comfort spectrum. Crisp-coated fried dishes, such as chips, or battered or bread-crumbed items, for example, are best enjoyed before their crisp exterior softens as they cool.

Temperature test
Compare the taste, texture and flavour of two thick slices of toast: both buttered straight from the toaster, but one eaten hot and the other eaten tepid.

Warm

As hot food cools to an enjoyable warm temperature, your perception of taste and flavour deepens and textures start to change. Cream-, egg-, butter- and starch-based sauces, as well as pulses and starchy ingredients, thicken as they cool, while crisp fried food softens and becomes chewy. As a result, they stay longer in your mouth, which increases your exposure to tastes and flavours and allows you to appreciate the finer nuances of different textures in comfort. Certain types of dishes lend themselves to being served warm – for example, hand-held foods, savoury tarts and baked fruit puddings. Others are served warm by default – for instance, savoury salads where a hot item, such as sautéed ducks' livers, is mixed into cold salad ingredients to create warm elements within the wilted leaves.

Temperature test
Compare the taste, texture and flavour of the Onion, Bacon and Soured Cream Tart (p.32), first eaten hot from the oven, then left until warm, then chilled.

Tepid

Temperature test
Compare the level of flowery notes you can detect within the Lavender Lemon Syrup (p.42) when it is hot and when it is tepid.

Tepidity is a tricky temperature for a cook as the eater is inclined to interpret lukewarm food as either careless neglect or, worse still, a blatant disregard for their safety. Bacteria in food multiply most between 5–63°C/40–145°F and room temperature (20°C/68°F) is their idea of heaven. Consequently, 'cold' food should never be left out longer than 1 hour. Nevertheless, tepid food can be utterly delicious. One reason why chocolate is widely believed to have such a pleasurable mouth feel, is that it melts at just below our body temperature. Anyone who has eaten freshly made sushi will know that the tepid temperature of the vinegared rice makes the raw fish feel more 'fleshy'. With tepidity, there are no distractions of heat or cold, only pure taste, pure flavour and an intense textural awareness.

Cold

Temperature test
Season the Spiced Sweetcorn and Lime Soup (p.213) while hot. Serve chilled, but reheat a tiny amount before serving, then compare the saltiness of the hot and cold soups.

Within recipe-writing circles, there is much debate as to whether something served at room temperature, such as the Chocolate Spice Biscuits (p.186), is cold. According to the *Oxford English Dictionary*, 'cold' means 'of or at a temperature perceptibly lower than that of the living human body; or at a relatively low temperature.' In other words, below 37°C/98.6°F. Thus, the said biscuit is cold, but then so too is a chilled Apple and Sorrel Mousse (p.184). Legally, cold food (as opposed to ambient food) must be kept at 8°C/47°F or below in the UK. One thing is certain, the colder the ingredient the less flavour you can perceive, and the less sweetness and the more salt you detect. Textures change as well: fat-based liquids thicken, such as oil-based dressings, vinaigrettes, and egg and cream liaisons; even syrups become more viscous.

Frozen

Temperature test
Before churning, set aside a small amount of the chilled Strawberry Ice Cream custard (p.188). Compare the taste, texture and flavour of the liquid and frozen creams.

A limited number of recipes are consumed frozen, mainly ice creams, parfaits, bombes, various forms of water ice and some canapés. Nevertheless, there is a surprising degree of variability in texture and degree of freezing. Shaken cocktails, for example, can be viscous with tiny ice crystals, while milkshakes can be more textural and slushy. If a frozen dish contains fat, it will coat your mouth in a distinctive buttery way and create lingering tastes and flavours as it melts. Restaurants often use liquid nitrogen to fast-freeze both sweet and savoury liquids. This creates smaller ice crystals, which give the frozen liquid an ultra-smooth texture. Domestic freezers are usually held at -18°C/-0.4°F. The colder the food, the less flavour is released and the less you can detect many sweet, sour and bitter tastes.

Hot

Focusing on temperature allows you to see recipes in a new way and can open up interesting avenues of creativity. Hot food, for example, is traditionally served on the hotter side of warm, to avoid the risk of burning. However, the hotter the dish, the less flavour we can detect, which begs the question as to what the benefits are to serving a piping-hot dish, aside from legal reasons? Anyone selling hot food in Britain must keep it at 63°C/145°F or above for health and safety reasons, and reheated food must reach at least 82°C/180°F for 10 minutes, to kill potentially harmful bacteria.

Traditionally, hot food has been seen as being more nutritious and reviving than cold. Even today, many employment contracts, such as for doctors working on-call in Britain, include the right to hot food. While it is true that eating hot food is physically warming and psychologically comforting, it is not necessarily more nutritious. Some have argued it takes more calories to digest cold food, but there is no nutritional difference between eating a cooked dish hot or cold.

The answer lies in our past. It's hard to appreciate the once all-pervading chilliness of life, where the level of frigidity meant that you sensed even the faint heat from a candle flame. Practically minded cooks created recipes to warm and insulate the eater from the cold, such as sweetened hot drinks, soups, stews, pies and puddings. Many were calorific, high in sugar, fat and starch – it takes energy to keep warm.

Central heating and an urban indoor-centric life have transformed our culinary needs and changed our diet. Today, what is widely regarded as hot food is mainly cooked for its symbolically comforting nature, rather than its heat-giving qualities. Every chef knows that a hearty Rich Beef Pie (p.128) or Fruity Steamed Pudding (p.162) will fly out of the kitchen on a wild autumn day.

Thus, from the modern cook's perspective, hot food is served as much for its psychological benefits, as its capacity to warm. This in turn leads to the question as to what makes a recipe comforting? This is subjective, but in my view soft unctuous textures and homely references are an essential element, such as with the Persian Sour Lentil Soup (p.26) and the Pork and Spinach Meatballs (p.160).

Glühwein seems silkier and less sweet when drunk piping hot

Glühwein

Makes 6 glasses

Convivial hot drinks have been drunk across Northern Europe for centuries. A dish of hot rum punch or mulled ale would be called for at every inn in England. Enjoyed by a blazing fire, the bowl of spiced and sugared alcohol would be assembled by one of the drinkers and often heated by the insertion of a red hot poker. Scandinavians still enjoy glögg, a sweetened spiced wine with its distinctive raisins and almonds at the bottom of each glass; and no Christmas fair across Germany and Austria would be complete without glühwein (photographed on p.157) to keep out the frost.

Choose a reasonable-quality fruity wine for this recipe – just because it's sweetened and spiced doesn't mean you should drink cheap rubbish that will give you a headache.

2 star anise

1 small cinnamon stick

4 cloves

4 strips finely pared orange zest

4 strips finely pared lemon zest

1 bottle of Merlot red wine

3–4 tbsp caster (granulated) sugar, or to taste

1 tbsp good white rum

Tie the star anise, cinnamon and cloves in a small clean piece of muslin (cheesecloth) – if you don't have any muslin, just add loose. Place in a non-corrosive saucepan with the finely pared orange and lemon zest and wine. Set over a low heat and slowly bring up to just below boiling point. Do not let the mixture bubble. Remove from the heat and leave to infuse for 15 minutes.

Return to the heat, again taking care not to let it bubble, remove the spices and citrus zests (if preferred) and sweeten to taste. Finally, add the rum and serve immediately in mugs or special glühwein glasses with handles. If you don't have any, make sure your guests have protective napkins. Glasses must be heated beforehand with hot water to stop them from cracking when the hot wine is poured in.

Note
Fast-cool a very small amount of hot glühwein on ice and compare the taste and flavour between the hot and chilled versions.

Peppered Venison Steaks

Serves 6

All meat benefits from resting a little after cooking to ensure it's succulent, so this recipe is on the cooler side of hot. However, black pepper contains a pungent chemical called piperine, which – as Harold McGee explains in his book *On Food & Cooking* – causes certain sensory nerves in the mouth to become hypersensitive to ordinary sensations such as touch and temperature. Even breathing can seem like the inhalation of a cool breeze if you've bitten on a lot of black pepper. This dish is delicious eaten with Chips (p.164).

850 ml/29 fl oz/3½ cups good-quality Chicken Stock (p.47)

3 tbsp black peppercorns

1 tbsp plain (all-purpose) flour

fine sea salt

2 x 450 g/1 lb venison loins, each cut into 6 medallions

4 tbsp extra-virgin olive oil

6 tbsp brandy

200 ml/7 fl oz/generous ¾ cup dry white wine

85 g/3 oz/6 tbsp chilled unsalted butter, diced

Place the chicken stock in a wide saucepan and boil vigorously until reduced by two-thirds. Set aside.

Preheat the oven to 90°C fan/110°C/225°F/gas mark ¼.

Roughly crush the peppercorns in a mortar or under a rolling pin. Place them in a shallow dish with the flour and a pinch of salt. Mix together. Coat the venison medallions in the peppercorn mix, pressing them well into the meat.

Set 2 non-stick frying pans (skillets) over a medium-high heat. Add 2 tbsp of the olive oil to each pan. Once very hot, add 6 venison medallions to each pan. Sear briskly on all sides for 2 minutes or until well coloured.

You now need to flambé the venison – remove the first frying pan away from your extractor fan. Add half the brandy and set alight. Once the alcohol has burned off, transfer the steaks onto a plate and keep warm in the oven. Repeat the process with the other frying pan.

Pour half of the wine into each pan, stirring vigorously to loosen any sediment or peppercorns. Boil until the wine has reduced to a few tablespoons, then tip into the saucepan of reduced chicken stock. Season to taste and bring to the boil. As soon as it tastes good, reduce the heat to low and whisk in the butter. Do not let it boil or the butter will separate. Serve with the venison steaks.

Pork and Spinach Meatballs with
Spicy Tomato Sauce x 2

Serves 4

This is a dish that will make you feel you could hike up a mountain, albeit after a bit of digestion. Comfortingly hot, stewed dishes tend to have plenty of sauce that is filled with soft-textured goodies which can be eaten with a fork. The best taste even better the day after cooking. The sauce here can be made a day or two ahead and the dish itself can be reheated when needed.

For the tomato sauce

650 g/1 lb 7 oz tomatoes

5 tbsp extra-virgin olive oil

2 fat garlic cloves, peeled

1 onion, finely diced

1 tsp dried chilli flakes

500 ml/18 fl oz/generous 2 cups good-quality Chicken Stock (p.47)

2 x 400-g/14-oz cans black beans, drained and rinsed

salt and freshly ground black pepper

For the pork meatballs

7 tbsp extra-virgin olive oil

1 onion, finely diced

1 garlic clove, finely chopped

250 g/9 oz baby spinach, washed

500 g/1 lb 2 oz minced (ground) pork

55 g/2 oz soft white breadcrumbs

finely grated zest of 2 lemons

Begin by making the sauce. Preheat the oven to 180°C fan/200°C/400°F/gas mark 6.

Place the tomatoes in a single layer in a roasting pan. Toss in 2 tbsp of the olive oil and roast for 15 minutes, then add the garlic cloves and continue to roast for a further 40 minutes, or until they've collapsed into a soft caramelized mess.

Meanwhile, set a wide saucepan over a medium-low heat. Add 3 tbsp olive oil and gently fry the onion for 10 minutes, then mix in the chilli flakes and continue to fry for 5 minutes, or until the onions are soft and golden. Set aside until the tomatoes are ready.

Remove the tomatoes from the oven and, once they're cool enough to handle, peel and discard the skins. Squash the roasted garlic and tomatoes together and tip into the sautéed onion pan. Loosen any caramelized bits from the pan with some of the chicken stock and pour into the pan along with the remaining stock. Season to taste, then return the pan to a medium-high heat and boil for 10 minutes. Add the beans, reduce the heat and simmer for 5–10 minutes.

To make the meatballs, set a frying pan (skillet) over a medium-low heat. Once hot, add 3 tbsp of the olive oil, followed by the finely diced onion and garlic. Fry gently for 10 minutes, or until soft and golden, then tip into a mixing bowl.

Drop the spinach into a saucepan of boiling unsalted water. As soon as it wilts, drain into a colander and cool under cold running water. Squeeze dry with your hands and finely chop. Mix into the softened onions with the minced pork, breadcrumbs and lemon zest (omit the zest initially if you're following the citrus flavour test on p.59) and season to taste. Fry a small patty in the frying pan to check the seasoning. Taste and adjust as necessary.

Set a clean plate beside you and roll the pork mixture into 24 ping-pong-sized balls.

Place a large clean frying pan over a medium-high heat. Once hot, add 3 tbsp olive oil and a single layer of meatballs. Fry briskly for 5–6 minutes, shaking the pan regularly to ensure that the meatballs are well coloured on all sides. Remove to a plate, add another 1 tbsp oil to the pan and repeat the process until all the balls are browned. Mix into the beans, cover and simmer for 15 minutes. Serve piping hot.

Note
For an umami-boosted variation add 115 g/4 oz finely diced, dry-cured back bacon to the pork mixture. Omit the chilli in the sauce, but add 1 bay leaf and a small piece of Parmesan rind with the beans, substituting cannellini beans for black beans.

Fruity Steamed Pudding with Madeira Sauce

Serves 8

This is the perfect dish for a cold rainy day. There are few dishes as warming as a British steamed pudding – they are still regarded as an ultimate comfort food. The original and heartiest versions were made with suet and studded with dried vine fruit, but in the nineteenth century, slightly lighter recipes were developed with the invention of raising agents and the liberal use of different types of fruit and sugar. I've adapted the two methods to create a lighter modern version. The Madeira sauce originates from the nineteenth century and adds a further warming glow to the eater.

55 g/2 oz/⅓ cup raisins

55 g/2 oz/⅓ cup sultanas (golden raisins)

55 g/2 oz/generous ⅓ cup currants

55 g/2 oz/generous ⅓ cup chopped mixed candied peel

3 tbsp brandy

175 g/6 oz/¾ cup unsalted butter, softened, plus extra for greasing

175 g/6 oz/¾ cup plus 2 tbsp light brown muscovado sugar

½ tsp mixed spice

finely grated zest of 2 lemons and juice of 1 lemon

3 medium eggs, lightly beaten

175 g/6 oz/1⅓ cups self-raising flour, sifted

85 g/3 oz/1½ cups fresh white breadcrumbs

115 g/4 oz peeled, cored and roughly grated cooking apple

Place the raisins, sultanas, currants, candied peel and brandy in a sealed container and shake. Ideally leave for 4–5 days (although 24 hours will suffice), mixing regularly.

Take 8 x 150 ml/5 fl oz/⅔ cup pudding basins. Using the bottom of a basin as a template, draw 8 circles on some baking parchment. Use the top of a basin to draw 8 more circles. Liberally butter the basins, then line the bottom of the basins with the small discs. Cut 7 squares of foil large enough to be fitted over the basin tops.

Preheat the oven to 200°C fan/220°C/425°F/ gas mark 7.

In a large bowl, beat the butter, sugar, mixed spice and lemon zest until pale and fluffy, then beat in half the beaten eggs. Fold half the flour into the butter mixture, followed by the remaining eggs, breadcrumbs, juice of 1 lemon, and grated apple. Finally, fold in the remaining flour and the macerated dried fruit with any liquid.

Divide the mixture between the pudding basins – the mixture will need a little space at the top as it rises slightly on cooking. Cover each with a disc of parchment and then a square of foil, tucking the foil around the rim of the basins to neatly form a baggy seal. Place the basins in a small roasting pan. Pour in enough boiling water to come over halfway up the sides of the basins. Cover the pan with foil and cook in the hot oven for 1 hour.

Remove the puddings from the oven and leave to rest for 5 minutes. The sponge will shrink back slightly, making it easier to turn out.

For the sauce

250 ml/9 fl oz/1 cup rich
(sweet) Madeira

85 g/3 oz/6½ tbsp caster
(granulated) sugar

1½ tbsp arrowroot

3 tbsp cold water

juice of 1 lemon

Meanwhile, make the sauce. Put the Madeira and sugar in a small saucepan and bring up to simmering point. Place the arrowroot in a small bowl and gradually stir in the cold water, followed by the lemon juice, until you have a smooth white paste. Slowly stir the hot Madeira into the arrowroot before returning the mixture to the saucepan. Set over a low heat and keep stirring until it has thickened and turned clear.

Turn out each pudding, removing the baking paper as you do so. Serve liberally drizzled with the hot sauce.

British Chips

Serves 4

Certain fried foods, such as chips (fries) or Sweet Potato Fritters (p.148), benefit from being served as hot as is comfortable to eat, as their starchy interiors gradually lose their fluffy texture as they cool. Toss these thin golden chips in fine sea salt when they're almost too hot to handle, then test it out. Those who love soggy British chips will, of course, disagree. Happily, there is no such thing as right or wrong in cooking – only personal taste – so if you're a soggy chunky chip person, please ignore my words, cut your chips thicker and serve them warm, not hot.

4 large floury potatoes, such as King Edwards

corn oil, for deep-frying

fine sea salt

Peel the potatoes and cut into thin chip-sized batons. Place in a large bowl of cold water and leave to soak for 30 minutes to remove the excess starch.

Heat the oil in a deep-fat fryer to 150°C/300°F. If you don't have a deep-fat fryer, pour in enough oil to reach one-third of the way up the sides of a large, heavy-based saucepan and clip a thermometer onto the side of the pan.

Drain the chipped potatoes and pat dry on some paper towels. Cook in batches, so that the oil retains its temperature as the potatoes 'blanch'. Fry the potatoes until they have a crisp uncoloured skin with a soft centre – this will take around 4 minutes. Remove from the oil and shake off any excess oil before spreading them out to cool on paper towels. Once cold, either set aside, or – if you're prepping well ahead – chill until needed. Then bring up to room temperature before cooking.

To serve, heat the oil to 180°C/350°F and cook the blanched chips in batches for about 3 minutes, or until golden and crisp. Drain on paper towels, tip into a mixing bowl and salt liberally, before dropping a pile of chips onto each plate.

Warm

The majority of so-called hot dishes today are served warm. This allows the eater to experience the subtleties of taste, flavour and texture, while still enjoying the pleasure of consuming warm food in the comfort of their toasty home.

Obviously, as you eat, food continues to cool and change texture. Serving a combination of dishes at different temperatures will alter your perception. Monitor your reactions and consider alternatives. Do you like cold cream poured on to the warm, as opposed to hot, Apricot and Raspberry Sponge Pudding (p.66), for example, or would you prefer a warm Custard (p.174) to prevent the pudding from becoming tepid? How does warm food make you feel? Does eating Roast Chicken with Cannellini Bean Salad (p.170) make you feel relaxed and holiday-ish or dissatisfied and vaguely hungry?

Don't forget to take into account that magical semi-illicit zone of nibbling, where you eat once-hot leftovers while clearing a meal, or dip into something that is technically meant to be served cold. I can never wait for freshly baked bread to fully cool. The temptation to test the crusty end with freshly spread butter melting into its moist crumb is just too much. Similarly, I find myself dipping warm Brussels sprouts in the last of the gravy when I'm clearing the Christmas dinner. They just taste too good to resist. Is it possible to convey such sensations in a normal meal? Would my guests feel the same, if I offered them Staffordshire Oatcakes (p.173) straight from my pan and handed them the butter?

Once you've established a mental temperature map of your eating habits, start to experiment with different combinations of temperature, texture, taste and flavour. Explore types of dishes that are particularly well suited to being served warm, such as emulsified butter sauces, and dishes made with pulses and grains. Examine how much or how little your perception of taste, flavour and texture varies according to the temperature and consider how you could intensify your experiences.

Steamed Vegetables with Tarragon Butter Sauce

Serves 4

Butter liaisons have to be served warm, as opposed to hot, otherwise the butter will separate and the texture will become curdled. Once cold, the mixture changes texture once again and loses its velvety appeal as the butter solidifies.

Butter sauces can be made richer with the addition of egg yolks, as in Hollandaise or Béarnaise sauce, or they can be stabilized with the addition of a little cream, as here. You can use a wide variety of liquids as the base, including citrus juice, vinegar (and water), cider, vermouth and reduced stock. The liquid can be infused with a wide variety of flavourings, from herbs to spices.

You can vary the selection and amount of steamed vegetables for this dish according to the season. You might include any of the following: baby leeks, cauliflower florets, new potatoes, young beetroot (beets), inner celery stems or mini-turnips.

For the vegetables

16 stems asparagus

12 sprigs sprouting broccoli

175 g/6 oz sugar snap peas, top and tailed

12 spring onions (scallions), trimmed

12 baby carrots, peeled and trimmed

For the butter sauce

6 sprigs tarragon

1 small shallot, finely diced

2 black peppercorns

425 ml/15 fl oz/1¾ cups dry white wine

3 tbsp double (heavy) cream

250 g/9 oz/1 cup plus 2 tbsp cold unsalted butter, diced

fine sea salt

Prepare the vegetables: wash the asparagus stems in plenty of cold water to loosen any sand from their tips. Trim them, cut off any woody inedible parts and, using a potato peeler, pare the lower part of the stems. Repeat the process with the broccoli sprouts. Wash and trim the other vegetables, leaving small sprigs of green leaves on the carrots.

Now make the sauce. Place 3 sprigs of tarragon in a small saucepan with the shallot, peppercorns and white wine. Boil vigorously until reduced down to about 3 tablespoons. Remove from the heat, discard the peppercorns and tarragon sprigs, and add the cream.

Finely chop the leaves from the remaining 3 sprigs of tarragon and set aside until nearly ready to serve.

Shortly before serving, bring the cream up to the boil and allow to thicken slightly, then reduce the heat to a simmer and gradually whisk in the butter. Do not let the sauce boil at this stage or it may split. Stir in the chopped tarragon leaves and season to taste. Transfer to a thermos flask to keep warm until ready to serve, or place the saucepan in a much larger pan of just-boiled water.

Set a 2-tier steamer over a high heat. As soon as the water is boiling, fill the first tier of the steamer with the carrots. Cover and steam for 2 minutes, then add the asparagus to the carrots, cover and steam for a further 1 minute, then add the broccoli stems, spring onions and sugar snap peas to the second tier. Cover and steam for about 5 minutes.

Remove the vegetables to plates lined with paper towels. Working quickly, pat the vegetables dry and divide between 4 warm plates. Pour the warm butter sauce into 4 small soufflé pots and serve immediately, letting your guests use their fingers to dip the warm vegetables into the warm sauce.

Note
Compare the mouth feel of this emulsified butter sauce with the sauce where the tarragon and lemon are beaten into a compound butter and left to melt on salted salmon (p.19).

Freekeh, Chickpea and Tomato Pilaff

Serves 4

This simple dish challenges preconceptions about temperature by tasting equally good hot, warm or cold. I normally serve it warm with grilled lemon chicken for supper, before adding lemon and parsley to the leftovers the next day to make a lunchtime salad. Freekeh are green wheat grains that have been roasted. They can be bought whole or cracked. If you combine the soft-textured grains with other soft textures, such as chickpeas (garbanzo beans) or chunks of roasted aubergine (eggplant), you will convey a sense of comfort to the eater.

280 g/10 oz/1½ cups whole green freekeh

4 tbsp extra-virgin olive oil

200 g/7 oz shallots, finely sliced

1 fat garlic clove, finely chopped

2 tsp cumin seeds

450 g/1 lb ripe tomatoes, peeled and diced

2 tsp Spanish sweet smoked paprika

2 x 400-g/14-oz cans chickpeas (garbanzo beans), drained and rinsed

450 ml/16 fl oz/scant 2 cups boiling water

3 tbsp finely chopped parsley leaves

salt and freshly ground black pepper

If serving tepid or cold

1 tbsp extra-virgin olive oil, or to taste

1 tbsp lemon juice, or to taste

Soak the freekeh in cold water for 20 minutes.

Meanwhile, set a saucepan over a low heat. Once hot, add the oil, followed by the sliced shallots, garlic and cumin seeds. Gently fry for 10 minutes, or until soft and golden.

Place the tomatoes in a bowl, cover with boiling water and lightly cut the skin of each tomato. After 2 minutes, drain, peel and chop the tomatoes.

Add the smoked paprika to the onions, cook for 1 minute, then stir in the chopped tomatoes. Season with salt and pepper, then cook briskly for 5–10 minutes, or until the tomatoes form a thick paste.

Strain and rinse the freekeh thoroughly under cold running water. Shake dry and stir into the tomatoes. Add the chickpeas and boiling water. Bring to the boil, cover, then reduce the heat to low. Simmer gently for 25 minutes or until the freekeh is tender and the liquid is absorbed. The time can vary a lot, depending on how dry (old) the freekeh is. Once tender, take the pan off the heat and leave to rest, covered.

When you're ready to serve, mix in the chopped parsley. If serving tepid or cold, I often add a little extra olive oil and some lemon juice to taste.

Blackened Salmon with Pineapple Salsa

Serves 4

I've written this recipe to illustrate how you can use a number of different stimuli to create a warm recipe. In this case, you have the burning sensation from the capsaicin in the hot smoked paprika, which coats the blackened salmon. The fish is served hot from its pan, but it quickly cools to warm as it is eaten with the cold (room temperature) sweet and sour pineapple salsa. Crucially, this too contains chilli – adding a further sense of heat within the mouth. The end result is an exciting dish to eat – it's a favourite supper in the Kapoor household. I usually serve it with steamed and buttered Charlotte or Ratte potatoes, and salad leaves lightly dressed with lemon and olive oil.

2 tbsp hot (or sweet) smoked Spanish paprika

4 tsp dried garlic granules

4 x 140 g/5 oz salmon fillets

5–6 tbsp cold-pressed sunflower oil

½ fresh pineapple (you need 175 g/6 oz flesh)

2 tbsp lime juice

¼ Thai chilli (or to taste), finely chopped

salt and freshly ground black pepper

Note
It is known that capsaicin suppresses our perception of sweetness, bitterness and umami, but not sourness and saltiness.

Mix together the paprika and garlic granules with some salt and pepper in a shallow bowl. Place the salmon fillets skin-side down on a work surface. Slip a knife between the skin and the flesh of each salmon fillet and carefully slice so that you remove the skin. Discard the skin. Coat the salmon fillets in 3 tbsp of the sunflower oil, then dip each in the spice mixture so that they are thoroughly coated in an oily spicy mix. Set aside.

Cut away the pineapple's skin and remove its eyes. Cut out the central core and finely dice the pineapple flesh. You need about 175 g/6 oz flesh. Place in a small bowl with the lime juice and a little chilli. Mix together and season to taste. Remember that the heat of the chilli will increase the longer it sits in the salsa.

When you are ready to serve, heat a large non-stick frying pan (skillet) over a medium-high heat. Once hot, add 2–3 tbsp sunflower oil, then add the spiced fish steaks flesh-side down. Fry briskly for 2 minutes or until seared and blackened, then turn and cook for 3–4 minutes or until the fish is just cooked through. Plate the fish, partially topping each with pineapple salsa.

Roast Chicken with Cannellini Bean Salad

Serves 4

I originally devised this recipe as an easy-to-make weekend meal for *The Sunday Times*. It is a classic example of a warm salad, in that the hot bacon and heat-retentive cannellini beans are mixed into salad leaves and served with the warm roast chicken.

1.5 kg/3 lb 5 oz free-range, corn-fed chicken

2 lemons

a few thyme sprigs

2 tbsp extra-virgin olive oil

200 g/7 oz smoked back bacon, trimmed of fat and diced

2 garlic cloves, finely chopped

2 x 400-g/14-oz cans cannellini beans, drained and rinsed

2 bunches chives

2 romaine hearts, washed

2 bunches watercress, washed and trimmed

salt and freshly ground black pepper

Preheat the oven to 180°C fan/200°C/400°F/gas mark 6.

Place the chicken in a roasting pan that can also be used on the hob. Rub the chicken all over with the juice of half a lemon. Tuck the semi-squeezed lemon half inside the chicken's cavity with the thyme sprigs. Season the bird with salt and pepper and rub with the olive oil.

Roast in the centre of the hot oven for 30 minutes, then turn the bird over, so it is lying on its breast. Roast for a further 1 hour. It's cooked if the juices run clear when the thickest part of the thigh is pierced with a skewer.

Transfer the cooked chicken to a serving dish, roughly wrap in foil and leave to rest in a warm place. If necessary, pour off any excess juice from the roasting pan, leaving about 3 tbsp chicken fat, and set over a medium-high heat. Add the bacon and fry briskly for 5 minutes or until it's cooked and turning crispy. Add the garlic, fry for 2 minutes, then mix in the drained rinsed beans. Once hot, remove from the heat, mix in the chives and season to taste with the juice of half a lemon, salt and pepper.

Carve the chicken into rough pieces. Rip the lettuce hearts into easy-to-eat chunks and place in a large mixing bowl with the watercress sprigs. Mix in the hot beans, toss thoroughly and divide between the plates. Top with chunks of carved chicken and serve with a lemon cut into quarters.

Does eating warm food make you feel relaxed or hungry?

Hot or cold sauces alter the perception of warm foods

Staffordshire Oatcakes

Makes 10 oatcakes

Staffordshire oatcakes are very addictive, but they have become a rarity outside of the Midlands and the North of England. Thankfully, Felicity Cloake developed a recipe for them in her 'How to make the perfect ...' column in *The Guardian*. My recipe is a slight adaptation of hers.

These can either be served hot out of the pan while you continue to cook the rest, or made ahead and reheated under a hot grill (broiler), either from room temperature or from frozen. They freeze well and make an excellent breakfast, lunch or tea. They're particularly good eaten liberally buttered, but you could serve them with smoked salmon and crème fraîche, or with blueberry sauce (p.109), but without the black pepper.

900 ml/31 fl oz/scant 4 cups tepid water

2 tsp active dried yeast

250 g/9 oz/scant 2 cups finely ground oatmeal

100 g/3½ oz/scant ¾ cup strong wholemeal (bread) flour

100 g/3½ oz/scant ¾ cup strong white (bread) flour

1¼ tsp fine sea salt

cold-pressed sunflower oil, for frying

unsalted butter, to serve

Pour about 100 ml/3½ fl oz/generous ⅓ cup of the tepid water into a small bowl and sprinkle on the yeast.

Mix the oatmeal, flours and salt in a large bowl. Once the yeast starts to froth and smell alive pour it into the oatmeal mix. Using a wooden spoon, gradually stir in sufficient tepid water to make a smooth, thick, but pourable batter. Cover and leave in a warm place for 1 hour, or until the batter is bubbly and clearly rising. Transfer to a jug (pitcher).

Set a large heavy-based non-stick frying pan (skillet) over a medium-high heat. Once hot, pour a little oil into the pan and rub the pan with a thick layer of paper towels. Pour some batter into the centre of the pan, letting it spread out to a pancake about 15 cm/6 inches in diameter and no thicker than 5 mm/¼ inch (ideally a little less). As the batter cooks, the bubbles will form small holes. Once the batter has set and is flecked golden underneath, flip it over with a palette knife or fish slice and continue to cook until the other side is golden. It should take about 4 minutes in all.

Set aside on a plate, keep warm under some foil or a clean kitchen towel. Repeat the process until you have finished the batter. Serve warm with lots of butter.

Basil Custard

Serves 6

The benefit of adding sweetness via a sauce is that it both dilutes and sweetens your main dish. Thus, an intense sweet-and-sour-tasting plum pie will seem to be sweeter and less sour, similarly a bitter-sweet steamed chocolate pudding will appear to be more creamy and sweet in taste. This is lovely eaten with raspberries.

425 ml/15 fl oz/generous 1¾ cups full-fat (whole) milk

3 large sprigs basil

6 medium egg yolks

115 g/4 oz/⅔ cup caster (granulated) sugar

150 ml/5 fl oz/⅔ cup double (heavy) cream

Place the milk and the basil sprigs in a saucepan. Set over a medium heat and scald by bringing just up to boiling point, so that the liquid trembles with the first tiny bubbles but doesn't erupt into a boil. Remove from the heat, cover, and leave to infuse for 30 minutes.

If you want to serve cold, place some ice in a large bowl with a small amount of cold water. If hot, have a thermos flask ready.

Whisk together the egg yolks and sugar until pale. Reheat the milk and, once very hot, but not boiling, slowly whisk into the egg yolks. Strain the mixture into a clean saucepan. Set over a low heat and, using a wooden spoon, stir the custard continuously until it becomes as thick as runny double cream and almost holds a trail. This will take about 25 minutes. Do not let the custard boil or get too hot, or it will split. If the custard gets too hot, keep stirring but remove the saucepan from the heat until it cools sufficiently to return to the heat.

Once the custard has thickened, stir in the double cream and keep stirring until it is hot, then serve immediately or transfer to the thermos. If you want to serve the custard cold, add the cream and plunge the pan into the iced water to quickly cool the custard.

Note

Experiment with other custard flavourings. Replace the basil with one of the following: a spilt vanilla pod, a broken cinnamon stick, 6 cardamom pods, 1 bay leaf, or a few sprigs of lavender.

Tepid

Serving tepid food should be approached with caution. It is the most visceral of all temperatures and can cause a sense of unease in those who are culturally conditioned to eating hot or warm food. The eater has no distractions from the texture and will experience maximum taste and flavour. Thus, any error will quickly reveal itself.

That being said, it can also be the most enjoyable temperature to eat certain dishes, as you can appreciate every aspect more intensely. Where possible, season your tepid dish when it has cooled, to ensure that you have the correct level of salt or sweetness, and flavour it more lightly than a chilled dish, as you will detect much finer nuances of smell. You must also treat fat more carefully, as your palate will detect any solidification, which can be unpleasant if it feels granular, such as tiny dense droplets of melted butter or bacon fat.

As your sensitivity is increased, it is worth experimenting by contrasting textures with tastes in tepid dishes. Eaters commonly associate sour tastes with hard, sharp textures, for example, so you could contrast this perception by serving the Peach and Basil Tapioca (p.183), where the delicate sweet-sour taste of the fruit juice is released by soft, slippery tapioca.

Contrasting temperatures, such as by serving a hot dish with a tepid dish, can also be utterly delicious. A simple example might be to accompany the Spiced Pea and Potato Frittata (p.176) and some crusty bread with a cup of piping hot tomato soup. The unexpected always makes you experience something more intensely.

Spiced Pea and Potato Frittata

Serves 4

This is a good dish to appreciate the benefits of tepidity. If you serve this hot, the potatoes seem at odds with the cooked egg. If you serve it too cold, the potatoes feel unpleasantly damp and frigid compared to the dense-textured egg. Serve it tepid and the silky potatoes merge seamlessly into the omelette, while the sautéed onion and potato taste deliciously sweet. And, if that were not enough, the chilli and ginger release tempting notes of capsaicin and sweet spicy zingerone (from the cooked raw ginger), to make each mouthful very tempting.

3–4 tbsp extra-virgin olive oil

450 g/1 lb waxy potatoes, such as Nicola, peeled and cut into 1-cm/½-inch dice

1 small onion, finely diced

1 tsp peeled and finely chopped fresh ginger

1 green chilli (or to taste), finely chopped

115 g/4 oz/scant 1 cup frozen or fresh petits pois

6 medium eggs, roughly beaten

4 tbsp finely grated Parmesan

salt and freshly ground black pepper

Set a 25-cm/10-inch non-stick frying pan (skillet) over a medium-low heat. Add 3 tbsp olive oil and, once hot, add the diced potatoes and season with salt and pepper. Fry gently for 10 minutes, stirring occasionally, until the potatoes are half cooked.

Mix in the onion, ginger and chilli and continue to fry gently for 10 minutes, stirring occasionally, until the onions are soft and golden. Finally, add the frozen or fresh peas and cook for another 5 minutes.

Once the potatoes are tender, season the beaten eggs and pour into the frying pan. Give it a good shake, so that the egg is evenly distributed amongst the vegetables. Sprinkle with the Parmesan and, as soon as the eggs begin to set, loosen the edges with a palette knife. Cook over a low heat for 10–15 minutes, or until the mixture is just set.

Cover the pan with a large plate and invert it so that the omelette slips out. If necessary, add a further 1 tbsp olive oil to the pan and, once hot, slip the omelette back into the pan so that you cook the reverse side for a further 5 minutes, or until cooked through. Slide on to a plate.

Serve when tepid, but do not leave it more than 1 hour at room temperature.

The Most Delicious Chicken Sandwich

Serves 2

Some dishes are tepid by default. This recipe comes from my first book, *Modern British Food* (1995), and is still a favourite Sunday night supper. You could, of course, chill the sandwich, but the bread and chicken would become more dense and the cucumber and lettuce soggy. Instead, by squashing the warm chicken into the bread, its juices soak into the soft bread, while the cucumber retains its slight post-salting chewiness and the lettuce remains crisp. Serve with cornichons and potato crisps as, not only do they taste gorgeous together, they also add even more textural interest.

2 sprigs thyme or lemon thyme

finely grated zest and juice of 1 lemon

2 tbsp extra-virgin olive oil

1 garlic clove, finely chopped

2 chicken breasts, skinned

¼ cucumber, peeled and thinly sliced

1 Little Gem (Boston) lettuce

3 spring onions (scallions), trimmed

1 French baguette (you need a 40-cm/16-inch length loaf)

4 tbsp Mayonnaise (p.44), or to taste

salt and freshly ground black pepper

Note

The fatty texture of the mayonnaise will make the flavours linger in your mouth.

Pull the leaves off the thyme sprigs and place in a small bowl with the lemon zest and juice, 1 tbsp olive oil and garlic. Lightly season.

Remove the small fillet from each chicken breast and add to the marinade. Then trim each breast and, slicing at an angle, cut into 4 pieces. Mix into the marinade and leave to marinate for 20 minutes while you prepare the other ingredients.

Lightly salt the thinly sliced cucumber and set aside. Separate, wash and dry the lettuce leaves. Finely slice the spring onions at an angle. Trim the ends off the French baguette and cut into 4 sections, each about 10 cm/4 inches in length. Slice each section open lengthwise – leaving it attached on one side like a book. Open each up and spread both cut sides with mayonnaise (top and bottom) before sprinkling the bottom half with spring onions. Carefully lay the cucumber slices on the upper half.

Set a cast-iron griddle pan over a high heat. Once very hot, oil the chicken pieces and sear them for 3 minutes on one side, then turn over and cook for 2 minutes, then reduce the heat to low and cook for a further 3 minutes, until golden and cooked through. Remove to a plate and slice through the thicker pieces of chicken. Arrange a single layer of cooked chicken on top of the spring onions (adding any juices), then slip the lettuce leaves on top and press the sandwich closed. Squash firmly and serve immediately.

Crispy Duck, Mint and Noodle Salad

Serves 4

- -

As with the Chicken Sandwich (p.177), this recipe mixes together warm and cold (room temperature) ingredients to create a highly textural tepid dish. It's worth comparing the two dishes to appreciate how sensitive you become to the different textures when food is tepid; in this case the slightly dry, sesame-dressed rice noodles, crisp cucumber, crunchy duck fat and tender duck flesh.

For the duck

1½ tsp fine sea salt

1 tsp Chinese five-spice powder

4 duck breasts, each about 175 g/6 oz with skin on

For the salad

1 Thai chilli, or to taste, finely sliced

6 spring onions (scallions), trimmed and finely sliced into matchsticks

1 bunch chives, roughly sliced

a handful of mint leaves, finely shredded

1 cucumber, peeled, seeded and cut into matchsticks

225 g/8 oz dried instant rice vermicelli noodles

6 tbsp toasted sesame oil, or to taste

125 ml/4 fl oz/½ cup hoisin sauce, thinned with 1 tsp warm water

You need to prepare the duck 8 hours in advance. Mix together the salt and spice. Remove the skin from the duck breasts and score the outer surface of the skin in fine diamonds. Trim the meat. Rub the salty spice into the skin and meat. Arrange in a single layer on 2 plates – don't cover as you need it to dry out – and chill for 8 hours.

Shortly before serving, preheat the oven to 200°C fan/220°C/425°F/gas mark 7.

Pat dry the duck breasts and skin. Cut the skin into 1-cm/½-inch thick slices.

Set a dry frying pan (skillet) over a medium heat. Add the duck skin and cook for 5 minutes, turning regularly. The skin will start to release its fat. Add the duck breasts to the pan and fry briskly for 5 minutes, turning once. Transfer the skin and breasts to a non-stick roasting pan. Add some of the duck fat to keep the meat moist and roast for 10 minutes. Remove and rest for 10 minutes.

To make the salad, place the finely sliced chilli, spring onions, chives, mint and cucumber matchsticks in a large mixing bowl.

Prepare the noodles by soaking them in a bowl of boiling hot water for 3 minutes, or follow the instructions on the packet. Drain thoroughly and mix into the salad with the sesame oil – add extra if needed. Finely shred the duck skin. Set to one side. Finely shred the lean duck fillets.

Working quickly, divide the noodle mixture between 4 shallow soup bowls. Place a pile of shredded duck breast on top of each serving of noodles, then top with the shredded skin. Spoon the hoisin sauce around the outer edge and serve immediately. The salty duck and hoisin sauce means the noodles require no extra seasoning.

Does your sensitivity to taste, flavour and texture increase as food cools?

Plum Tarte Tatin

Serves 4

Many ingredients become firmer as they cool and cooked fruit is no exception. Tarte tatins are often served piping hot with ice cream, but I find them most enjoyable when they're eaten barely warm. That way, the caramelized butter has cooled to create a delicious sticky sauce, while the fruit has lost its steam to reveal its buttery texture as it soaks into the flaky puff pastry. Serve this intense tasting tart for pudding or tea.

It's easiest to make the full 225 g/8 oz puff pastry (p.126) and freeze half the dough. Remember that the weight of home-made pastry always refers to the amount of flour used in the recipe. The weight of shop-bought pastry usually refers to the final pastry weight.

½ quantity home-made puff pastry (p.126)

plain (all-purpose) flour, for dusting

55 g/2 oz/scant ¼ cup unsalted butter, softened

55 g/2 oz/generous ¼ cup granulated sugar

500 g/1 lb 2 oz Victoria plums, halved and stoned

Preheat the oven to 180°C fan/200°C/400°F/gas mark 6.

Roll out the pastry on a lightly floured surface. Then, using a plate that is slightly larger than a 18-cm/7-inch oven-proof cast-iron frying pan (skillet) as a template, cut out a circle of pastry, lightly prick with a fork and chill in the refrigerator.

Using your fingers, press the butter onto the base of your oven-proof pan until it coats it evenly. Sprinkle the sugar evenly over the butter. Tightly pack the plum halves in concentric circles in the pan, ensuring that their rounded skin side is pressed into the sugar.

Place over a medium-high heat and cook for about 8 minutes, or until the mixture caramelizes. As soon as the sugar has caramelized, remove from the heat and quickly press the pastry circle onto the plums, pushing the edges down around the inside of the pan. Immediately place in the centre of the hot oven.

Bake for 30 minutes or until the pastry is a beautiful golden colour and well risen. Remove from the oven and allow to rest for 5 minutes. Then, take a slightly larger plate, press against the pastry and invert the pan, giving it a good shake. The tart should slip out, juices and all. It can be served hot, warm or cold, but is at its best tepid.

Cold

As the insightful Mrs Leyel wrote in her book *Picnics for Motorists* in 1936: 'The art of arranging cold meals is to choose dishes that are better cold than they would be hot ....' This immediately sets the cook to thinking in a new temperature-led way. Mrs Leyel's picnic menus illustrate that 'cold' can refer to ambient, frigid and frozen temperatures, with dishes as varied as mousse of chicken liver with caraway straws, cucumber and gherkin salad, and banana ice cream. However, in this book, cold refers to anything below 37°C/98.6°F, but above freezing.

Her point, however, is a good one. How often do we question whether a dish is improved by being served cold and, if so, how cold? Take the Chilled Noodles with Prawns (p.40). The coldness transforms the ginger soy-dressed ingredients into a tempting dish, the sophistication of which would be lost if it were eaten warm or tepid.

Remember that while your perception of taste and flavour is virtually the same for tepid and ambient food, chilled food is different. The colder the food, the more your sensitivity to most sweet, sour and bitter tastes is reduced, while your perception of salt is increased. This affects salty-tasting umami ingredients, such as soy sauce and Parmesan. Normally, umami ingredients enhance your sense of sweet tastes, but with chilled dishes salty, savoury tastes will dominate.

Textures also change as they get colder, particularly fat-based textures, which will solidify. Chill the Plum Tarte Tatin (p.180) and you will find that the pastry becomes dense and firm and the buttery plum juices solidify. The same is true of sponges, dressings, soups, cold meats, terrines and custards.

Setting aside such practicalities for a moment, you should also consider why you are serving cold food. Is it to ease the workload of the kitchen or is it to refresh and stimulate the eater? Is it context dependent? For example, compare eating a few choice cherries served chilled on a beautiful plate at the end of a meal, to sharing a bag of ambient cherries on a picnic. In other words, constantly question which temperature would best enhance your dish.

Smoked Salmon Pâté

Serves 4

Traditional British fish paste, or pâté as it later became known, relies on being lightly chilled to develop its creamy texture. If you eat it straight from the food processor, its soft airy texture melts too quickly in the mouth, revealing pulverized fish suspended in butter rather than a silken buttery whole.

This is equally good spread onto hot toast (p.52) or canapés, particularly when topped by sliced cornichons.

90 g/3¼ oz/6 tbsp unsalted softened butter

a large pinch of cayenne pepper

a pinch of freshly ground black pepper

2 tbsp lemon juice, or to taste

200 g/7 oz sliced smoked salmon

2 tbsp double (heavy) cream

Place the butter, cayenne pepper, black pepper and lemon juice in a food processor. Process until the butter is fluffy. Add the smoked salmon and double cream and briefly whiz until the salmon just forms a paste. If you over-process, the salmon will become sticky. Taste and adjust the seasoning – you shouldn't need any salt, but you may need more lemon juice. Fill 4 x 100 ml/3½ fl oz/scant ½cup china soufflé dishes. Cover and chill until needed.

Peach and Basil Tapioca

Serves 4

This makes a tantalizing late-summer pudding that can be served tepid or chilled. Your mouth will fill with the herbal grassy-flavoured basil and floral peach, as the chilled tapioca slips around your mouth.

The peaches are kept unpeeled as their skin releases a faint hint of bitterness and turns the purée a beautiful blush rose. The texture is slightly rougher, but if you want to make it ultra-silky, push through a sieve before mixing.

Seed tapioca pearls can be bought online from health food delis, but take care to buy 'seed pearls' as these hold their shape when cooked.

500 g/1 lb 2 oz white or yellow peaches

1 large sprig basil

juice of ½ lemon

115 g/4 oz/⅔ cup caster (granulated) sugar

100 g/3½ oz/⅔ cup seed tapioca pearls

Quarter, stone and roughly chop the peaches. Place in a non-corrosive saucepan with the basil, lemon juice and sugar. Cover and set over a low heat, stirring occasionally, until the peaches start to release their juice and the sugar has dissolved. Simmer for about 10 minutes or until soft.

Remove from the heat, discard the basil and purée the peaches with a hand-held blender or in a food processor. Set aside until needed.

Bring 500 ml/17 fl oz/2 cups water to the boil in a heavy-based saucepan. Stir in the tapioca and keep stirring until the mixture starts to simmer, then reduce the heat to low and cook very gently for 30 minutes, stirring regularly, until the tapioca has swelled into translucent spheres.

Remove from the heat, transfer to a mixing bowl and stir in the peach purée. Leave until tepid, then spoon into glasses and either serve or chill and then serve.

Apple and Sorrel Mousse with Sugared Blackberries

Serves 4

When refrigerators were first introduced into Britain, there was a proliferation of recipes for sweet and savoury iced soufflés, mousses and creams. Most required gelatine, which is usually chilled – marshmallows (p.112) being an exception. The result was a creamy airy concoction that slowly released its tastes and flavours as the gelatine melted in the mouth, as can be experienced with this jade-green mousse. It tastes similar to gooseberry mousse with slightly more sappy notes, which are magical when combined with musky (room temperature) blackberries.

Today, chefs have myriad different forms of algae-based gelatines, which set into many different types of textures, from dense, sliceable jellies to caviar-like spheres of jellified liquid.

You can make this recipe without the sorrel. If so, add 1 tbsp lemon juice to the apples before cooking and 3 tbsp Calvados to the apple purée.

450 g/1 lb cooking apples, such as Bramleys

100 g/3½ oz sorrel leaves, washed

12 g/scant ½ oz leaf gelatine

115 g/4 oz/scant ⅔ cup granulated sugar

150 ml/5 fl oz/⅔ cup double (heavy) cream

2 medium egg whites

To serve

450 g/1 lb blackberries

1–2 tbsp caster (granulated) sugar

Peel, core and roughly slice the apples. Place in a non-corrosive saucepan with 4 tbsp water and cover. Set over a medium heat and stir occasionally until the apples begin to release some juice, after about 4 minutes. Then reduce the heat and simmer for a further 6 minutes, or until the apples have reduced to a pulp.

Meanwhile, prepare the sorrel leaves by stripping away and discarding their stalks before roughly shredding their leaves. Mix into the hot apple pulp and cook for 2 minutes or until the leaves collapse into a khaki green mess. Remove from the heat.

Place the gelatine in a bowl. Cover with some cold water and soak for 5 minutes. Drain the water from the gelatine and stir into the hot apple and sorrel. Once the gelatine has melted, add the sugar and purée the apple mixture with a hand-held blender or in a food processor.

Transfer to a large bowl and leave until tepid, then chill. As the mixture cools, it will begin to set. You need to keep an eye on it – once in the refrigerator it only takes about 30 minutes. As soon as the apple purée reaches a floppy consistency, similar to softly whipped double cream, whisk the cream until it forms soft peaks and fold into the setting apple mix.

Using a clean, dry whisk immediately whip the egg whites until they too form soft peaks. Fold them into the apple mixture and transfer to a pretty serving bowl, cover and chill.

When you're ready to serve, toss the blackberries in the sugar. Spoon out the mousse and add some sugared blackberries to each plate.

Note
Compare the mouth feel of this fat-dependent mousse with the fat-free Rhubarb and Rose Water Jelly (p.106). Both are chilled sweet and sour puddings – does the flavour linger longer in your mouth with one?

Chocolate Spice Biscuits

Makes 16 biscuits

Biscuits (cookies) belong to the wonderful world of ambient foods. Who can resist the biscuit tin when it's time for a morning coffee or a late night snack? I've created this recipe to play with the contrast of the chocolate melting in your mouth, as you release the buttery, spicy flavours from the hard biscuit.

cold-pressed sunflower oil, for greasing

115 g/4 oz/¾ cup plus 2 tbsp self-raising flour

a pinch of fine sea salt

½ tsp bicarbonate of soda (baking soda)

1 tsp ground ginger

1 tsp ground cinnamon

1½ tsp mixed spice

30 g/1 oz/2½ tbsp light brown muscovado sugar

55 g/2 oz/scant ¼ cup unsalted butter

55 g/2 oz/scant 3 tbsp golden syrup

115 g/4 oz good-quality dark (bittersweet) chocolate, roughly broken

Preheat the oven to 180°C fan/200°C/400°F/gas mark 6. Lightly grease 2 non-stick baking sheets and set aside.

Sift the flour, salt, bicarbonate of soda and spices into a large bowl. Mix in the sugar.

Melt the butter and golden syrup together in a saucepan over a low heat. Do not let them boil. Then, using a wooden spoon, stir the warm butter into the spiced flour. As soon as it is mixed, discard the spoon and, using your hands, mould into a dough. Turn out and shape into a sausage.

Cut the sausage into 16 pieces. Roll each piece into a small ball, then lightly flatten each ball and place on the prepared baking sheets, allowing each biscuit some space to spread as it cooks.

Bake for about 10 minutes, or until golden brown and covered in cracks, but still soft. Do not let them turn too dark or they will taste bitter. Remove from the oven and leave for a few minutes on the baking sheet to cool and harden slightly. Transfer to a wire cake rack and leave until cold.

Once the biscuits are cold, put the chocolate in a bowl that will neatly fit over a pan of just-boiled water that is off the heat. You will need to replace the boiling water at least once to allow the chocolate to melt.

Once the chocolate has melted, use a teaspoon to coat the top of each biscuit with chocolate. Then return to the cooling rack. Once the chocolate has fully set you can transfer the biscuits to a serving plate or biscuit tin.

Frozen

The cook enters a different world of sensory perception when they prepare frozen food. It's a world where tastes change, textures alter and flavours are suppressed, until the food is sufficiently warmed in the mouth.

However, developments in technology, in particular access to liquid nitrogen and the Pacojet, have enabled restaurants to serve incredibly fine-textured frozen ices with the flick of a switch. The Pacojet micro-purées frozen ingredients into crystals an undetectable 2 microns in size. Chefs use the latter to make the likes of ultra-smooth beetroot (beet) sorbet and fluffy horseradish snow.

As a result, frozen elements have become a commonplace component in both sweet and savoury restaurant dishes. They are hard to achieve at home without such technology, so domestic cooks tend to limit themselves to traditional frozen sweet recipes. These can be divided into water- and fat-based frozen puddings and slushy semi-frozen drinks.

The texture of domestic frozen dishes is dependent on both the culinary method and the correct balance of sugar to water or fat. Too much sugar, alcohol or salt will prevent freezing. It's therefore important to start with a clear idea of the texture you wish to achieve and the impact you want to create. Are you looking for the slow, lingering appeal of dipping into a luscious ice cream, such as the Chocolate Nori Ice Cream (p.74), or the tingling burst of a granita (p.189)?

Modern recipes often advocate strong, punchy flavours for frozen concoctions, but in the past many of the recipes tasted surprisingly delicate, as can be discovered in Mrs Marshall's definitive *The Book of Ices* (1885), with recipes for frozen Apple Ice Water and Bergamot Ice Water.

The key lies in allowing the flavours to be slowly released as the mixture melts in your mouth. In *The Secret of Scent* (2006), Luca Turin illustrates perfectly how temperature can change flavour: 'Put some strawberries and ice in a blender, give the mixture a twirl until the ice is finely crushed, wait for ten seconds, then take the lid off and smell. What you get is hard-boiled eggs, because the strawberries contain light, sulphur-containing compounds that alone manage to struggle free at this low temperature.' If you've tried this, now place a spoonful of the iced strawberries in your mouth and wait and see what happens.

In my view, it's important to keep frozen recipes as simple as possible. The eater's dulled senses will gain greater pleasure from the slow development of a dominant flavour. Extraneous textures, such as nuts, or wafers, should be added in moderation, otherwise they become a distraction. Nor do I enjoy the common custom of serving ice cream with a hot dish – for example, sticky toffee pudding with vanilla ice cream. I find both the temperature contrast and the resulting tepid food unpleasant, but then, food is highly subjective.

Strawberry Ice Cream

Serves 4

Home-made strawberry ice cream is DELICIOUS. This recipe (doubled up and photographed on p.235) uses double cream and lots of egg yolks to make a classic high-fat custard that retains its creamy texture when frozen. The alcohol makes it softer and more scoopable. (For the banana version, see the note on p.148.)

300 ml/10 fl oz/1¼ cups double (heavy) cream

1 vanilla pod

225 g/8 oz strawberries, hulled

140 g/5 oz/scant 1¼ cup caster (granulated) sugar

juice of ½ lemon

3 tbsp eau de vie fraise or framboise or kirsch

4 egg yolks

Place the cream and vanilla pod in a medium saucepan. Set over a low heat and bring to the boil, then remove from the heat.

Purée the strawberries, with a hand-held blender or in a food processor, with 85 g/3 oz/scant ½ cup sugar. Add the lemon juice and eau de vie and set aside in a bowl large enough to hold the custard as well.

Whisk the egg yolks with the remaining sugar, until pale and fluffy. Slowly stir the hot cream into the egg yolks with a wooden spoon. Return the mixture to the pan.

Set over a low heat and, using a wooden spoon, stir continuously in a figure-of-eight motion until the cream thickens enough to coat the back of the spoon. This will take 10–20 minutes, depending on your confidence. Don't let it boil or the custard will split. If it feels as though it's getting too hot, just lift the pan off the heat and keep stirring. As soon as it is ready, strain the custard through a sieve into the strawberry purée. Mix well, cover and, once cool, chill in the refrigerator.

Churn the cold custard, according to the instructions for your ice cream machine, until it reaches a soft set. Transfer to a covered container and store in the freezer. Alternatively, pour into a shallow plastic container, cover and freeze. Beat with a fork every 40 minutes, or until you have a smooth, soft-set ice cream.

Note
You can reuse your vanilla pod. Rinse after use and, once dry, keep in the sugar jar for vanilla sugar.

Plum Water Granita

Serves 4

This fluffy pink cloud of ice crystals melts in your mouth to release a subtle plum flavour. It follows the Victorian concept of a refreshing dilute water ice, as opposed to a modern-style intense-tasting plum sorbet. Don't worry at the plum water's initial sweetness, it tastes less sweet once frozen.

Umeshu is a type of Japanese sour plum sake, but you can substitute it with Mirabelle eau de vie, if wished. This recipe takes time to make, so prepare the plum water the day before freezing and allow 4 hours of half-hourly stirring of the plum liquid. Make sure the freezer is set at -18°C/-0.4°F.

550 g/1 lb 4 oz cooking plums, quartered and stoned

115 g/4 oz/scant ⅔ cup granulated sugar

600 ml/20 fl oz/2½ cups boiling water

2 tbsp umeshu (plum sake) or Mirabelle eau de vie

Place the plums and sugar in a saucepan. Add the boiling water and set over a low heat. Stir until the sugar has dissolved, then simmer gently for 10 minutes, until the plums have collapsed into a frothy mass.

Tip the mixture into a sieve and leave to drip into a bowl for 3 hours. (Do not push the plums through the sieve, you can set them aside and serve them with yogurt or fromage frais for breakfast.)

Stir the umeshu or Mirabelle eau de vie into the strained plum juice and, once tepid, cover and chill in the refrigerator.

Transfer the cold plum water to 1 or 2 shallow containers, taking care that the liquid is no more than 2.5 cm/1 inch in depth. Place in the freezer for 30 minutes, then remove and, using a fork, scrape the frozen mixture around the edges into the liquid. Return to the freezer and repeat this every 30 minutes for 3–3½ hours, or until the mixture is a mass of icy crystals.

It is now ready to serve. Return to the freezer and check it's consistency about 15 minutes before serving. If it is too solid, leave at room temperature for 15 minutes, then scoop into glasses or bowls.

Raspberry Ice-Cream Sandwich

Serves 8

Contrasting textures can be used in frozen puddings, ranging from chocolate chips and crunchy nuts to sorbet ripples and sugary sponges. This ice cream is a semifreddo, which depends on whisked cooked Italian meringue and whisked double (heavy) cream for its air and stability during the freezing process. Ideally, you should use an electric whisk for this recipe.

This recipe makes double the semifreddo quantity needed, as it's much harder to make with only one egg white. Keep the excess for a special supper-time treat with extra raspberries. You can adapt this recipe to other fruits, such as (cooked) rhubarb or blackcurrants.

For the sponge
55 g/2 oz/scant ¼ cup unsalted butter, melted, plus extra for greasing

3 medium eggs

85 g/3 oz/scant ½ cup caster (granulated) sugar

85 g/3 oz/scant ⅔ cup plain (all-purpose) flour, sifted

For the raspberry ice cream
250 g/9 oz raspberries

1 tbsp lemon juice

2 tsp distilled orange flower water

300 ml/10 fl oz/1¼ cups double (heavy) cream, chilled

2 medium egg whites

225 g/8 oz/1 cup plus 2 tbsp granulated sugar

To serve
340 g/12 oz raspberries (optional)

Begin with the sponge. Preheat the oven to 170°C fan/190°C/375°F/gas mark 5. Grease a 20-cm/8-inch square cake pan and line the base with baking parchment.

Place the eggs and caster sugar in a large bowl and set over a pan partially filled with just-boiled water (off the heat). Whisk until the eggs double in volume and hold a trail for 5 seconds. Remove from the pan and continue to whisk until tepid.

Pour the melted butter around the edges and, using a flat metal spoon, fold into the whisked eggs. Sift the flour over the surface and gently fold into the mixture. Spoon into the prepared pan, give a tap to even out the surface and bake for 20–25 minutes, or until it has shrunk from the sides and springs back if lightly pressed. Remove to a wire cooling rack.

Once the cake is cold, turn out on to a sheet of baking paper and slice horizontally into two layers.

Meanwhile, make the raspberry ice cream. Purée the raspberries, with a hand-held blender or in a food processor, and push through a sieve into a bowl, discarding the seeds. Stir in the lemon juice and orange flower water. Chill, covered.

In a large bowl, whisk the cream until it forms soft floppy peaks.

Timing is crucial for the next stage. Place the egg whites in a clean dry bowl and have a clean dry electric whisk close to hand.

Clip a thermometer onto a small saucepan. Add the sugar and 150 ml/ 5 fl oz/⅔ cup water and set over a low heat, stirring regularly until the sugar has dissolved. Then increase the heat and boil vigorously until the mixture reaches hard ball stage (120°C/250°F on the thermometer).

Once the sugar syrup nears hard ball, start whisking the egg whites until they form stiff peaks. As soon as the syrup reaches hard ball, keep whisking the egg whites (at a high speed) while you pour a continuous thin stream of hot syrup into the egg whites. They will form billowy clouds of meringue as you whisk. Continue to whisk until the meringue feels tepid.

Using a metal spoon, fold the raspberry purée into the meringue mixture. Then immediately fold the pink meringue into the whipped cream. Transfer to a shallow container and place in the freezer for 30–60 minutes, or until it is soft frozen.

Lay the bottom cake layer (cut-side up) on a board lined with baking parchment. Spoon about half the lightly frozen ice cream mixture on top of the cake and smooth evenly using a palette knife. Sandwich together with the other cake layer (cut-side down) and press down gently and evenly. Lay another sheet of parchment on top and freeze for 2–3 hours.

To serve, trim the edges of the cake and slice into slim fingers. Arrange on individual plates. Once sliced, let it sit for a few minutes to soften slightly before serving. You can, if wished, garnish with extra raspberries.

Appearance

Appearance
Recipes

In the beginning
sources of inspiration

Construction
different approaches to food arrangement

Heightening expectation
the power of suggestibility

Instagram versus reality
losing the camera lens

Personal expression
cooking is an expression of self identity

Appearance

'To me, photography is the simultaneous recognition, in a fraction of a second, of the significance of an event as well as of a precise organization of forms which give that event its proper expression.'

THE DECISIVE MOMENT
by Henri Cartier-Bresson, 1952

The same is true of cooking. The final appearance of every dish you make is the result of your organization of taste, aroma, texture, temperature and shape to express a single moment in time.

In this last chapter, I want to explore the importance of vision. All cooks are taught that food should look appetizing. At one level, this relates to your ability to use colour, texture, spatial arrangement and crockery in an appealing manner. It also requires an understanding of the occasion and an appreciation of the surroundings and the light.

However, at a deeper level, it depends on your ability to convey a sense of time and place by your choice of seasonal foods and visual cues. Serve a hearty lentil soup in a beautiful, dark, rough-textured bowl, for example, and you will evoke winter with the tactile rustic look of the bowl and the warm colour of the soup; in the same way that a casual scattering of blackberries on a hazelnut meringue prompts thoughts of warm autumn days.

As cooking ends with the finished dish, so the act of eating begins with the visual impact of your food; but what is deemed tempting in one culture, may not appeal to another. The appearance of food is highly subjective. Americans apparently like brightly coloured food, particularly if offered on white plates, whereas Japanese diners prefer muted natural colours and subtle-toned dishes.

Over the years, food manufacturers and scientists across the world have tried to codify our reactions. How do we respond when we discover that the steak we've been eating is dyed blue, for example, and do we feel more or less hungry if we eat the same portion of food from a small or large plate? As you might expect, we react badly to blue-coloured steak as it suggests contaminated meat, and we feel more replete eating from a small plate.

Many of these trials have been inconclusive. Results tend to vary according to the age and cultural background of the subject. Will a red apple taste sweeter than a green apple? It depends on your experience of red and green apples. The same is true of colouring food and drinks red or green.

For centuries, culinary fashion has constantly changed in what is considered visually pleasing. To my knowledge, only Japanese chefs have tried to develop methodical guidelines to creating an aesthetically pleasing meal. Their origins lie in Buddhist thought and Japanese culture, but they are universally relevant.

The use of empty space is crucial. It creates an energetic tension between the food and the plate, and the plate and the surrounding utensils. Contrasting shapes can also be employed to create an agreeable visual tension – for example, a round dumpling on a square dish.

Different styles of food arrangement can be set before the diner at one time. Thus, amongst several, one dish of food might be neatly arranged, while another has an air of relaxed informality. Some schools of Japanese chefs have a tradition of serving odd numbers, which can be very pleasing. Sashimi, for example, might be presented in groups of three, five or seven slices.

Given that culinary fashions are as fickle as the world of couture, one has to accept that it's difficult to capture the natural beauty of food by defined methods. One minute only airy piles of food are considered chic, the next minute they've been replaced by neatly organized arrangements of precisely cut food. And to make matters worse, there are some dishes that never look attractive. It's hard, for example, to make beef stew look appealing. It takes an act of faith to eat such dishes, but if they taste good, appetite and experience overrules the eyes.

The best approach is to create your own culinary look. After all, your food is as much a statement of who you are, as your choice of clothes. The first step towards redefining how you present your cooking is to pause and look at every dish you eat. Don't look at it through a camera lens, instead focus on how it looks in real life.

Monitor your responses to the colour, texture, space, structure and visual contrast of every dish you see. Do you prefer the casual look of a bubbling home-made lasagne flopped on to a familiar dinner plate, for instance, or a daintily arranged restaurant dish of 'lasagne' where a square of pasta is delicately balanced on top of a luscious concoction and drizzled with sauce? How does each dish make you feel? Does your environment alter your perception and reaction?

The next step is to consider the occasion. Are you cooking a TV supper at home, preparing a dinner party or making a picnic, for example? Every meal has different requirements. The TV supper should be easy to eat on your knee and look appealing in a cosy setting. The dinner party might be lit by flickering candles and must appear sophisticated, regardless of whether its served from platters or ready plated; while the picnic will be viewed in bright sunlight and should look tempting when held in the hand.

The time of year will also alter your presentation. The changing colours of your seasonal ingredients, the type of recipe and the varying light will all influence the type of crockery and utensils that you choose. Wood and rough-textured glazes, for example, are associated with warmth and softness, so work well with cold-weather dishes; whereas glass is felt to be cooling and metals are perceived as cold and hard, which make them better suited for chilled hot-weather recipes.

No matter whether you're making an autumnal muesli or Crab and Avocado Tostadas (p.124), your aim must always be to express a moment in time that captivates the viewer before they taste a morsel of your food. It is, after all, the culmination of your creativity.

Appearance Notes

'One of the most important factors in good cooking is the presentation of the food. Dishes can be made to look irresistible by the right use of form, colour, and garnish, and clever dishing-up.'

PENGUIN CORDON BLEU COOKERY by Rosemary Hume and Muriel Downes, 1963

The subjective nature of appearance makes it a difficult topic to tackle. After much thought, I have divided the notes into the six categories that I always think about before making a dish. I then felt that it might be helpful to examine other aspects that can influence the appearance of a finished dish. These are designed to provoke thought, thus I've touched on subjects that range from how you start to conceptualize the look of a dish, to the impact of Instagram on ugly dishes.

Context

Context is everything. When you're planning what to cook, always take into account the practicalities of an occasion, including the environment, type of light and method of serving. Delicate airy salads, for instance, will be lost on a buffet table, whereas colourful, bold-shaped salads suitable for a fork will stand out amidst the array and still look good when plonked on a plate. Low-level lighting and shadows make dark dishes appear darker, and bright light exposes culinary errors and smudgy plates. Where possible, choose crockery and cutlery that will complement the mood you wish to create, remembering that touch is as important as sight. Only then can you construct the impression you're seeking to evoke, be it informal, evocative or glamorous.

Appearance test
Serve one slice of Picnic Fruit Cake (p.203) on a delicate china plate and another direct from a scrunched foil picnic wrapping. Does your perception of the cake's texture, taste and flavour vary?

Seasonality

Everyone carries a sense of seasonality within them, based on their environment and memories. From a visual perspective, you should try to mirror the changing seasonal colours, light and atmosphere in your food. The more you focus on seasonal ingredients, the more their colours will reflect the natural world – for example, creating pastel tones in spring and intense, bright notes in summer. Try using shallow utensils with delicate colours in spring, and more glass and white porcelain in summer, before moving to soft, warm-coloured, deeper utensils as winter approaches. Reflect the changing weather with different types of recipes, moving from refreshing, chilled dishes and salads in summer, to luscious, rich and warm concoctions in winter. Thus the creamy-toned, black-flecked Truffle Taglierini (p.73) served in a plain, deep bowl reflects the stark simplicity of winter.

Appearance test
Compare your reaction to seeing Brussels sprouts served with a summer dish of roast chicken salad compared to a winter meal of roast chicken.

Texture

Appearance test
Pile one portion of garlic and chilli spaghetti on a plate. Then, using tongs, curl a second portion into an airy pile on another plate, so that you get a sense of the individual strands. Compare.

Photographs of food come alive when a sense of texture is conveyed, such as with limpid drops of olive oil or crumbling pastry flakes. The same is true in real life. A careful use of texture can make food look much more appealing. Look at the predominant texture in your recipe and consider how you can enhance it. You can highlight individual textures by incorporating space into your final arrangement, for example, or you can introduce contrasting-textured ingredients such as in the Fennel, Pink Grapefruit and Chicory Salad (p.117). Homogenous textures, such as stews, and thick-sauced dishes, such as macaroni cheese or rice pudding, are tricky. Sometimes, it's best to be honest and – rather than disguise them – allow them to be what they are, with the merest hint of a garnish.

Colour

Appearance test
Turn the Rhubarb Jelly (p.106) brown by adding green food dye and see if your guests can correctly identify its flavour.

British cooks in the 1970s were counselled never to serve an all-beige or beige-brown meal. Such things were possible in those days and young cooks were advised to add colour (usually in the form of parsley) to prevent the eater's appetite from becoming dulled by the monotonous tones. Today, it's commonly believed that our perception of taste and flavour in food and drink can be enhanced by its colour and colour saturation – for example, a deep red strawberry is presumed to taste more intense than a pale pink strawberry. Research in this field has been inconclusive and contradictory, although it seems that that colour influences our ability to correctly identify a flavour. Better to approach the natural colours of your food as though you were an artist and combine them in an aesthetically pleasing manner.

Memory

Appearance test
Compare the reactions to serving the Strawberry Ice Cream (p.188) in ice cream cones to serving in small modern bowls.

Everything we make is an expression of who we are at that moment. It captures a small element of our past experiences, while at the same time becoming a memory in its own right. In other words, cooking constantly utilizes, evokes and creates memories. You can emphasize this aspect further by drawing on visual associations in the dish, remembering that they are always highly personal. Banana Flambé (p.97), for example, conjures up youthful winter nights for me. Take time to consider what a recipe means to you and draw on the elements that resonate with you. Highlight seasonal or retro tones, textures, colours, crockery and cutlery. It might be the subtle hint of rose petals strewn over a cake, or a statement, such as a bubbling gratin cooked in an old-fashioned orange Le Creuset dish.

In the Beginning

Inspiration for a dish can come in many forms. It might be triggered by the scent of tea drifting on the summer air, the spillage of flour upon a work surface, or the sight of silver-blue mackerel on a fish counter.

Such moments hold the essence of a recipe as it takes shape in your mind. How can you convey the shimmering beauty of the mackerel on an autumn day or capture the transient nature of the spilt flour? Would dusting pizza, bread or scone dough with flour capture the latter instant or would it detract from the final mouth feel?

It's important to step back and think about whether you can draw out these elements in your final dish. It's not an easy task. Sometimes it helps to start by looking at the physical structure of each ingredient. Which method of preparing a potato, for example, would best express the chilly minimal feel of a winter's day – the fragile shape of a golden crisp, the fluffy look of mashed potato, or the earthy appearance of a jacket potato?

It's also worth focusing on the actual moment you're trying to evoke, such as picking blackberries from a tangled autumnal hedge or the dreamy nature of a summer's afternoon when you catch the scent of tea. Seek out the colours, utensils and spatial arrangement that reflect the recipe's landscape and the weather and let the dish speak for itself.

Autumn Muesli

Serves 2

The inky purple of the blackberries and pretty greens of this recipe conjure up the exquisite tones of early autumn for me and carry the flavour of the mossy, damp, sweet-smelling air.

This particular version of muesli can only be eaten during the filbert (hazelnut) season in early autumn, when you can buy fresh filberts still encased in their leafy shells. Once cracked open, the nuts have no brown outer skin and are sweet and milky. However, you can adapt the recipe to the changing seasonal ingredients – moving to dried hazelnuts or walnuts and different fruit.

55 g/2 oz/generous ½ cup rolled (old-fashioned) oats

1 tbsp sunflower seeds

1 tbsp pumpkin seeds

15 g/½ oz/2 tbsp fresh filberts (hazelnuts) or cobnuts

½ dessert apple

115 g/4 oz/generous ¾ cup blackberries

200 ml/7 fl oz/generous ¾ cup full-fat (whole) milk, or to taste

a drizzle of good, light-flavoured runny honey (optional)

The night before breakfast, mix together the oats and sunflower and pumpkin seeds. Cover and set aside. Shell the nuts and keep them refrigerated.

The next morning, roughly slice the nuts, cut the apple into small dice and add with the blackberries to the oat mixture. Divide between two bowls and add milk to taste. I don't find it necessary to sweeten this dish, but others might, so offer a good runny honey, such as linden tree honey.

Peas in a Green Salad

Serves 4

Who wants to eat cooked peas when they taste so delicious raw? This simple salad represents the essence of early summer to me – exquisitely green with the sharp taste of lemon, bitter leaves and sweet peas conjuring up the woodland smells of my childhood. Try creating different variations, such as by adding delicate fungi notes with finely sliced button mushrooms, or creamy, lemony tones with crumbled feta cheese.

350 g/12 oz freshly picked, young peas in the pod (about 150 g/ 5½ oz shelled peas)

4 Little Gem (Boston) lettuces

1 bunch chives, roughly sliced

a handful of tender small mint leaves (optional)

2 tbsp lemon juice

3 tbsp extra-virgin olive oil

salt and freshly ground black pepper

Shell your peas into the salad bowl. Trim the lettuces (setting aside the outer leaves for a green soup). Separate, wash and dry the inner leaves, ripping the larger ones in half. Add to the peas with the sliced chives and mint leaves.

When you are ready to eat, add the lemon juice and olive oil to the bowl, lightly season and mix thoroughly. Add more lemon juice if necessary. Serve immediately.

If you are plating individual salads, use your clean hands to gently lift the leaves into an airy pile on each plate. The peas have a tendency to roll to the bottom of the salad, so scoop them with your fingers and gently drop them through each serving once you've plated the leaves.

Mackerel Teriyaki

Serves 4

The burnished look of the seared mackerel teriyaki captures autumnal tones.

3 tbsp naturally brewed
  soy sauce

1¾ tbsp sake

¾ tbsp mirin

2 tsp granulated sugar

4 medium-sized
  mackerel, filleted

1 tbsp fine sea salt

2 tbsp groundnut
  (peanut) oil

For the garnish

4 pickled ginger shoots
  or sliced pickled ginger
  roots, to taste

Add the soy sauce, sake, mirin and sugar to a small saucepan. Bring to the boil, then set aside.

Neatly trim each mackerel fillet to remove any discoloured parts and any tiny fin bones. Run your finger tips lightly along the flesh of each fillet to feel for the central pin bones; each time you feel one, pull it out with a pair of kitchen tweezers.

Take a clean tray that is large enough to hold the fish and evenly and lightly sprinkle the surface with half the salt. Lay the fillets skin-side down on the salt. Sprinkle them with the remaining salt. Chill for 30 minutes.

Bring a kettle of water to the boil, place a wire cooling rack in your clean sink and set a heatproof board by the sink (for your hot pan later).

Set a large heavy-based non-stick frying pan (skillet) over a high heat. Once hot, add the oil. When the oil is very hot, place the mackerel fillets in the pan, skin-side down. Use a large palette knife to keep moving the fillets about for about 30 seconds–1 minute, to prevent them from sticking to the pan. Turn each fillet and seal the flesh for another 30 seconds–1 minute, then take the pan over to the sink and carefully remove the half-cooked fillets to the cooling rack. Immediately pour the freshly boiled water over the fish to remove the excess oil.

Return the fillets, skin-side down, to the same oily pan, set over a medium heat and add the soy mirin mixture (teriyaki sauce). As soon as it begins to bubble, rotate the pan so that the fish become coated in the sauce.

Arrange the fillets, skin-side up, on 4 appetizer plates. Let the sauce bubble up in the pan, then spoon a little sauce over each fish. Garnish each plate with the ginger shoots or a small pile of pickled ginger roots. Serve immediately.

Baked Potato Soufflé with Smoked Haddock

Serves 4

This earthy-flavoured wintery supper looks beautiful accompanied by a red chicory salad tossed in mustard vinaigrette (p.39). You only need half a potato per person but you will need to bake your potatoes in advance.

2 floury baking potatoes, such as King Edward, Maris Piper (russet) or Wilja (about 225 g/ 8 oz each)

250 g/9 oz smoked haddock fillet

1 bay leaf

3 medium eggs, separated

3 tbsp double (heavy) cream

55 g/2 oz finely grated Comte cheese, plus 1 tbsp for sprinkling

unsalted butter, for greasing

salt and freshly ground black pepper

Preheat the oven to 170°C fan/190°C/375°F/ gas mark 5.

Scrub the potatoes clean, lightly prick with a sharp knife and bake for 1 hour, or until soft when pierced with a knife. Remove and leave until cool enough to handle.

Place the haddock fillet, skin-side down, in a shallow saucepan with the bay leaf and cover with cold water. Set over a medium-low heat and slowly bring up to a simmer. As soon as the fish is cooked, about 5 minutes, transfer the fillet to a plate. Leave until cool, then skin the fish, removing any bones as you separate the remaining flesh into small flakes. Cover and set aside.

Cut the cooled potatoes in half and scoop out their flesh – taking care to leave enough flesh for the potato skin to hold its shape. For the best results, push the scooped flesh through a ricer or the rough grater of a mouli legumes (food mill); otherwise, mash vigorously. You need 185 g/ 6½ oz/¾cup cooked flesh. Place the measured flesh in a large mixing bowl. Beat in the egg yolks, cream, finely grated cheese, and salt and pepper to taste.

Reheat the oven to 170°C fan/190°C/375°F/ gas mark 5. Butter a baking dish and arrange the potato skins in it.

Whisk the egg whites in a large, clean, dry bowl until they form soft peaks. Using a flat metal spoon, fold a large dollop of whisked egg white into the potato mixture, before gently folding in the remaining egg whites. Gently fold in the flaked fish and immediately spoon the mixture into the potato skins. You will need to pile the mixture up. Sprinkle with a spoonful of grated cheese and bake in the oven for 35 minutes, or until well risen and golden. Serve immediately.

Picnic Fruit Cake

Serves 10

Plump, warm-toned, dried fruits sit within the dense, dark crumb of this moist, loaf-shaped cake. It has no adornment, other than its simple wrapper. The style-conscious can wrap their slices in paper parcels, before slipping the sliced cake into their knapsacks or hampers.

You can make a lighter-coloured, honey-toned (sweeter) version of this recipe by replacing the black treacle with golden syrup and the whisky with calvados.

55 g/2 oz/generous ⅓ cup glacé cherries, halved

85 g/3 oz/⅔ cup chopped mixed candied peel

85 g/3 oz/⅔ cup currants

115 g/4 oz/generous ¾ cup sultanas (golden raisins)

115 g/4 oz/generous ¾ cup raisins

150 ml/5 fl oz/⅔ cup whisky

150 g/5½ oz/1 cup plus 2 tbsp plain (all-purpose) flour, sifted

heaped ¼ tsp bicarbonate of soda (baking soda)

85 g/3 oz/generous ⅓ cup unsalted butter, softened

85 g/3 oz/7 tbsp light muscovado sugar

½ tsp cinnamon

finely grated zest and juice of 1 lemon

55 g/2 oz/scant 3 tbsp black treacle

3 medium eggs, separated

In a large bowl, mix together the glacé cherries, mixed peel, currants, sultanas and raisins. Tip into a plastic container with a lid and mix in the whisky. Seal and set aside for 24 hours, giving the mixture the odd shake to remix.

Preheat the oven to 120°C fan/140°C/275°F/gas mark 1. Line a 900 g/2 lb non-stick loaf tin (pan) with 2 strips of baking parchment, so that all 4 sides are covered by the paper.

Sift the flour and bicarbonate of soda into a small bowl and mix thoroughly.

In a large bowl, beat the butter, sugar and cinnamon until fluffy. Add the lemon zest and juice, black treacle and the egg yolks. Beat thoroughly with a wooden spoon. Tip in the macerated fruit, scraping in its sticky juice, and mix in thoroughly. Then add the flour and mix thoroughly again.

Quickly whisk the egg whites until they form stiff peaks. Using a flat metal spoon, fold the egg whites into the cake mixture and immediately spoon the mixture into the lined tin. Place in the centre of the oven and bake for 2 hours, or until a knife or metal skewer inserted into the centre comes out clean.

Remove from the oven and turn out onto a cooling rack. Leave until cold, then wrap in foil until needed.

Construction

There are an infinite number of ways to arrange your food before serving. All depend on space, height, depth and contrast. From a visual perspective, elements of a meal can be categorized as flat, tall or deep. For example, a steak is essentially flat, whereas chips (fries) can be served flat or heaped into a pile. It's important to highlight the texture of each element, thus you become aware of the chips' shape and texture when piled up. In the same way, a bowl of soup can appear flat or deep, depending on whether you're looking at a single opaque surface of colour, or you can see ingredients floating in the the liquid, such as in Miso Soup (p.64).

We each have a unique artistic sensibility. You might see flat dishes as complex one-dimensional patterns, or as low-lying three-dimensional sculptures. A plate of finely sliced tomatoes, dotted with drops of oil and wild garlic flowers reflects the first approach, whereas the Smoked Trout on Rye open sandwich (opposite) illustrates the latter perspective.

How much space is set between each ingredient is also a matter of personal taste. Thus, the Mackerel Teriyaki (p.201) needs little, other than its garnish of pickled ginger shoots, to appear elegantly taut on its plate, whereas the Beetroot, Leek and Hazelnut Salad (p.207) is a complex tumble of leaves and shoots.

It helps to look at the structure of the dominant component of your dish and consider how it might be enhanced once on a plate or in a bowl. The Caramelized Onion and Beef Stew (p.127), for example, is brown and gloopy, despite the chunks of carrot and celeriac. However, its texture and colour is transformed into a tempting, rich concoction if you serve it with the contrasting, highly textural, bright-green leaves of spring greens (collards).

A wise cook will forget the latest culinary fashion and adapt the appearance of their food to their abilities and circumstances. Some chefs have a natural aptitude for tiny, jewel-like, food arrangements, whereas others are brilliant at creating glorious, naturalistic dishes. In the same way, it's only sensible to adjust your presentation to suit the utensils you have to hand, regardless of whether you're limited to white plates or a hodge-podge of old crockery.

Smoked Trout on Rye

Serves 2

Open sandwiches are essentially flat, albeit a little textured on the top. You can either regard them as an abstract pattern, or – as in this case – add a little height by your choice of toppings. In either case, only use edible garnishes that enhance the taste, flavour and texture of your dish. This makes a gorgeous filling lunch.

1 hot-smoked trout, skinned and filleted

1 tbsp lemon juice

1 tbsp peeled and freshly grated horseradish

2 tbsp crème fraîche

8 cornichons, drained and rinsed

½ small red onion, finely sliced into rings

a handful of small watercress sprigs, washed

3 thin slices dark rye bread

salt and freshly ground black pepper

Flake the trout flesh into a bowl, discarding any fine bones as you do so. Toss in the lemon juice.

In a small bowl mix together the horseradish and crème fraîche. Season lightly, as the smoked trout is salty. Mix into the smoked trout.

Prepare the remaining ingredients. Dry the cornichons on some paper towels and cut in half lengthwise. If you don't like strong onions, soak the finely sliced onion rings in a bowl of iced water for 15 minutes, then drain and pat dry on paper towels. Dry the washed watercress sprigs.

Take the 3 thin slices of rye bread, place a couple of watercress sprigs on each slice, then spoon on the smoked trout mixture. Cut each slice into a triangle and divide between two plates. Now insert more watercress sprigs along with the sliced cornichons, into the smoked trout of each triangle. Top with the onion rings and more watercress and serve with a small knife and fork.

A salad can be flat, tall or deep, with or without space …

Beetroot, Leek and Hazelnut Salad

Serves 4

Always be sensitive to the natural shape and texture of your ingredients. Consider the difference between eating quartered beetroot that follows the natural contours of the root and finely diced beetroot. The latter barely contains any flavour. In contrast, your tongue feels the textured layers of the quartered root, and your mouth is filled with its sweet earthy aroma.

450 g/1 lb raw beetroot (beets), trimmed

55 g/2 oz/scant ½ cup shelled hazelnuts

450 g/1 lb slender or baby leeks

85 g/3 oz mixed bitter salad leaves

1 tbsp finely chopped shallot

½ tsp good runny honey

2 tbsp white wine vinegar

6 tbsp hazelnut oil (or extra-virgin olive oil)

salt and freshly ground black pepper

Note
Compare the 'piled' arrangement of this salad with the flatter look of the Charred Leek Salad with Thyme Oil (photographed on p.67).

Preheat the oven to 180°C fan/200°C/400°F/ gas mark 6.

Wash and wrap the beetroot in foil and bake on a lower shelf in the oven for 1 hour, or until tender. Remove and leave to cool in the foil.

Meanwhile, spread the hazelnuts on a small baking sheet and roast them on a higher shelf in the oven for 10 minutes, or until fragrant. Leave to cool. Rub the nuts in a cloth to remove most of their brown skins. Roughly chop and place in a large mixing bowl. Set aside.

Trim the leeks, cut away their roots and the darkest part of their leaves. Remove their tough outer leaves and cut a cross in the pale green sections – to create a mop-like effect. Wash them thoroughly in a sink filled with cold water.

Bring a large saucepan of unsalted water to the boil and add the leeks. Boil briskly for 2–4 minutes, or until they are just tender. Drain and cool under cold running water, squeeze out the excess water and pat dry on paper towels.

Add the leeks and the salad leaves to the nuts. In a small bowl, whisk together the shallots, honey, vinegar and oil. Season to taste.

Peel the roasted beetroot, cut into attractive wedges and add to the leeks.

Once you're ready to serve, whisk the dressing again and pour over the salad. Lightly toss and adjust the seasoning, if necessary.

Divide the leek salad between four plates. To introduce height and light to each salad, carefully position the beetroot to support the salad leaves. Open up the leek tops so that they're like an upside-down octopus curling through the salad. Serve immediately.

Prawn Nori-maki

Makes 4 rolls and 32 pieces

Certain foods such as these nori-maki (nori-roll) sushi, require an ordered approach to presentation. I originally wrote this recipe for *Sainsbury's Magazine*. Although it's long, each stage is simple. You can vary the filling to your taste, but always use the freshest possible fish; otherwise use vegetables such as cucumber or Japanese thin omelette (seasoned with a tiny bit of sugar and salt). Cut your chosen filling, such as salmon fillet or peeled and seeded cucumber, into 5-mm/¼-inch thick strips.

For the sushi rice

5 tbsp rice vinegar

5 tbsp granulated sugar

4 tsp fine sea salt

250 g/9 oz/1⅓ cups Japanese sushi rice

8-cm/3¼-inch square of kombu (dried kelp)

325 ml/11 fl oz/1⅓ cups soft mineral water

For the nori-maki

12 king prawns (jumbo shrimp), cooked and peeled

4 sheets toasted nori seaweed

wasabi paste, to taste

For the hand vinegar

1 tsp rice vinegar, mixed with 3 tbsp cold water

To serve

naturally brewed soy sauce, to taste

pickled ginger, to taste

To prepare the sushi rice: put a few ice cubes in a large bowl with some cold water. Set a small metal bowl in the middle of the icy water. Mix the vinegar, sugar and salt in a small saucepan. Set over a low heat and stir regularly until the sugar has dissolved, then pour into the chilled bowl. Once cool, set aside.

Put the rice in a large bowl and place in the sink. Cover the rice with cold tap water and, using your hands, gently agitate the rice until the water becomes milky. Immediately pour off the water and keep repeating the process until the water is almost clear. Drain into a sieve and leave for 30 minutes.

Wipe the kombu with a damp cloth and slash it in a few places. Place the rice in a medium-small saucepan that has a tight-fitting lid. Add the soft mineral water and place the kombu on top of the rice. Cover and bring to the boil. Immediately remove and discard the kombu. Cover the rice, return to the boil, then reduce the heat to low and simmer for 10 minutes. Turn off the heat and leave, covered, for 25 minutes.

Ideally, ask someone to help you at this stage. Give them a fan or a folded newspaper. Spread the hot rice in a thin layer in a large bowl. Ask them to briskly fan the rice while you toss it in horizontal, cutting strokes with a flat wooden spatula. Keep the grains separate, don't mash them together. As you toss, gradually sprinkle 2–3 tbsp of the rice vinegar dressing over the rice. Check the taste and consistency as you do so – you don't want mushy rice. Once the rice is tepid, it is ready for use. Cover with a clean damp cloth.

Prepare your nori-maki filling. Slice each of the king prawns in half lengthwise, then in half widthwise.

Mix the hand vinegar in a small bowl – it helps prevent the sushi rice sticking to your hands.

Place 1 sheet of toasted nori, shiny-side down, on a bamboo rolling mat. Moisten your fingers with a little hand vinegar and, using your fingertips, lightly spread a quarter of the sushi rice in a thin, even layer over the nearest three-quarters of the nori sheet up to the edge (leaving the furthest quarter of the sheet uncovered). You'll need to keep rinsing your fingers with the hand vinegar.

Use your index finger to smear a thin horizontal line of wasabi paste across the centre of the rice. Arrange 3 of the sliced prawns on top of the wasabi line. Try to make the filling an even thickness without any gaps or lumps, as this will ensure that it will look good when sliced. The thicker your filling, the thicker your roll.

To roll: hold the line of ingredients firmly in place and, using your thumbs under the mat, lift up the nori and rice nearest to you and gently bring it over the filling, pressing it down as you continue to roll until you meet the end of the nori sheet. Hold the bamboo mat gently but firmly around the roll for 30 seconds to press the roll into shape.

Place the roll on a clean cutting board and remove the mat, making sure that the uncovered edge of the nori is underneath the roll. Repeat with the remaining ingredients to make 4 rolls in total.

Take a very sharp knife, wet its blade and slice the roll cleanly in half. Rinse the knife and cut each half into 4 pieces, rinsing the knife between each cut.

To serve: if you are serving these as lunch, allow 8 rolls per person. Place a tiny dipping bowl filled with soy sauce on each person's plate, along with a small heap of pickled ginger. Arrange the nori-maki, cut-side up, on each plate and serve immediately.

Greek Salad

Serves 4

In contrast to the height of the preceding Beetroot, Leek and Hazelnut Salad (p.207), this salad could be categorized as deep, if served in a bowl, as little space exists between its even-sized chunks of food and you look down into it. In such instances, remember Constance Spry's general advice on not serving heaped piles of food in *The Constance Spry Cookery Book* (1956), 'quite apart from appearance, it is difficult to serve without accident. It is maddening, because a dish perhaps has been over-filled, to get a portion of food on to one's favourite dress.' Enough said.

Simple recipes, such as Greek salad, need superlative ingredients to taste amazing. In other words, seek out the sweetest tomatoes, most flavoursome cucumber, the best olive oil, finest feta and very tastiest olives you can find, and you won't be able to stop eating it.

1 cucumber, peeled

400 g/14 oz flavoursome tomatoes

1 green (bell) pepper, quartered, seeded and diced (optional)

1 small red onion, diced

12 black or green olives, stoned and diced

2 tbsp lemon juice

4 tbsp extra-virgin olive oil

115 g/4 oz drained barrel-cured feta, roughly crumbled

salt and freshly ground black pepper

Cut the cucumber and tomatoes into similar-sized dice of your choice. I usually cut them around 2.5 cm/½ inch (but see p.100). Place in a bowl with the diced green pepper (if using), onion and olives. Add the lemon juice and the olive oil to taste, then mix in the crumbled feta. Finally, season the dish to your taste and leave to sit until you're ready to serve, then remix and decant to your chosen bowl or platter.

Note
Try mixing this recipe without any salt. Amazingly, the salty olives and feta cheese make the other ingredients taste even more exciting than when salted.

Lime Jelly with Raspberries

Serves 8

There is something ethereal about looking through translucent food, regardless of whether you are observing a gleaming green olive lying within a dry martini or raspberries suspended in a wobbly jelly (jello). Play with adding different ingredients to this jelly, such as tiny elderflowers or snippets of the tiniest tarragon leaves.

300 g/10½ oz/1½ cups granulated sugar

15 g/½ oz fine leaf gelatine

200 ml/7 fl oz/generous ¾ cup freshly squeezed lime juice (about 6–8 limes)

150 g/5½ oz/generous 1 cup raspberries

Put the sugar and 400 ml/14 fl oz/1¾ cups water in a saucepan, set over a low heat and stir occasionally until the sugar has dissolved. Remove from the heat.

Put the leaf gelatine in a bowl and cover with cold water. Soak for 5 minutes, then pour off the cold water and add the gelatine to the hot syrup. Stir briefly to ensure it has fully melted.

Strain the measured lime juice through a fine sieve into the gelatine syrup, stir and transfer to a jug (pitcher), then cover and set aside until tepid.

Place 3 perfect bright red raspberries in each of 8 x 125 ml/4 fl oz/½ cup jelly moulds. Half-fill each of the moulds with the liquid jelly mixture and place in the refrigerator. Leave the remaining liquid jelly mixture in the jug to stand at room temperature.

Once the jelly has soft-set, in about 1 hour, fill each mould to the brim with the remaining liquid jelly mixture. This stops the raspberries from floating to the top of the jelly mould. Chill for 6 hours or until firmly set.

To serve, dip each jelly mould into a bowl of very hot water for a couple of seconds, pat the mould dry and turn out by inverting onto a small plate.

Note

Compare eating this jelly with and without runny double (heavy) cream. The fat in the cream will alter your perception of its taste.

Heightening
Expectation

Never underestimate the power of suggestibility. You can heighten the eater's pleasure by subtly emphasizing certain visual aspects of food, such as colour, seasonality and cultural/social references – for example, Hallowe'en, Chinese New Year or a birthday.

Research shows that colour affects people's ability to correctly identify the flavour of food and drink. Heston Blumenthal famously illustrated this by serving two tiny tablets of red and orange jelly on a large white plate in his Michelin-starred restaurant, The Fat Duck, in Britain. Each guest was advised to taste the orange first, yet no hint of orange could be detected as it melted in the mouth, much to the bewilderment of many diners. It was made from golden beetroot, whereas the red jelly was made from blood oranges.

Conversely, if you eat food that is coloured according to its anticipated taste, as in an orange-tasting, orange-coloured jelly, you will appreciate it more intensely. Obviously, you should only do this naturally, not by adding colourings. You can also use colour contrast to emphasize a colour – for instance, the green leaves of the lettuce highlight the burnished gold and brown tones of the Honey Chilli Chicken in Lettuce Leaves (p.214).

Everyone has an emotional connection to the seasons and, by referencing the changing seasons in your finished dish, you will instantly create a sense of anticipation, happiness or wistfulness in the diner. Japanese chefs will try to create all three emotions through a meal, by introducing ingredients that are coming into season and going out of season, as well as those that are at their peak.

There are many ways that you can introduce seasonality, some of which have already been discussed (p.196). However, another way is to highlight the natural beauty of your food. Before you begin to cut your raw ingredients, gently run your hands over them – where appropriate, slice in sympathy with their natural contours. Thus, you sense the supple beauty of a mackerel and the curvaceous nature of a beetroot.

Drawing on cultural references is a further extension of seasonality. Who does not feel a thrill when served mini roast squash at Hallowe'en, or a pretty quails' egg salad at Easter?

Spiced Sweetcorn and Lime Soup

Serves 6

This lovely soup takes on a beautiful yellow colour once puréed, which will amplify the eater's expectation of its 'sweet corn' flavour. Since it can be served hot, warm or chilled, experiment with presenting it in different types of bowl, from cooling glass to warming rough pottery.

4 tbsp extra-virgin olive oil

2 medium onions, roughly diced

3 stems celery, roughly diced

1 garlic clove, roughly diced

½ or 1 Thai chilli, or to taste, finely diced

12 sweetcorn cobs (yields 950 g/2 lb 2 oz kernels)

30 g/1 oz bunch of coriander (cilantro), washed

500 ml/18 fl oz/generous 2 cups good-quality Chicken Stock (p.47)

juice of 1 large lime

100 ml/3½ fl oz/generous ⅓ cup crème fraîche, optional

salt and freshly ground black pepper

Set a saucepan over a low heat. Add the oil and, once hot, add the diced onions, celery, garlic and chilli. Fry gently for 15 minutes, or until soft.

Strip the corn cobs of their outer leaves, pull away their fine hairs and wash. Clear your chopping board, then stand each cob on its stem end and carefully cut away the kernels from the cob. They go everywhere. Gather them into a bowl and discard the cobs.

Strip the coriander leaves from their stems. Wrap the leaves in damp paper towels and store in the refrigerator (they're for the garnish). Finely chop the stems, then stir into the softened onion, followed by the corn kernels. Fry, stirring occasionally, for about 6 minutes, or until the corn has softened slightly. Mix in the stock and 700 ml/24 fl oz/3 cups water. Do not season at this point. Increase the heat to high, cover and bring up to a boil, then reduce the heat to medium-low and simmer for 40 minutes, or until the vegetables are meltingly soft.

Liquidize the soup in a food processor or using a hand-held blender, then pass through a coarse sieve into a clean pan.

This soup can be served hot, warm or chilled. Season to taste at your chosen temperature. If you are serving hot, only add the lime juice after reheating the soup, otherwise add the lime juice to the cool or tepid soup. Divide between 6 soup bowls. If you're garnishing the bowls, add a swirl of crème fraîche and/or a scattering of the reserved coriander leaves, roughly chopped.

Honey Chilli Chicken in Lettuce Leaves

Serves 4

I originally wrote this recipe for my first book, *Modern British Food* (1995). All of the ingredients should be cut to a similar cashew-nut size. Once cooked, they glisten gold, red, green and pale brown. However, by serving it in the lettuce leaves you heighten the colour contrast and sharply focus the eater's attention by serving it in an unexpected way. That said, it's not an easy dish to eat with the lettuce, although it does taste very good. If you can't find tiny chillies, you can use ½ tsp chilli flakes – but, obviously, it won't look quite as pretty.

You can serve this as a starter, but it also makes a lovely supper with steamed rice and Sesame Soy Spinach (p.50) or sweet-sour cucumber salad (p.21).

4 chicken breasts, skinned and boned

1 small egg white

1 tbsp cornflour (cornstarch)

2 garlic cloves, finely chopped

2 tbsp runny honey

2 tbsp rice (or white wine) vinegar

2 tbsp naturally brewed soy sauce

12 spring onions (scallions), trimmed

4 tbsp groundnut (peanut) oil

115 g/4 oz/1 cup unsalted cashew nuts

12 tiny dried red chillies

8 cup-shaped inner Iceberg lettuce leaves

Cut the chicken into 1-cm/½-inch chunks. Beat the egg white with the cornflour and then mix into the chicken with half the garlic. Cover and chill until needed.

Mix together the honey, vinegar and soy sauce. Set aside. Cut the spring onions into similar-sized lengths to the chicken.

When ready to serve, set a large non-stick frying pan (skillet) over a medium-high heat. Add 1 tbsp of the oil, add the cashew nuts and stir-fry constantly until they turn pale gold. Using a slotted spoon, quickly remove the nuts to a small bowl.

Add the remaining oil to the hot pan, followed by a single layer of the chicken pieces. Fry for 2 minutes, or until golden, then flip over and cook for a further 1–2 minutes. Using a slotted spoon, remove to the bowl with the cashew nuts. Repeat this process with the remaining chicken.

Add the chillies with the remaining garlic and the spring onions to the hot pan. Rapidly stir-fry for a few seconds, then return the nuts and chicken to the pan, before stirring in the honey-soy mixture. Stir quickly to coat all the ingredients, bring the sauce up to the boil, then immediately spoon the mixture into the lettuce leaves, allowing 2 leaves per person.

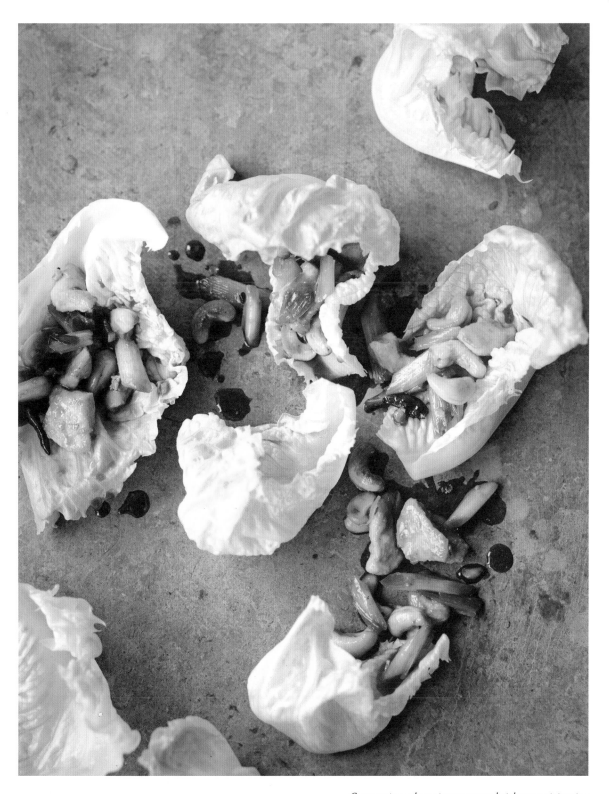

Contrasting colours is one way to heighten anticipation

Muted, rough-textured plates enhance the autumnal look

Soft Hazelnut Meringue with Blackberries

Serves 6

In Britain, hazelnuts and blackberries immediately conjure up autumn and that wistful feeling that summer is coming to end. Nothing more is needed to add to the taste, texture and flavour of this dish.

55 g/2 oz/scant ½ cup blanched hazelnuts

1½ tsp cornflour (cornstarch)

6 medium egg whites

250 g/9 oz/1⅓ cups caster (superfine) sugar

1½ tbsp white wine vinegar

icing (confectioners') sugar, sifted, for dusting

For the topping
300 ml/10 fl oz/1¼ cups double (heavy) cream

500 g/1 lb 2 oz blackberries

2 tbsp icing sugar (confectioners' sugar), sifted

Note
Compare the texture of this meringue with the uncooked Lime and Rose Marshmallows (p.105). This melts more quickly in the mouth, compared to the chewy nature of the marshmallow.

Preheat the oven to 180°C fan/200°C/400°F/gas mark 6.

Place the blanched hazelnuts on a small baking sheet and roast for 7 minutes, giving the sheet the odd shake, until lightly coloured. Remove and turn out onto a plate to cool.

Reduce the oven temperature to 130°C fan/150°C/300°F/gas mark 2. Line the bottom and sides of a shallow 30 x 20 cm/12 x 8 inch Swiss roll tin (jelly roll pan) with baking parchment.

Tip the cold hazelnuts into a food processor with the cornflour and grind in short bursts, until they form a fine meal. Don't over-process or the nuts will turn into a paste.

Put the egg whites into a large, clean, dry bowl and whisk until they form soft peaks. Whisk in a third of the sugar and, as soon as the egg whites begin to look more glossy, whisk in another third, followed by the remaining third. When the meringue is really thick and glossy, fold in the nuts and the vinegar with a flat metal spoon.

Spread the mixture evenly in the lined tin. Bake for 20 minutes, or until soft but slightly bouncy. Remove from the oven and leave to rest on a wire cake rack for a few minutes.

Liberally dust a larger sheet of baking parchment with icing sugar. Gently tip the meringue onto the parchment and peel the baking paper from its underside. Leave to cool.

Shortly before serving, cut the meringue into 6 squares and place each on a dessert plate. Place the double cream in a bowl and whisk until it forms soft peaks. Spoon a floppy spoonful over each meringue slice. Scatter each with the blackberries and dust with icing sugar.

Saffron Rice

Serves 2

One of the simplest ways to heighten expectation is to introduce a complementary coloured dish to accompany the food you're serving. This can come in many forms, from the structure and colour of a beautiful salad, to different-coloured rice, as here. In every case, it heightens the eater's perception of the main dish. Test this out by serving the rice with the Seared Tuna (p.230) or the Lamb Rogan Josh (p.82). See the photograph on p.83.

As a basic rule for cooking basmati rice, always add double the volume of liquid to rice; in other words, use 1 cup of rice to 2 cups of liquid, for 2 people.

1 tbsp extra-virgin olive oil

1 fat shallot, halved and finely sliced

170 g/6 oz/1 cup basmati rice

a pinch of saffron

a pinch of fine sea salt

Set a small saucepan over a low heat. Add the oil, followed by the shallot, and gently fry for 5 minutes, or until soft and golden. Stir in the rice and cook for 3 minutes, or until the rice looks slightly translucent.

Meanwhile, in a small bowl or mortar, mix together the saffron threads and salt. Grind the saffron under a teaspoon or with the pestle, until it forms a powder. Tip into the rice and add 425 ml/ 15 fl oz/generous 2 cups water. Cover, bring to the boil and immediately reduce the heat to low. Simmer for 15 minutes, then turn off the heat and leave for 5 minutes. The rice is ready when it is fluffy and just past al dente. All the liquid should have been absorbed.

Note
You can add an umami taste to this dish by replacing the water with Chicken Stock (p.47); this in turn will amplify the sweet, salty and umami taste of the food it's accompanying.

Instagram
Versus Reality

Social media has changed how people see food. The desire to capture an ever-wider audience by posting up photographs of every moment, has resulted in distorting our sense of reality. Many would-be foodies share an idealized version of meals that is unrelated to what we eat and how food actually looks in the physical world. Display a luscious-looking chocolate cake, for example, and the chances are you'll have a zillion hits. Post up a roast fowl looking a bit bird-like, and – no matter how good it tastes – the response will be much smaller. Within the magazine world, home economists dread the mandatory Christmas roast turkey shoots. There are some ingredients, including turkey, that don't lend themselves to the camera's lens. Your only hope is to add some clever copy or work seriously on trying to make it look more appealing.

Unsurprisingly, some aspiring food bloggers, Instagrammers, et al, prioritize appearance rather than taste. Their photographs can look amazing and, naturally, such images influence the common perception of what is attractive, even when it tastes a bit dodgy. A harmless example is the current fashion for scattering gleaming red pomegranate seeds over everything. Pomegranate seeds are delicious in the right context, but it's questionable whether their bitter-sweet taste and wet texture adds to the taste, flavour and mouth feel of the many salads, main courses and puddings they garnish.

Nor is it just domestic cooks who are affected. As the power of social media has grown, so restaurants have shifted their focus from traditional journalists to those who have the biggest online audience. Young chefs must now define their food by devising a number of photogenic signature dishes, which they hope will go viral. How many can afford the luxury of creating less-photogenic dishes? How many would dare serve something that looks less than appealing, such as a wonderful-tasting – but brown – Tuscan wild boar stew? In Italy, it's presented unadorned – the eater's appetite wetted solely by its savoury aroma. Good food doesn't have to look fantastic. The following recipes are there to test your preconceptions of what makes food attractive.

Cheat's Nasi Goreng? Add an egg!

Serves 2

Eggs are almost as loved on social media as cakes, which makes this colourful dish perfect for would-be Instagrammers. Although this recipe is not authentic, it still tastes gorgeous. Despite the recipe length, it's very easy to make.

Ideally, you should make the rice a few hours in advance, so that it is cold before frying. Hot rice added to the frying pan becomes greasy. You can substitute sliced chicken breast (stir-fried separately with some extra spice) for the prawns (shrimp) or even combine them to make a hearty dish.

115 g/4 oz/⅔ cup basmati rice

300 ml/10 fl oz/1⅓ cups cold water

4 tbsp cold-pressed sunflower oil

1 medium egg, beaten with a tiny pinch of salt

3 slices back bacon, cut into lardons

1 small onion, finely sliced

1 garlic clove, finely diced

1 small Thai chilli, finely diced (optional)

1 medium carrot, peeled and cut into pea-sized dice

½ tsp shrimp paste (kapi)

1 tsp Malaysian asam pedas curry paste or sambal bajak

55 g/2 oz/scant ½ cup frozen petits pois

1 tbsp naturally brewed soy sauce

1 tbsp mirin

1 tbsp sake

200 g/7 oz cooked North Atlantic prawns (shrimp)

To serve

1 tbsp cold-pressed sunflower oil

2 medium eggs

2 flavoursome tomatoes, sliced

¼ cucumber, peeled and finely sliced

2 lime wedges

a handful of coriander (cilantro) leaves

a pinch of fine sea salt

Continued on p.222

Eggs and bright colours are popular on social media

Place the rice in a small saucepan, add the cold water (double the volume of rice), cover, and bring to the boil. Reduce the heat to low and simmer for 15 minutes. Take off the heat and leave covered until cold.

Prepare all of the ingredients before you start to cook.

Set a large non-stick frying pan (skillet) over a medium heat. Add 1 tbsp of the oil and, once hot, add the beaten egg. Cook the thin omelette for 30 seconds, flip over and lightly cook the other side for a few seconds. Remove to a plate. Once cool, roll up and finely slice.

Add the remaining 3 tbsp oil to the pan, increase the heat and add the bacon. Fry briskly for 2 minutes, until lightly coloured. Lower the heat and add the onion, garlic and chilli. Fry gently for 5 minutes, or until they begin to soften, then add the carrot. Cook for 2 minutes, then mix in the shrimp paste and spice paste and fry for 3 minutes. Add the frozen peas, soy sauce, mirin and sake. Increase the heat and bubble vigorously until the liquid has evaporated. Mix in the cold rice, sliced omelette and prawns. Keep stir-frying until everything is evenly coated in the spicy mixture and piping hot. Divide the fried rice between 2 plates or shallow bowls.

To serve, place a clean non-stick frying pan over a medium-high heat. Once hot, add the oil and crack the eggs into the pan. While they are cooking, lightly salt the sliced tomato and cucumber and arrange around the fried rice. Place a fried egg in the middle of each plate, garnish with the lime wedges and scatter with coriander leaves. Serve immediately.

Roast Partridge with Watercress

Serves 4

Certain dishes look beautiful in reality, despite the fact that they're not naturally photogenic. Many roast fowl belong to this category. Traditionally, in Britain, the cook often garnished the said bird with a liberal bunch of watercress. Aside from the fact that watercress tastes delicious with game, it also looks very pretty when served in glimmering candlelight.

4 oven-ready partridges

1 lemon

a small bunch of thyme

1 tbsp runny honey

salt and freshly ground black pepper

55 g/2 oz/scant ¼ cup unsalted butter, softened

4 slices thin rindless streaky bacon

For the gravy
150 ml/5 fl oz/⅔ cup dry white wine

150 ml/5 fl oz/⅔ cup good-quality Chicken Stock (p.47)

For the garnish
1 large bunch of watercress, washed and trimmed

Preheat the oven to 200°C fan/220°C/425°F/ gas mark 7.

Wipe the birds clean with a damp cloth and remove any tiny feathers. Roughly squeeze the juice from the lemon into a large bowl before quartering the lemon and stuffing a piece into each bird with some thyme. Add the honey to the lemon juice, then add the birds to the bowl and thoroughly coat in the mixture.

Season each bird and arrange in a small flame-proof roasting pan. Place a small nut of butter in each cavity, before smearing their breasts with the rest of the butter. Wrap each partridge in a bacon jacket.

Roast in the hot oven for 20 minutes, then remove the bacon and keep to one side. Baste the birds thoroughly and roast for 8 more minutes.

Transfer the birds from their roasting pan to a warm serving dish – tipping each bird up as you do so, so that all their lemony juices are poured into the pan. Keep the birds warm by loosely wrapping in some foil.

To make the gravy, place the roasting pan over a medium-high heat and add the wine and bacon jackets. Boil vigorously, scraping any crusty bits from the base of the pan as you do so. Once the wine has reduced by three-quarters, add the chicken stock and boil until reduced by half. Strain and serve with the partridge, garnished with the watercress.

Tomato and Cheese Lasagne

Serves 4

- -

Some baked dishes, such as lasagne, are not the most photogenic. Happily, lasagne remains a firm favourite with many families. Try this amazingly light vegetarian version with home-made 'green' pasta to test your photographic skills. Don't be put off by the length of the recipe – it's worth the effort, releasing myriad flavours as you eat. The tomato sauce can be made a day or two in advance and the lasagne can be assembled several hours in advance.

For the tomato sauce

3 tbsp extra-virgin olive oil

225 g/8 oz shallots, finely diced

2 garlic cloves, finely chopped

1 tsp dried chilli flakes

900 g/2 lb ripe tomatoes, peeled and chopped

3 sprigs basil

a small piece of Parmesan rind

salt and freshly ground black pepper

For the pasta dough

1 medium egg

30 g/1 oz bunch flat leaf parsley, leaves only, washed and dried

100 g/3½ oz/generous 1 cup Italian '00' white flour, plus extra for dusting

Set a heavy-based saucepan over a medium heat. Add the olive oil, followed by the sliced shallots, garlic and chilli flakes. Gently fry for 15 minutes, until soft, then add the tomatoes, basil and Parmesan rind. Reduce the heat and simmer gently for 1½ hours, until thick and flavoursome. Remove the basil and Parmesan rind and purée the mixture with a hand-held blender or in a food processor. Strain the sauce through a sieve into a bowl. Season, set aside until cool, then chill, covered, until needed.

To make the pasta, put the egg and parsley leaves in a food processor. Process until finely chopped. Add the flour, briefly process, then tip out and knead into a ball. Wrap in clingfilm (plastic wrap) and chill for 1 hour (or longer).

Prepare the cheese: Pat dry the mozzarella and roughly grate into a bowl. Mix with 115 g/4 oz/1¾ cups of the finely grated Pecorino, the ricotta, finely grated lemon zest and thyme. Season with black pepper and chill, covered, until needed. Keep the remaining Pecorino separate.

On a lightly floured work surface, roll the pasta into a thin rectangle. Feed it through the widest roller setting of a pasta machine. Refold it into 3 layers and re-roll. Repeat the process, then narrow the pasta machine to the next setting and repeat the process. Narrow the machine setting again and repeat the process. Continue passing the pasta sheets through ever-narrower settings, until it feels silky and you can almost see your hand through the sheet. Cut the sheets in half as they become too long to handle comfortably. Hang each finished sheet to dry a little (over the back

For the cheese

250 g/9 oz buffalo
mozzarella, drained

140 g/5 oz/generous
2 cups finely grated
Pecorino Sardo

250 g/9 oz/generous
1 cup ricotta

finely grated zest of
1 lemon

1½ tsp finely chopped
thyme

Note

Try this verdant-
flavoured pasta in
other dishes, such
as wild mushroom
pappardelle: cut
the rolled dough
into strips, dust in
semolina, loosely
arrange on a
semolina-dusted tray
and leave to dry for
about 20 minutes,
before covering with
a clean cloth.

of a wooden chair for example), while you roll the remaining pasta.

Cut the pasta sheets to fit your lasagne dish (about 20 x 20 x 5 cm/8 x 8 x 2 inches).

Bring a large pan of salted water to the boil. Have a bowl of iced water close by. Drop 2–3 sheets of pasta into the boiling water and cook for 30–40 seconds, then remove to the cold water. As soon as they're cool, place on a clean cloth and pat dry. Repeat the process as you build up the lasagne layers in your dish.

Spread a thin layer of the tomato sauce on the bottom of your lasagne dish. Cover with a single layer of lasagne sheets, trimming them to fit your dish, if necessary. Spread with half the cheese mixture.

Cover with another layer of pasta, followed by half the remaining tomato sauce and all the cheese mixture. Cover with pasta and top with the remaining tomato sauce. Sprinkle with the reserved grated Pecorino and cover the dish with foil. It can be chilled at this stage.

Preheat the oven to 180°C fan/200°C/400°F/gas mark 6.

Bake the lasagne for 40 minutes, removing the foil halfway through cooking. The top should be flecked gold and bubbling hot.

Chocolate Tiffin x 2

Makes 12 pieces

There are certain dishes that everyone loves, regardless of what they look like. Chocolate tiffin (photographed p.240), which is also called chocolate refrigerator cake, is one of those recipes. Many cooks add brightly coloured ingredients to liven it up, such as glacé cherries, chopped candied peel and pistachios; however, my version here is unashamedly dark with its roast nuts and stem ginger. If you can't get hold of delicious crunchy oat Hobnob biscuits (unthinkable), use plain digestive biscuits (graham crackers) instead.

55 g/2 oz/scant ½ cup blanched whole almonds

45 g/1½ oz/⅓ cup blanched whole hazelnuts

30 g/1 oz/scant ¼ cup shelled pistachios

30 g/1 oz/¼ cup walnut halves

85 g/3 oz/⅔ cup finely chopped soft prunes

85 g/3 oz/generous ½ cup stem (preserved) ginger in syrup, drained, rinsed and finely diced

225 g/8 oz plain Hobnob biscuits (see note above)

200 g/7 oz good dark chocolate, such as Valrhona Caraibe

5 tbsp golden syrup

210 g/7½ oz/scant 1 cup unsalted butter

Note

For an orange version, replace the ginger with chopped mixed candied peel and add the finely grated zest of 2 oranges.

Preheat the oven to 180°C fan/200°C/400°F/gas mark 6. Line the bottom and sides of a shallow 30 x 20 cm/12 x 8 inch baking sheet with baking parchment.

Place the blanched almonds and hazelnuts on a small baking sheet with the shelled pistachios. Roast for 7 minutes, giving the sheet the odd shake, until lightly coloured. Remove and tip onto a chopping board to cool.

Once cool, add the walnuts and roughly chop the nuts into raisin-sized pieces. Place in a large mixing bowl. Add the chopped prunes and diced stem (preserved) ginger to the nuts.

Crush the biscuits into small chunks, either with your hands or with a rolling pin, and tip into the nuts. Using your hands, mix thoroughly so that all the ingredients are evenly distributed.

Put the chocolate, golden syrup and butter in a small pan. Set over a low heat and stir occasionally until the mixture has melted. Pour the warm mixture into the nut and biscuit mixture. Stir until well mixed then spread evenly into the lined baking sheet. Pat down firmly and chill in the refrigerator until set.

To serve, lift the paper out of the sheet and cut the mixture into your chosen shapes: rectangles, squares or even triangles. Peel off the paper and serve on a pretty plate.

Personal Expression

Cooking is as much an expression of self-identity, as your choice in clothes. It takes time to find your own culinary style. Most cooks initially reflect their early influences, such as family, favourite cookbooks and television cookery programmes. Young chefs, meanwhile, learn to plate food according to the taste of their head chef. Gradually, as your culinary knowledge deepens, so your taste and vision develops.

Your character will always dictate how you present your food. Flamboyant or shy, messy or neat – it will inevitably be expressed in your cooking. After all, every aspect of preparation affects the final dish, from how you cut your vegetables to whether you wipe clean the rim of a gratin dish before baking. I struggled for years to make neat-looking tarts and pies until I finally accepted that I am a naturally free-form (messy) type of cook. I realized that it was better to work with my nature than fight against it.

Your choice of recipes also dictates how you present your food. Often, many of the dishes we cook are an expression of who we are, as Claudia Roden so beautifully writes in *A Book of Middle Eastern Food* (1968): 'I was a schoolgirl in Paris then. Every Sunday I was invited together with my brothers and a cousin to eat ful medames with some relatives. This meal became a ritual. Considered in Egypt to be a poor man's dish, in Paris the little brown beans became invested with all the glories and warmth of Cairo, our home town, and the embodiment of all that for which we were homesick.'

It is worth looking at the types of recipes you like to cook and seeing if there is a common thread that runs through them. It allows you to push your boundaries and branch into other areas of cooking. Since I cannot depict your food, here are a few recipes that typify my home cooking. My dishes tend to be slightly messy, often colourful, but – hopefully – always delicious.

Miso-Dressed Noodles with Aubergine and Green Beans

Serves 2

This earthy-flavoured, soft-textured aubergine (eggplant) and soba noodle dish is eaten at room temperature as a light lunch or starter. The bright green beans and spring onions (scallions) contrast in both colour and texture.

For the noodles

1 aubergine (eggplant), about 250 g/9 oz

115 g/4 oz fine green beans, topped and tailed

100 g/3½ oz Japanese soba (buckwheat) noodles

2 spring onions (scallions), trimmed and finely sliced

For the dressing

2 tbsp white sesame seeds

2 tbsp aka red miso

1 tbsp caster (granulated) sugar

1 tbsp mirin

Preheat the oven to 200°C fan/220°C/425°F/gas mark 7.

Stab the aubergine all over with a sharp knife and bake for 45 minutes, or until soft. Remove and set aside until cool enough to handle.

To make the dressing, place the sesame seeds in a small dry frying pan (skillet), set over a low heat and keep stirring for about 7 minutes, or until the seeds turn a pale brown and release their fragrance. Tip into a mortar and grind to a rough paste. Grind in the miso paste, followed by the caster sugar and mirin. Mix thoroughly and divide equally between 2 medium-sized mixing bowls.

Drop the trimmed beans into a pan of unsalted boiling water and cook for 4–5 minutes, or until just tender but still bright green. Drain and cool under cold running water. Pat dry with paper towels and set aside.

Peel the warm aubergine, discarding the skin and stem. Slice the flesh into bean-length shreds and mix into one bowl of miso dressing.

Add the soba noodles to a pan of unsalted boiling water and cook according to the packet instructions, until al dente – usually about 5 minutes. Drain and rinse thoroughly under the cold tap. Shake well and mix into the second bowl of miso dressing. Coat thoroughly, then mix in the green beans and the miso-coated aubergine. Divide between 2 serving bowls and garnish with the finely sliced spring onion.

Paprika Chicken and Black Bean Stew

Serves 3

Personal style often focuses on favourite ingredients, culinary methods and lifestyle – for example, I love smoked paprika, cumin seeds, pulses and fresh tomatoes, and, having been a chef for many years, I have a great fondness for TV suppers. Try serving with the Saffron Rice (p.218) or soft corn tortillas.

5 tbsp extra-virgin olive oil

1 small onion, finely diced

1 garlic clove, finely diced

¼ tsp cumin seeds

1 tsp Spanish smoked sweet paprika

400 g/14 oz fresh tomatoes

1 x 400-g/14-oz can black beans, drained and rinsed

2 large boneless chicken breasts, skinned

1 tbsp plain (all-purpose) flour

2 x 110-g/4-oz Revilla chorizo de Pueblo, thickly sliced (optional)

200 ml/7 fl oz/generous ¾ cup cold water

salt and freshly ground black pepper

To serve

1 small avocado, quartered, peeled and stoned

3 tbsp soured cream or natural Greek yogurt

a handful of coriander (cilantro) leaves, roughly chopped

Set a medium saucepan over a low heat and add 3 tbsp of the olive oil, the onion, garlic and cumin seeds. Fry gently for 10 minutes, or until soft. Add the paprika and cook for a further 2 minutes.

Meanwhile, put the tomatoes in a bowl, cover with boiling water and, using a sharp knife, lightly stab the skin of each tomato. Leave for 2 minutes, then drain, peel and chop the tomatoes.

Add the chopped tomatoes to the onions and fry briskly, stirring regularly, until they form a thick purée, about 10 minutes. Mix in the drained beans and remove from the heat.

Trim the chicken breasts of any fat or bloody bits and cut into easy-to-eat chunks. Season the flour in a small bowl. Toss the chicken pieces in the flour.

Heat a non-stick frying pan (skillet) over a high heat. Add the remaining olive oil and, once hot, add the floured chicken pieces to the pan. Fry briskly for 2–3 minutes, until the chicken is coloured on all sides. Move the chicken pieces to the black beans.

Reduce the heat to low under the frying pan and fry the sliced chorizo (if using) for 1 minute on each side, or until lightly coloured and much of its fat has been released. Transfer to the chicken and beans. Stir the water into the beans so that you have a thick sauce. Season to taste and simmer gently for 10 minutes, or until the chicken is just cooked.

Reheat when you're ready to serve. Cut the avocado into dice, lightly salt and garnish each portion of beans with a spoonful of soured cream, topped with diced avocado and a scattering of coriander leaves.

Seared Tuna with Tomato, Bean and Avocado Relish

Serves 6

This is a classic example of using brightly coloured food to suggest exciting tastes and textures – in this case with the sweet, tart and spicy tomato and bean relish. You can amplify this effect by serving the dish with Saffron Rice (p.218). This relish is equally good eaten with the Blackened Salmon (p.169).

For the bean relish

2 red (bell) peppers, quartered and seeded

450 g/1 lb cherry tomatoes

2 tbsp white wine vinegar

6 tbsp extra-virgin olive oil

1 Thai chilli, or to taste, finely diced

1 medium red onion, diced

6 tbsp roughly chopped coriander (cilantro) leaves (from a medium-sized bunch)

2 x 400-g/14-oz can kidney beans, drained and rinsed

2 ripe avocados

salt and freshly ground black pepper

For the tuna

2 tbsp extra-virgin olive oil

6 x 175 g/6 oz tuna steaks

Begin by making the relish. Turn the grill (broiler) to high. Place the pepper quarters skin-side up under the grill and cook until their skin blisters and blackens. Remove to a small bowl, cover with a plate and leave to steam until cool enough to peel.

Put the cherry tomatoes in a bowl, cover with boiling water and, using a sharp knife, quickly make a small incision in the skin of each tomato. Leave for 2 minutes, then drain and peel the tomatoes.

Halve or quarter the tomatoes and place in a large mixing bowl. Mix in the vinegar, olive oil and salt and pepper to taste, with the diced chilli, red onion, chopped coriander and beans.

Cut the peeled peppers into kidney-bean-sized dice. Mix into the tomatoes and adjust the seasoning to taste.

When you are ready to serve, quarter, stone and peel the avocados, then cut into bean-sized dice and mix into the relish.

Preheat 2 oven-top griddle pans over a high heat or wait until the charcoal on a barbecue is glowing hot and white. Oil the tuna steaks, season with salt and pepper and arrange on the griddle pans or barbecue. Cook for 2–3 minutes on each side (if they're about 2-cm/¼-inch thick), carefully moving them every minute or so to sear them with golden-brown diamond grill marks. The tuna is cooked when it retains a faint pinkness in the centre. It will continue to cook when removed from the heat. Slice each tuna steak and serve with the relish.

Your character will always dictate how you serve your food

Summary Fruit Salad

Serves 6

Throughout the summer, I make this simple pudding. The mix of fruit varies according to what soft fruit is available, but is characterized by the intense colours and fragrant, fruity scents of summer.

If you have time, serve it with the pale yellow Basil Custard (p.174), as its scent emphasizes the herbal fragrance of midsummer. If you're lucky enough to have access to a blackcurrant bush, substitute currant leaves for basil in the custard, as they will infuse it with a wonderful lemony flavour.

350 g/12 oz strawberries, hulled and halved

1 tbsp lemon juice

55 g/2 oz/3½ tbsp caster (granulated) sugar, or to taste

2 tbsp kirsch (optional)

250 g/9 oz cherries, halved and stoned

115 g/4 oz redcurrants, stripped from their stalks

350 g/12 oz raspberries

To serve

cold Basil Custard (p.174) or double (heavy) cream

Mix the strawberries, lemon juice, half the sugar and all the kirsch in a large bowl, before mixing in the cherries and currants.

Shortly before serving, mix in the raspberries and add more sugar, if necessary.

Serve with the basil custard or cream. If plating, spoon a heaped small pile of fruit salad into a shallow bowl. Pour the custard around – not on – the fruit in the empty area of the bowl. Repeat with the remaining bowls.

Nori Water Biscuits

Makes about 30 biscuits

Even the plainest of foods can be beautiful. These salty, umami-tasting, crisp savoury biscuits are very addictive, and – to my eyes at least – look equally attractive spread out on a plain plate, snuggled into a small basket or packed for a picnic. Eat with the finest unsalted butter you can find.

1 tsp cold-pressed sunflower oil, for greasing

5 g/⅛ oz toasted nori sheets

225 g/8 oz/1¾ cups plain (all-purpose) white flour, sifted, plus extra for dusting

1 tsp baking powder

½ tsp fine sea salt

55 g/2 oz/scant ¼ cup cold lard, diced

100 ml/3½ oz/generous ⅓ cup very cold water

Preheat the oven to 160°C fan/180°C/350°F/gas mark 4. Lightly grease 2 non-stick baking sheets.

Using a pair of scissors, snip the nori into small pieces. Put the snipped nori, plain flour, baking powder and salt into a food processor. Process until the nori is cut into fine fragments. Add the diced lard and briefly process until the mixture forms tiny crumbs. Tip into a mixing bowl.

Add the cold water and mix into a firm dough. Turn out, briefly knead, and cut in half. Lightly flour your work surface and roll out the first half into a very thin sheet, as thin as you can go without the dough breaking. Stamp out the biscuits using a 7-cm/2¾-inch diameter pastry cutter and transfer to the baking sheets. Repeat with the remaining dough. Knead together the trimmings and repeat until you've finished all the dough.

Prick the biscuits with a fork and bake in the hot oven for 25–30 minutes, or until pale golden and crisp. Transfer to a wire rack and leave until cold. Store in a biscuit tin and eat with butter or cheese.

Bibliography

Ghillie Başan, *Mezze: Small Plates to Share*, Ryland Peters & Small (2015).

Heston Blumenthal, *The Big Fat Duck Cookbook*, Cape Press Ltd. (2008).

Linda B. Buck, 'Unraveling the Sense of Smell', Nobel Lecture (December 8, 2004).

Henri Cartier-Bresson, *The Mind's Eye Writings on Photography and Photographers*, Aperture (1999).

Jayaram Chandrashekar, et al, 'The Receptors and Cells for Mammalian Taste', *Nature*, Vol. 444 (16 November 2006).

Savitri Chowdhary, *Indian Cooking*, Andre Deutsch (1954).

Alan Davidson, *The Oxford Companion to Food*, Oxford University Press (1999).

Dale DeGroff, *The Craft of the Cocktail*, Proof Publishing Ltd. (2003).

David A. Embury, *The Fine Art of Mixing Drinks*, Faber & Faber Ltd. (1958).

Josephine Emlee, *Cooking for Texture*, Faber & Faber (1957).

M.F.K. Fisher, *The Art of Eating*, Pan Books Ltd (1983).

Patience Gray, *Honey from a Weed*, Prospect Books (1986).

Philip D. Howes, et al, 'The Perception of Materials Through Oral Sensation', PLoS ONE DOI (2014).

Deh-Ta Hsiung, *Chinese Cookery Secrets: How to Cook Chinese Restaurant Food at Home*, Paperfronts (1993).

Rosemary Hume and Muriel Downes, *Penguin Cordon Bleu Cookery*, Penguin Books (1963; revised edition 1977)

Dan Jurafsky, *The Language of Food*, W.W. Norton & Company (2014).

Sybil Kapoor, *Citrus and Spice: A Year of Flavour*, Simon & Schuster (2008).

Sybil Kapoor, *Modern British Food*, Michael Joseph (1995).

Sybil Kapoor, *Taste: A New Way To Cook*, Mitchell Beazley (2003).

Sybil Kapoor, 'The Unspoken Language of Food', *Oxford Symposium, Food and Language, Proceedings of the Oxford Symposium on Food and Cookery 2009*, Prospect Books (2010).

C.F. Leyel, *Picnics for Motorists*, George Routledge & Sons Ltd. (1936).

Hsiang Ju Lin, Tsuifeng Lin, *Chinese Gastronomy*, Thomas Nelson and Sons Ltd (1969).

Giorgio Locatelli, *Made in Italy: Food and Stories*, Fourth Estate (2006).

Ruth Lowinksy, *Lovely Food: A Cookery Notebook*, The Nonesuch Press (1931).

Mrs A. B. Marshall, *The Book of Ices* (1885), Smith Settle (1998).

Harold McGee, *McGee on Food & Cooking: An Encyclopedia of Kitchen Science, History and Culture*, Hodder and Stoughton (2004).

Ole G. Mouritsen and Klavs Styrbaek, *Mouthfeel: How Texture Makes Taste*, Columbia University Press (2017).

Mary Norwak, *English Puddings Sweet & Savoury*, Grub Street (1996).

Edouard de Pomiane, *Cooking in Ten Minutes*, Bruno Cassirer (1948).

Apicius Redivivus (Dr Kitchiner), *The Cook's Oracle*, John Hatchard (1818).

Claudia Roden, *A Book of Middle Eastern Food*, Penguin (1970).

Edmund T. Rolls, 'The Neural Representation of Oral Texture Including Fat Texture', Journal of Texture Studies (2011).

Jeremy Rounds, *The Independent Cook*, Barrie & Jenkins (1988).

Margaret Shaida, *The Legendary Cuisine of Persia*, Penguin Books (1994).

Gordon M. Shepherd, *Neurogastronomy: How the Brain Creates Flavor and Why It Matters*, Columbia University Press (2012).

Susan Spaull and Lucinda Bruce-Gardyne, *Leiths Techniques Bible*, Bloomsbury (2003).

Constance Spry and Rosemary Hume, *The Constance Spry Cookery Book*, Weidenfeld and Nicolson, (1956; revised edition 1971).

Yukikko Takahashi (editor), *Dashi and Umami: The Heart of Japanese Cuisine*, Eat-Japan/Cross Media Ltd (2009).

K. Talavera, et al, 'The Influence of Temperature on Taste Perception', Cellular and Molecular Life Sciences (December 2006).

David Thompson, *Thai Food*, Pavilion Books Ltd. (2002).

Yoshio Tsuchiya, Masaru Yamamoto, *A Feast for the Eyes: The Japanese Art of Food Arrangement*, Kodansha International Ltd. (1980).

Shizuo Tsuji, *Japanese Cooking: A Simple Art*, Kodansha International Ltd (1985).

Luca Turin, *The Secret of Scent: Adventures in Perfume and the Science of Smell*, Faber and Faber (2006).

Andrew Whitley, *Bread Matters*, Fourth Estate (2006).

Strawberry Ice Cream (p.188)

Index

Acknowledgements

Many people have influenced me, although some may not be aware that their food, words or books have led me on a journey that has shaped my thoughts and ultimately led to this book. In particular, I would like to thank Heston Blumenthal, Kyle Connaughton, Yoshinori Ishii, Rene Redzepi and Claudia Roden. There are times when a recipe cannot be improved, so many thanks to Ghillie Başan, Felicity Cloake, Deh-Ta Hsiung and Andrew Whitely for generously allowing me use your recipes. Thank you too to Helena Lang, for allowing me to reprint my Sainsbury's magazine sushi recipe. Other friends who have helped include Roopa Gulati and Brigitta Paramanathan. I must also thank everyone in Pavilion, in particular, Katie Cowan for giving me a free reign, Stephanie Milner for being my very patient editor, Caitlin Leydon and Bella Cockrell for all their work, and Helen Lewis and Michelle Mac for their inspired design. A very big thank you too to Linda Tordoff for the wonderful illustrations, Keiko Oikawa for the beautiful photographs, Cynthia Inions for all the props (I wanted to take them home), Polly Webb-Wilson and Hattie Arnold for their fantastic food styling (and a regular supply of cardamom buns). Lastly, I would like to thank my husband for his constant love and support.

Chocolate Tiffin (p.226)